Lean Six Sigma:
Combining Six Sigma Quality with Lean Speed

Lean Six Sigma:

Combining Six Sigma Quality with Lean Speed

Michael L. George

McGraw-Hill

New York Chicago San Francisco Lisbon London
Madrid Mexico City Milan New Delhi San Juan
Seoul Singapore Sydney Toronto

McGraw-Hill

A Division of The **McGraw·Hill** *Companies*

11 12 13 DOC/DOC 0 9 8 7 6 5 4

ISBN 0-07-138521-5

Library of Congress Cataloging-in-Publication Data applied for.

Production services provided by CWL Publishing Enterprises, Madison, WI, www.cwlpub.com. For McGraw-Hill, the sponsoring editor is Richard Narramore.

Printed and bound by R.R. Donnelley & Sons Company.

This publication is designed to provide accurate and authoritative information in regard to the subject matter covered. It is sold with the understanding that neither the author nor the publisher is engaged in rendering legal, accounting, or other professional service. If legal advice or other expert assistance is required, the services of a competent professional person should be sought.
> —*From a Declaration of Principles jointly adopted by a Committee of the American Bar Association and a Committee of Publishers*

McGraw-Hill books are available at special quantity discounts to use as premiums and sales promotions, or for use in corporate training programs. For more information, please write to the Director of Special Sales, McGraw-Hill, 2 Penn Plaza, New York, NY 10128. Or contact your local bookstore.

 This book is printed on recycled, acid-free paper containing a minimum of 50% recycled de-inked fiber.

Contents

Preface   ix

Part One. The Lean Six Sigma Value Proposition   1

1. Lean Six Sigma: Creating Breakthrough
Profit Performance   3
The Roadmap to Higher Shareholder Value   4
The Lean Six Sigma Secret   8
The Lean Six Sigma Value Proposition   9
Lean Six Sigma and MRP   13
The Power Is in the Total Process   13
To Learn More   14

2. Six Sigma: The Power of Culture   15
Critical Success Factors for Six Sigma   17
Predicting Team Success, Preventing Team Failure   23
The Six Sigma Process and Improvement Tools   24
The Role of Six Sigma as a Metric   31
The Key Is in the Culture   32
Key Messages of Six Sigma   32
To Learn More   32

3. Lean Means Speed   33
Is This Lean?   34
The Essentials of Lean   35
The Lean Metric: Cycle Efficiency   36
Velocity of Any Process   49
Knowing Where to Focus: The 80/20 Rule   51
Using a Value Stream Map to Find the 20% Waste   51
The Major Lean Improvement Tools   56
The Lean Enterprise   59
Epilogue on Ford   59
The Laws of Lean Six Sigma   60
To Learn More   60

**4. Creating Competitive Advantage with
   Lean Six Sigma**   61
   The Need for Executive Engagement   62
   Value Stream Selection à la Warren Buffett   71
   Competing with Lean Six Sigma   76

**Part Two. The Lean Six Sigma Implementation
   Process**   79

**5. Initiation: Getting Commitment from Top
   Management**   85
   Laying the Groundwork   87
   Leadership Engagement   87
   The Next Moves   92

6. Infrastructure and Deployment Planning   93
   Plan Components and Typical Timelines   94
   The Detailed Deployment Plan   96
   A. Process Focus   96
   B. Organizational Structures   98
   C. Measures   110
   D. Rewards and Recognition   113
   E. Infrastructure Tools   115
   Completing the Deployment Plan   116

7. Kickoff: Establishing the Vision Company-Wide   117
   Structure of the Transforming Event   118
   A. CEO Presentation   119
   B. Design Team Presentation   120
   C. "Testimonials" from Experienced Companies   120
   D. Simulation   120
   E. Launch Preparations   122
   The Cascade of Transforming Events   122
   Achieving a Company-Wide Vision   123
   Only the Beginning ...   123

**8. Selecting the Right People—and the
   Right Projects**   125
   Selecting Black Belt Resources   126
   Selecting Projects   127
   The Language of Project Selection   129
   Who Does What   130
   Diagnostic Processes for Project Identification   131
   Top-Down Project Identification   132
   Bottom-Up Project Identification   144

Grouping and Screening Ideas 146
Project Definition and Scoping 148
Final Project Selections 153
Projects Suitable for Lean Six Sigma 155
Selecting the Right Resources and Projects 156

9. Predicting and Improving Team Performance 157
Understanding Individual Performance 158
Preferred Team Roles as Predictors of Team
    Success or Failure 159
Applying Belbin's Research 162
The Importance of Team Leadership 163
Implications for Black Belt Training 165

**10. Implementation: The DMAIC
Improvement Process** 167
The Context of Improvement 168
The DMAIC Process and Its Tools 170
A Walk Through DMAIC 173
Developing Focus: The DMAIC Filter 177
Big Gains with Simple Tools: Two Examples 178
Implications for Black Belt Training 181

11. Implementation: The DMAIC Tools 182
Define Tools 183
Measure Tools 185
Analyze Tools 199
Improve Tools 203
Control Tools 222
Using the Lean Six Sigma Tools 224

12. Institutionalizing Lean Six Sigma 226
Institutionalization 228
Planning for Each Business Unit Launch 232
The Executive's Role 232
Emphasizing the Ultimate Goals 234

Part Three. Leveraging Lean Six Sigma 235

13. Total Supply Chain Acceleration 237
Part A: Accelerating Your Internal Supply Chain 238
Part B: Extending the Enterprise to Suppliers 257
Part C: The Downstream Pull System 266

14. Lean Six Sigma Logistics 270
Inventory and Strategic Goals 271
Inventory and The Cost of Production 273

Fundamental Logistics Cost Drivers 278
Lean Manufacturing, Raw Materials, and
    Inventory Management 280
Implementing Lean Logistics 281
Challenges of Lean Logistics 288

15. Design for Lean Six Sigma **290**
The Case for Applying Lean Six Sigma
    to the Design Process 292
Improving Design Velocity 296
Design for Lean Six Sigma 303
Final Thoughts on Lean Six Sigma and
    Product Development 307

Index **309**

Preface

I n 1996, General Electric CEO Jack Welch praised Six Sigma as "the most important initiative GE has ever undertaken." Yet despite widespread success with Six Sigma, two years later Welch articulated one shortfall (GE Annual Report, 1998):

We have tended to use all our energy and Six Sigma science to "move the mean" to ... reduce order-to-delivery time to ... 12 days.... The problem is, as has been said, "the mean never happens,' and the customer ... is still seeing variances in when the deliveries actually occur—a heroic 4-day delivery time on one order, with an awful 20-day delay on another, and no real consistency.... Variation is evil.

Welch's statement was prompted by a growing awareness that time is nearly as important an improvement metric as is quality—and that reducing process lead times and variation in the time it takes to complete a process has just as much potential for improving a company's performance as reducing variation in quality.

Sometimes we regard our customers like the man who has one foot in the fire and the other in a block of ice: on average, he should be comfortable! But obviously the range of temperatures is intolerable—just as unpredictable delivery time is to our customers.

Most of the methods and tools associated with Six Sigma do not focus on time; they are concerned with identifying and eliminating *defects*. Any savings in time that result from Six Sigma projects are often a by-product of defect reduction and of the general problem-solving methodology. That's why, in GE's 2000 Annual Report (dated February 2001), Jack Welch announced a additional goal for GE: reducing the variation in lead time (which he refers to as "span"):

Today we have a Company doing its very best to fix its face on customers by focusing Six Sigma on their needs. Key to this focus is a con-

cept called "span," which is a measurement of operational reliability for meeting a customer request. It is the time window around the Customer Requested Delivery Date in which delivery will happen.

Welch positioned the focus on span as an *addition to* Six Sigma, not a replacement for it. *Quickly* and *reliably* reducing process lead time—which also reduces overhead cost and inventory—is the province of an entirely different set of principles and validated tools known as Lean methods. Use of Lean tools turbocharges the rate of reduction of lead time and manufacturing overhead and quality cost. Welch has thus provided yet another key insight to improve corporate performance (and we wish him well in his post-GE endeavors).

How are companies other than GE faring with continuous improvement initiatives? Data on the impact of continuous improvement programs like Six Sigma in service industries is hard to come by; however, the December 2000 issue of *Industry Week* included a survey of manufacturing companies that scored themselves against world-class performance metrics. Over half the firms had not achieved 98% on-time delivery and three-quarters had not been able to reduce manufacturing lead time by even 20% over the last five years. Scrap and rework costs exceeded 1% of sales for 77% of the respondents. These rates of improvement, even by self-evaluation, are quite slow—which is surprising, since subjective self-evaluations could be expected to err on the favorable side!

While such surveys are provocative, anyone dedicated to improvement knows that we need to look at objective data. Since my interest is rooted in driving "hard" financial results from improvements in process quality and lead times, I looked into ways that I could get data on world-class metrics from a company's financial statements. Internal quality levels are not reported by most companies; however, you *can* calculate the average delivery time by dividing work in process and finished goods inventory data from the financial footnotes in corporate 10-K reports by the cost of goods sold. Digging through the footnotes is a painstaking process, but I had my staff do it for a sample of 170 manufacturing companies for the years 1995 and 2000. We then calculated the percent improvement since 1995 and compared it with the *Industry Week* survey.

As you can see, average lead time has shown very little improvement. For about half the firms, lead time performance has in fact *declined* over the five-year period. As we will later see, if process *speed* has declined, generally so has process *quality*.

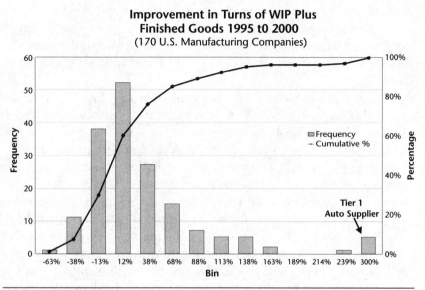

Figure 0-1. Histogram of percent improvement in lead time (170 companies)

On the positive side, a significant number of companies achieved an increase in WIP and finished goods turns of more than 100%—and several more than 300%. In "statistics-speak," data that departs from a normal distribution like this generally indicates that there are two populations: those that effectively apply Lean Six Sigma principles and those that don't. (I suggest you do the calculation to benchmark your firm against your leading competitors.)

These results show that the *Industry Week* survey was valid to the extent it could be tested. We must conclude that the principal population of companies is in fact improving at a very slow average rate. But take special note of the improvement shown by the tier-one auto supplier, a former division of United Technologies Automotive, at the far right in Figure 0-1. This 300% improvement rate was achieved in less than two years., We will use the case study to show how a company can improve at a very rapid rate if *both* Lean and Six Sigma tools are employed.

THE SYNERGY OF LEAN AND SIX SIGMA

Why are companies improving at such a slow rate, even when there is such a huge emphasis on improvement techniques like Six Sigma and Lean? What can they learn from GE or the tier-one auto supplier case study? Six Sigma does not directly address process speed and so the lack of improvement in lead time in companies applying Six Sigma methods alone is understandable. These companies also generally achieve only modest improvement in WIP and finished goods inventory turns.

But Lean methods alone aren't the answer either: Many of the firms that have shown little improvement in inventory turns have in fact attempted to apply Lean methods. It appears that, while many of the people at these companies understand Lean, they just aren't effective in implementing it across the corporation at a rapid rate. The companies achieve some remarkable successes ... but only in small areas. The data shows that improvement across the corporation as a whole remains slow without the Six Sigma cultural infrastructure.

An executive whose company is making rapid progress *now* said they started with Six Sigma, then spent several months trying to reduce lead time, ... only to realize they were reinventing Lean! In other words, no matter where you start—with Lean or with Six Sigma—you'll be driven to invent or learn the other half of the equation if you want to achieve high quality, high speed, and low cost. When a company uses both Lean and Six Sigma simultaneously, dramatic improvements across the corporation are achieved much more rapidly, and indeed we will prove that this combination is in fact a prerequisite for rapid rates of improvement.

So what is Lean Six Sigma?

Lean Six Sigma is a methodology that maximizes shareholder value by achieving the fastest rate of improvement in customer satisfaction, cost, quality, process speed, and invested capital.

The fusion of Lean and Six Sigma is required because:

- Lean cannot bring a process under statistical control.
- Six Sigma alone cannot dramatically improve process speed or reduce invested capital.

THE PURPOSE OF THIS BOOK

The purpose of this book is to show that the combination of Lean and Six Sigma—when focused on the highest-value projects and supported by the right performance improvement infrastructure—can produce remarkable results and is the most powerful engine available today for sustained value creation. We will provide case studies to illustrate how these results are achieved.

Some people have described Lean Six Sigma as "doing quality quickly," which may seem counter-intuitive at first. Intuition tells us that the faster we go, the more mistakes we make. If that were the case, trying to speed up a process would only result in lower quality. But Lean Six Sigma works not by speeding up the workers or the machines, but by *reducing unneeded wait time* between value-added steps. As James Womack has pointed out, "The most basic problem is that Lean flow thinking is counter-intuitive."[1]

This book closes that intuition gap with knowledge, both experiential and quantitative, and shows how Lean and Six Sigma methods complement and reinforce each other. It also provides a detailed roadmap of implementation so you can start seeing significant returns in less than a year.

Is Lean Six Sigma only suited for the factory? Absolutely not. Lean Six Sigma concepts are extremely powerful in improving the quality and speed of all types of transactional processes, including sales and marketing, quotations/pricing/order processing, product development, hotel check-in, mortgage applications, financial/administrative, and human resources. Transactional processes must also be improved in manufacturing companies, as they enable the manufacturing process. In fact many companies are finding that there is tremendous value-creation opportunity in attacking these processes simply because they have been overlooked in the past.

This book will provide insight into the application of Lean Six Sigma to both the manufacturing operations and the less-data-rich service and transactional processes.

Part One describes the **Lean Six Sigma Value Proposition**—how combining Lean and Six Sigma provides unprecedented potential for improving shareholder value.

Part Two discusses the **Lean Six Sigma Implementation Process**—how to prepare your organization for Lean Six Sigma and the steps for implementation.

Part Three is devoted to **Leveraging Lean Six Sigma** by extending its reach both within and beyond your corporate boundaries.

As you'll see in Part One, Lean Six Sigma—unlike other improvement methodologies—is clearly tied to shareholder value creation—an endeavor that must be led by the CEO or COO. Lean Six Sigma therefore demands strong leadership by its very nature. Companies that allow each division to "go its own way" will not achieve the results that are possible when unified leadership focuses all the parts of the organization on the same priorities.

LOOKING FOR A COMPETITIVE EDGE?

The fact that most companies are improving at a very slow rate can be a great competitive advantage to your company *if you find a way to exploit the opportunity.* This book lays out a strategy you can use to capitalize on the slowness of your competitors. These methods are already being used and widely endorsed by companies such as Caterpillar, GE, Honeywell, International Truck, ITT Industries, NCR, Northrop Grumman, Lockheed Martin, Rockwell, Raytheon, and many others. Should you decide that Lean Six Sigma is the most appropriate improvement process for your corporation, you will be in the best of company!

Notes

1. James P. Womack and Daniel T. Jones, *Lean Thinking* (New York: (Simon & Schuster, 1996), p. 23.

ACKNOWLEDGMENTS

Many people have made significant contributions to the development of this book, and I am pleased to acknowledge their work:

Jack Welch, who proved what CEO engagement could achieve;

Warren Buffett, who showed how to prioritize Lean Six Sigma projects;

Taiichi Ohno, who created the Toyota Production System;

Professors Jim Patell and Mike Harrison (Stanford Graduate School of Business), who made queuing theory a practical tool for application to Lean Six Sigma;

Dr. W. Edwards Deming and Dr. Genichi Taguchi, who made Statistical Process Control and Design of Experiments practical quality tools.

It has been my pleasure to study their work and achievements and to include their contributions within *Lean Six Sigma.*

And the most important acknowledgement is to my wife, **Jackie,** who has been a source of love and strength in the victories and vicissitudes of an adventurous life.

Part One

The Lean
Six Sigma
Value Proposition

Lean Six Sigma: Creating Breakthrough Profit Performance

Put yourself in the place of the CEO of a tier-one auto supplier (a former division of United Technologies Automotive[1]) whose business was barely earning its cost of capital in a really tough market. First and foremost, you've got to regain your Ford Q1 quality rating to remain in the game. You have been shipping brake hose fittings that are failing, a customer's critical-to-quality issue, which is creating containment costs for you and your customers. You have been notified that if you don't correct this problem, you will lose your largest customer. Marketing has told you that Ford wants to be able to order any of 168 products with only a two- to three-day lead time to support its own Lean initiative. To achieve such capability, your company will have to dramatically improve your currently abysmal on-time delivery performance. You also have to *reduce cost* by at least 5% per year to generate a superior return on invested capital (ROIC) and keep up with price reductions demanded by the market.

This firm clearly needed to improve quality and delivery time at a very rapid rate. To meet this challenge, this company chose

Lean Six Sigma. How does Lean Six Sigma deliver results so much faster than either Lean or Six Sigma? Here's the first clue:

"It's hard to be aggressive when you don't know who to hit."
—Vince Lombardi

The "who to hit" question facing this CEO was *what specific improvements should be executed and in what order* to achieve these goals? This question is the key breakthrough of Lean Six Sigma that was not, and could not, be understood by those who separately advocated only Lean or only Six Sigma.

The Principle of Lean Six Sigma: *The activities that cause the customer's critical-to-quality issues and create the longest time delays in any process offer the greatest opportunity for improvement in cost, quality, capital, and lead time.*

Always solve or contain first the external quality problems that affect the customer. The internal quality, cost, inventory, and lead time problems will manifest themselves in the time delay they cause.

What does quality have to do with time delay? They aren't quite two sides of the same coin, but quality and time share a close relationship: the surprising fact is that 10% scrap can slow down a factory by 40% (something we'll get into in more detail later in this book). What does slow process velocity have to do with quality? Faster velocity multiplies the speed with which quality tools reduce defects.

The questions that Lean Six Sigma can uniquely answer, which neither Six Sigma or Lean alone can, are:

- To which process steps should we first apply Lean Six Sigma tools?
- In what order, and to what degree?
- How do we get the biggest cost, quality, and lead time improvements quickly?

It is the synergy of Lean and Six Sigma together that has helped companies to reduce manufacturing overhead and quality cost by 20% and inventory by 50% in less than two years.

THE ROADMAP TO HIGHER SHAREHOLDER VALUE

It has been my experience that the slow rate of corporate improvement described in the Preface is not due to lack of knowledge of Six Sigma or Lean. Rather, the fault lies in making the transition from theory to implementation. Managers need a step-by-step, unambiguous roadmap of improvement that leads to predictable results. This roadmap provides the self-confidence, punch, and power necessary for action and is the principal subject of this book.

The tier-one auto supplier provides a case study of the speed of results that can be achieved when management has a Lean Six Sigma roadmap. As described above, the company needed to decide where to focus its energies to dramatically reduce process lead time and defects.

The first step was to apply a Six Sigma tool known as mistake proofing to the testers, which made it impossible for a defective part to be shipped to the customer. Thus, defective parts could at least be contained and would no longer by shipped to the customer.

The next challenge was to determine which workstations (steps in the process) were injecting the longest time delay into the process, so those delays could be eliminated using Lean and Six Sigma tools. Time delays can be determined by spreadsheet calculations for simple processes, as will be described in Chapters 3 and 13. For complex processes, the determination can be made by loading Materials Requirements Planning (MRP) data into supply chain acceleration software.[2] Here, MRP data was used to calculate the delay caused by each of 100 workstations.

The output from these calculations (Figure 1-1) shows the reduction of delay time that would result by applying Lean Six Sigma tools on the highest priority sources of delay. How do you identify the priorities? In this case, just 10 workstations out of the 100 created nearly 80% of the delay in the total process lead time. These 10 are referred to as *time traps*. This small number of troublemakers reinforces the well-known Pareto principle that the majority of problems (often 80% or more) come from a "vital few" causes (20% or less of the potential sources). Experience shows that this is true of *any* factory or process where the amount of value-added time (as judged by the customer) is less than 5% of the total process lead time.

The Top 10 Time Traps in Figure 1-1 are listed in descending priority of the time delay they inject into the process. The first bar shows the original 12 days delivery time. Each subsequent bar shows what the new lead time would be if the company made the specific improvement to the process at a given workstation.

You see that time trap analysis identifies improvements like "Mistake-Proof Tester" (a Six Sigma tool) and "Setup Reduction at Flare" (a Lean tool) and "DOE at Brazing" (a Six Sigma quality tool). The lesson was clear to this company: to meet their goal of improving

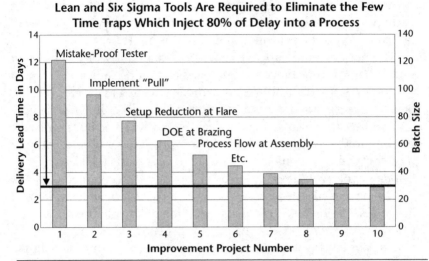

Figure 1-1. The top 10 time traps

quality and reducing lead time from its current 12+ days to two or three days—in under a year—they would need to combine Six Sigma tools (to reduce variation and eliminate *process defects*) with Lean tools (to increase *process speed*).

How well did the combination of Lean Six Sigma work? Look at Figure 1-2. As you can see, the variation in delivery time ("span," in Jack Welch's term) was dramatically reduced. Moreover, the variation

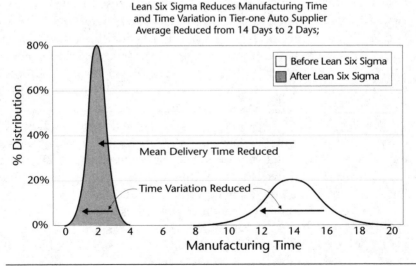

Figure 1-2. Tier-one supplier results from Lean Six Sigma

in process speed fell in direct proportion to the average speed increase. Using both Lean and Six Sigma, the company achieved Six Sigma quality levels (3.4 defects per million opportunities) on parameters that were critical to quality (CTQ) to Ford and allowed them to regain their Q1 rating.

Within two years, the shorter delivery time and improved quality led to a doubling of operating margin and revenue because the company kept winning substantial market share from their slower competitors. In that same time period, the company:

- Reduced manufacturing lead time from 14 days to 2 days
- Increased WIP inventory turns from 23 to 67 per year
- Reduced manufacturing overhead and quality cost by 22%
- Increased gross profit margin from 12% to 19.6%
- Increased operating margins from 5.4% to 13.8%
- Increased ROIC from 10% to 33%
- Attained Six Sigma quality levels on CTQ parameters

Conclusion: Rapid improvement requires both Lean and Six Sigma.

The lessons illustrated by the tier-one auto supplier have been borne out time and again in company after company. They are what led to the definition of Lean Six Sigma presented in the Preface:

Lean Six Sigma is a methodology that maximizes shareholder value by achieving the fastest rate of improvement in customer satisfaction, cost, quality, process speed, and invested capital.

The fusion of Lean and Six Sigma is required because:

- *Lean cannot bring a process under statistical control.*
- *Six Sigma alone cannot dramatically improve process speed or reduce invested capital.*

To make dramatic improvement in cost, quality, and responsiveness, a company must eliminate customer critical-to-quality issues and delays due to time traps using both Lean and Six Sigma tools. Otherwise, it will make the slow progress of the majority of companies that was described in the Preface.

Figure 1-1 reflects improvement specific to that company; the number and type of time traps will vary by industry and by situation. A similar analysis of a consumer products company determined that it could reduce finished goods inventory from $500 million to $300 million just by implementing a Lean tool known as "pull systems." Given the uncertain lending situation for corporate borrowers, reducing the revolving debt by $200 million dollars can be very important.

As you will soon see, knowing your time traps opens up a whole new universe of corporate performance.

THE LEAN SIX SIGMA SECRET

The amazing gains achieved by companies like this tier-one supplier arise from a key Lean Six Sigma insight:

> **Conclusion:** Most material in a manufacturing process spends 95% of its time waiting ... waiting for someone to add value to it or waiting in finished goods inventory.... By reducing this wait time by 80%, manufacturing overhead and quality cost can be reduced by 20%, in addition to the benefits of proportionally faster delivery and lower inventories.

These insights hold true for all processes, not just manufacturing.

One of the reasons cost is reduced by lead time reduction is that *slow processes are expensive processes.* Slow-moving inventory must be moved, counted, stored, retrieved, and moved again, and may be damaged or become obsolete. Slow-moving finished goods must be sold at "promotional prices" at a loss of margin. Expediters and stockroom personnel must deal with these problems. If a quality problem erupts, a large amount of inventory is in jeopardy of scrap and rework. A larger plant and more equipment and people must be used for a given capacity. These costs are often called the *hidden factory.*

The hidden factory consumes resources and people and produces nothing of value to the customer. Its costs are hidden within manufacturing overhead and the cost of poor quality (COPQ), which are typically two to four times that of direct labor and are *caused* by long process lead times and variability. Attacking these costs through *lead time* reduction offers enormous *cost reduction* leverage. Additionally, faster lead times quite often generate revenue growth, as customers do more business with the faster, more responsive supplier.

Just how important is manufacturing overhead and COPQ? The pie chart in Figure 1-3 shows the distribution of costs as a percentage of revenues for the top 1000 U.S. manufacturing companies.

If there is strong management support, a company can reduce manufacturing overhead and quality costs by 20% by the end of the first or second year. Increasing the operating margin by 4–7% of revenue in less than two years is a reasonable target for most companies. Lean Six Sigma directly attacks these costs more effectively than any previous improvement methodology because it comprehends both quality and speed.

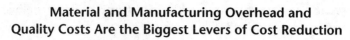

**Material and Manufacturing Overhead and
Quality Costs Are the Biggest Levers of Cost Reduction**

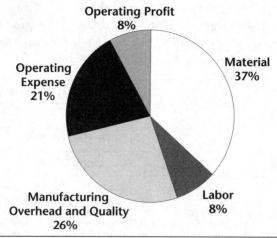

Figure 1-3. The cost levers

The distribution within the pie will differ by industry. For a man-ufacturer of high-tech electronic equipment, manufacturing overhead and labor amounted to only 12% of revenue. Why would such a com-pany be interested in Lean Six Sigma? One wanted to reduce delivery time from 10 days to two days, which yielded a revenue growth of 15%. It also had a very large cost-of-poor-quality problem.

However, don't think that Lean Six Sigma attacks only manufac-turing overhead and COPQ. As stated above, Lean Six Sigma can be used to improve velocity in *any* process, be it product development, order entry, fulfillment, design changes, customer services—thereby creating value in *all* sections of the pie.

THE LEAN SIX SIGMA VALUE PROPOSITION

Ask yourself these questions:

- Do customer value-added activities consume less than 5% of my total process time?
- What competitive advantage would I have if I could deliver in 50%-80% less time?
- What financial benefit would result from a 20% reduction in man-ufacturing overhead and quality cost?
- What cash infusion/debt reduction would result from a 50%-80% reduction in work in process (WIP) and finished goods inventory?

■ What revenue growth would result from reducing delivery time and time-to-market?

Gains in all of these areas are part of the Lean Six Sigma value proposition: the many ways in which use of Lean Six Sigma can contribute to improved shareholder value. Table 1-1, for example, shows benefits seen by the tier-one auto supplier.

Operating Margin	from 5.4% to 13.8%
Capital Turnover	from 2.8 to 3.7
ROIC	from 10% to 33%
Enterprise Value	increased 225%
EBITDA	increased 300%
Economic Profit = ROIC % - WACC %	from -2% to 21%
Manufacturing Lead Time	from 14 days to 2 days
Work-in-Process Inventory Turns	from 23 to 67 turns per year
On-Time Delivery	from 80% to > 99.7%
Quality Performance (External CTQ)	from 3σ to 6σ

Table 1-1. Operational and economic benefits of Lean Six Sigma seen by the tier-one supplier

As this company learned, Lean Six Sigma was the ideal tool for increasing shareholder value. It increases operating profit and decreases inventory and cap expenditures, thus increasing the numerator and decreasing the denominator. For the tier-one auto supplier, Lean Six Sigma efforts increased ROIC from 10% to 33%.

These results can be generalized even further, based on typical gains made to the cost levers shown in the previous pie chart (Figure 1-3), as shown in Table 1-2.

You will notice that these stretch goals are virtually identical to GE's that we discussed in the preface. The WIP+Finished Goods inventory turns can typically be doubled or tripled (more on this in Chapter 3). The percentages in Table 1-2 are based on an assumption of *no increase in revenue*. But many companies do increase sales. After all, becoming the best supplier in your industry in terms of quality, delivery, and innovation generally conveys increase in market share!

These kinds of gains have a direct impact on one of the key drivers

	% of Revenue		% Cost Reduction
	Current	Future	
Revenue	100%	100%	

Direct Costs
  Material
  Labor
  Overhead & Quality
	30%
	10%
	25%
		28.5%
		10.0%
		20.0%
			5%
			0%
			20%

Cost of Goods Sold	65%	58.5%	10%
Gross Profit	35%	41.5%	
General & Administrative	10%	10%	0%
Marketing	10%	10%	0%
Interest			
Other	5%	5%	0%
Operating Profit	**10%**	**16.5%**	

Table 1-2. Lean Six Sigma value proposition

of shareholder value for corporations—*return on invested capital (ROIC)*. One of the pillars of Lean Six Sigma is understanding the connection between shareholder value creation and specific improvements in the business. To build this connection, a value creation "line of sight" is established between projects and the key drivers of value creation—ROIC and revenue growth. This connection is supported by empirical stock market data[3] I have added at the end of the chapter compiled on the top 340 U.S. companies (with permission of McKinsey & Company). The premium multiple the stock market pays above book value (ratio of market to book value) was plotted versus revenue growth and economic profit (EP) (defined as return on invested capital % minus the weighted average cost of capital %), which in turn contributes to an increase in shareholder value, as shown in Figure 1-4.

You will notice that ROIC—the ratio of profit to invested capital—is the strongest driver of high stock market multiples of book value (indicated by the steep rise as ROIC increases). Revenue growth is a strong second.

The relationship between ROIC and revenue growth can be rolled up into one number: *net present value (NPV).*[4] Throughout this book you'll see NPV used to help select *priority* projects, because a high

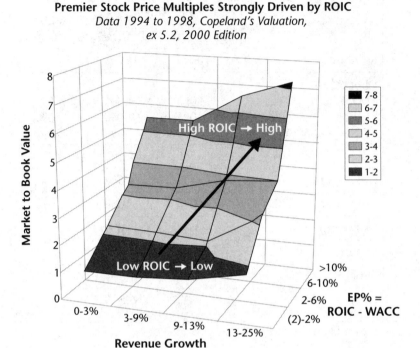

Figure 1-4. The empirical link between ROIC, growth, and stock price: "the value mountain"

NPV indicates the likelihood that improvement will contribute to shareholder value. NPV can be applied at many levels: to overall value streams (the sets of activities that transform a customer opportunity into a delivered outcome) or to individual projects. In the tier-one auto example, all products were produced in the same value stream (the production of brake hoses). When a company possesses multiple product lines or markets, it must select which value stream to improve first, and one of the best indicators is NPV. In fact, we recommend you select value streams for improvement based on the potential increase in net present value, confident that these projects will make the greatest contribution to shareholder value.

But are we putting too much emphasis on financial metrics at the expense of customer value? Not at all! The Voice of the Customer is represented within the value creation that leads to increased revenue retention and growth rates of the company.

So how does Lean Six Sigma deliver on its value proposition? The essential elements of the Lean Six Sigma process provide the framework (see Part Two for details):

1. Increasing shareholder value requires higher ROIC and growth, both of which roll up into one number: net present value (NPV).
2. Value streams for improvement should be selected based on potential increase in NPV.
3. Once a value stream has been selected, customers' critical-to-quality issues and the time traps (less than 20% of the activities) should yield project ideas.
4. Projects are selected based on the highest rates of return (the benefit-to-effort ratio).
5. The projects are then attacked using the Lean Six Sigma improvement tools.

LEAN SIX SIGMA AND MRP

One reason why Lean Six Sigma can deliver results faster is that it uses data stored in MRP systems to locate time traps and define what kind of improvement is necessary. This gives "eyes" to the improvement process. Many who advocated Lean or Six Sigma separately were somewhat aloof about MRP systems. ERP systems have been criticized by some advocates of Lean because they claim it "pushes" unneeded material into the line, causing congestion and poor flow. Lean Six Sigma makes use of the ERP "order point" to trigger releases from the pull system (Chapter 13) to prevent congestion. Thus MRP systems are enablers of Lean Six Sigma, which in turn creates a significant return on investment on these systems.

THE POWER IS IN THE TOTAL PROCESS

Though each piece of the Lean Six Sigma process can add value to your organization, the real gains will come from seeing the methods as a complete process that help you determine and implement clear direction from the board room to the frontline office or factory floor.

Earlier in the chapter, we showed that *slow* processes are *expensive* processes. As it turns out, slow processes are generally low-quality processes as well. In fact, time and quality are intimately linked, just as Lean and Six Sigma are inextricably linked as partners in cost reduction, lead time, and quality improvement. A firm that does only one will be driven to the other—or will simply fail to make rapid progress, since it will have to effectively invent the other process on the fly.

Why do you need Lean Six Sigma? Superior speed, quality, and cost are the engines driving productivity and revenue growth and sustained competitive advantage. Because of its speed in reducing process lead times, quality defects, cost, and invested capital, Lean Six Sigma provides common direction from the organizational leaders to managers and employees.

Understanding the Lean Six Sigma value proposition is a prerequisite for understanding what Lean Six Sigma really is and how to use it to greatest advantage. As you'll see in the next three chapters, there are essential cultural structures—such as true management engagement—and tools that are necessary for effective implementation. When these pieces are in place, Lean Six Sigma's relentless pursuit of product quality and process speed leads to corporate success and to personal success for the people who contribute to that journey. In a recent conference, Lockheed Martin summed up current thinking in the title of its presentation: "It's not Lean or Six Sigma, it's not Lean then Six Sigma, it's Lean and Six Sigma."

TO LEARN MORE

- Chapter 2 provides an overview of what Six Sigma contributes to the picture; Chapter 3 does the same for Lean methods.
- Chapter 4 shows how the elements of Six Sigma and Lean create a more powerful improvement engine.
- Part Two provides a review of and directions for the implementation of Lean Six Sigma.

Notes

1. The tier-one auto supplier was a former division of United Technologies Automotive, renamed Preferred Technical Group. The financial results cited are from the S1 Registration Statement.
2. For example, ProfiSight Technologies, www.profisight.com, protected by U.S. Patent 5,195,041, and 5,351,195.
3. *Valuation: Measuring and Managing the Value of Companies,* Copeland, Koller, and Murrin, 2000.
4. *Takeovers, Restructuring, and Corporate Governance,* J. Fred Weston, Kwang S. Chung and Jung A. Siu, Second Edition, 1998, p. 198.

Chapter 2

Six Sigma:
The Power of
Culture

Quality is the most important factor in business.
—Andrew Carnegie

A ndrew Carnegie understood the importance of quality and the elimination of variation as a competitive weapon. The cost of ore was based on the mine's reputation rather than measurement and critically determined the cost and capital of the company. A few years after he had hired a German chemist, Dr. Fricke, he remarked: "Nine-tenths of the uncertainties of pig-iron making were dispelled under the burning sun of his chemical knowledge. ... What fools we had been! But then there was this consolation: we were not as great a fool as our competitors, who said they could not afford to hire a chemist.... We had almost the entire monopoly of scientific management."

One of the critical lessons you learn from Carnegie was his personal *engagement* in the quality and manufacturing process and his personal selection of managers who would transform his goals into *action through continuous improvement and innovation.* In a very real sense, the Six Sigma culture and infrastructure is the embodiment of these principles in a form that any company can implement. While Carnegie's tombstone simply gives his name and dates of birth and death, at one point he suggested an epitaph he felt would be appropriate and captured his management philosophy: "Here

15

lies a man who was able to surround himself with men far cleverer than himself."

The only component of Six Sigma that Carnegie missed, to his dismay, was including his workers as part of the team. The essential difference between Six Sigma and all other prior initiatives is in the culture. Six Sigma was the first initiative that demanded the engagement of the CEO and P&L managers. It was the first to require them to commit 1% of the workforce to receive four weeks of training and their subsequent full-time commitment to improvement projects as black belts. Finally, Six Sigma was also the first to tie specific gains to quality improvements, asserting that each black belt should be able to contribute between $250,000 to $1,000,000 of increased operating profit per year.

Thus Six Sigma was the first improvement initiative that tied a level of investment to a clear profit return, the language a CEO can understand.

Anyone who has worked within a Six Sigma-driven organization knows Six Sigma isn't just an "improvement methodology." It is ...

- A **system** of management to achieve lasting business leadership and top performance applied to benefit the business and its customers, associates, and shareholders.
- A **measure** to define the capability of any process.
- A **goal** for improvement that reaches near-perfection.

The sigma level numbers often associated with Six Sigma represents the capability of a core business process, as measured in *defects per million opportunities*:

Sigma Level	Defects per Million Opportunities	Yield
6	3.4	99.9997%
5	233	99.977%
4	6,210	99.379%
3	66,807	93.32%
2	308,537	69.2%
1	690,000	31%

The "per million opportunities" aspect of the Six Sigma metric is critical because it allows you to compare the capability of widely different processes. The sigma metric makes sure that simpler processes, which have fewer steps and fewer chances for something to go wrong,

aren't given an advantage over more complex processes. (Having 20 errors in a four-step process is a higher *rate* of defects than having 50 errors in a 40-step process.)

The source of defects is almost always linked to *variation* in some form: variation in materials, procedures, process conditions, etc. (As you'll see, Lean Six Sigma expands the scope of variation to include *time*: missed deadlines, variability in lead times, and so on.) That's why the fundamental thesis of Six Sigma is that *variation is evil* because a high level of variation means customers will not get what they want—with all that that implies for retention, marketing efficiency, and revenue growth.

The system needed to achieve Six Sigma creates a culture characterized by:

Customer centricity: The knowledge of what the customer values most is the start of value stream analysis.

Financial results: No project or effort is undertaken unless there is evidence indicating how much shareholder value will be created. The goal is for each black belt to deliver an average of $500,000 of improved operating profit per year.

Management engagement: The CEO, executives, and managers are *engaged* in Six Sigma. They have designated responsibilities for overseeing and guiding Six Sigma projects to make sure those projects stay focused on organizational priorities.

Resource commitment: A significant number, typically 1% to 3% of the organization's staff, is devoted to Six Sigma efforts full-time and other employees are expected to participate regularly on projects.

Execution infrastructure: The hierarchy of specific roles (such as black belts and master black belts) provides ways to integrate Six Sigma projects into the "real work" of the organization and sustain the rate of improvement.

Let's expand on each of these important characteristics.

CRITICAL SUCCESS FACTORS FOR SIX SIGMA

Customer Centricity

The Six Sigma culture is *customer-centric*; its goal is to delight customers. The quality of a product or service is measured from the customer's perspective, by its contribution to their success. This customer focus comes through the Six Sigma drivers:

Voice of the Customer: What the customers say they want.

Requirements: Voice of the Customer input that is translated into specific, measurable elements.

Critical to Quality (CTQ): Requirements that are most important to customers.

Defect: Failing to deliver to a customer's CTQ.

Design for Six Sigma: Designing products and processes based on customer requirements.

The gaps between what customers desire and what you can currently deliver are the areas where significant value can be created for both supplier and customer. Thus Six Sigma is focused on addressing these gaps, increasing operating profit, and becoming part of the DNA of the company and its operations.

Six Sigma provides the discipline to help companies go beyond an anecdotal understanding of customer wants and needs to specific requirements-driven process metrics. This changes behavior from firefighting to disciplined improvement based on customer satisfaction.

Every defect in a process not only reduces quality but creates a time delay, generates an additional cost, and produces an associated loss of operating profit. The actual cost of defects depends, of course, on the process.

Here's an example. For the tier-one auto supplier described in Chapter 1, the cost of a brake hose "leaker" was not only the cost of rework, but also the cost of Q1 status with Ford, the potential loss of revenue, and the cost of potential product liabilities. These leakers were a critical-to-quality defect (when compared with other defects that affected the product's appearance only and were of no importance given the position of the product in the vehicle). Therefore, the benefit of improving quality to prevent leakers both dictated the choice of the value stream where the company should focus its improvement resources and went far beyond the savings from less rework and scrap.

This example demonstrates why the goal of Six Sigma is to uncover as many defects as possible—especially those that are critical to quality. In the words of Kiichiro Toyoda, the founder of Toyota, "Every defect is a treasure"—*if* the company can uncover its cause and work to prevent it *across the corporation*. This customer-centric culture is appropriate in an economy of intense global competition where the customer is supreme and has a multitude of alternatives to fulfill their needs.

Financial Results

At the heart of Six Sigma is a focus on financial results that reflects lessons learned the hard way. Total Quality Management (TQM), the principal quality initiative that immediately preceded Six Sigma, often positioned the need to solve quality problems as a moral imperative. With most TQM programs, there was no clear way of prioritizing which quality projects should receive the highest priority; an almost religious fervor caused projects to be carried out regardless of cost to the corporation or value to the customer. TQM was often led by people who had a modest understanding of the drivers of shareholder value and tended to invent their own metrics.

All that changed with Six Sigma, where financial performance is paramount.

This is not meant in criticism of the hard-working quality professionals who made great strides to make TQM successful. The CEO was seldom involved and to the P&L managers, TQM was regarded as ancillary to making money and a cross that management had to bear in the full knowledge that *"this too shall pass."*

In TQM's defense, it had complete success in the few cases in which it anticipated the culture of Six Sigma, i.e., customer centricity, financial results, management engagement, resource commitment, and execution infrastructure. In fact, the quality tools of Six Sigma and TQM are nearly identical. But while TQM has probably gotten a bum rap to some extent, a CEO can afford no patience with ineffective initiatives—which TQM efforts too often were.

Six Sigma speaks the language of the CEO. That's why Six Sigma is quite explicit about financial benefits expected from each and every effort. Black belts and champions are expected to contribute between $250,000 and $1,000,000 of incremental operating profit each year (and/or capital reduction times the cost of capital).

These expectations tie Six Sigma to the financial goals of the company as no other improvement process has before it. There are some up-front costs: a lot of time and money is invested in the training and startup phase. But a well-designed Lean Six Sigma process more than pays its costs during the first year of implementation.

Management Engagement

Back when TQM was the buzzword of the day, I well remember an incident at one of the greatest companies in America, with revenue of over $15 billion. The CEO, a truly outstanding executive, brought in the widely respected Dr. W. Edwards Deming, certainly a prime mover in the quality movement, for a two-day session to train all the senior executives. The CEO told his executives he was totally committed to the process and expected their complete attention and support in the ongoing program. He further insisted that every manager watch the 16-hour videotape of Deming's lecture, and introduced Deming. The CEO then immediately departed the meeting. A senior manager who attended that meeting told me that "commitment flew out the window" with him. People made fun of Deming's acerbic style and signed the clipboard log as having watched the videos when they had actually only scanned the outside of their cases.

This CEO no doubt properly felt that he had *endorsed* TQM and was probably surprised when nothing happened as a result of Deming's lectures. Given the hindsight of 15 years of experience, we can all now agree that endorsement is inadequate.

In contrast, one of the brightest applications of TQM occurred at Iomega in 1992. The company has had many ups and downs and operates in a very tough environment. In 1991 it was in a down period and under great cost pressure. It then took about 16 days to produce their Bernoulli Box mass storage device. The president, Fred Wenninger, was an advocate of TQM and Lean, which he had applied at Hewlett-Packard. He was actively *engaged* in the process, assigned about 20 people full time to the process, and supported the training of 250 other employees. In less than nine months, the lead time had dropped from 16 days to less than three days. The company's overhead and quality cost fell dramatically, margins rose, and the company's stock price nearly doubled.

This approach was really a precursor of what we now know as the Six Sigma culture: an infrastructure needed for success anchored by strong management involvement. In fact the word *engaged* management is due to Wenninger.

As noted, the problem with the first company was that TQM offered very little of interest to a CEO; there were seldom explicit financial results that could be linked to a CEO's annual or strategic goals. Many TQM efforts were implemented on blind faith that "things would get better" if quality improved. The problem was not the *people*; it was the *process*.

Six Sigma has changed all this with its emphasis on financial results that make it clear what executives will gain and have gained through their continued involvement. As with TQM, however, the results are self-evident: the biggest gains have been made in companies where executives are an integral part of Six Sigma deployment.

Resource Commitment

Typical full-time commitment of personnel to Six Sigma efforts is roughly 1% of the company's population, though I've seen situations where it reached 3% because there were sufficient opportunities for achieving significant gains. But far more important than the *number* of people is the *quality* of the commitment. Black belts and champions must be full time to achieve sustainable results. Six Sigma requires that champions and black belts be selected based on their potential for becoming the future leaders of the corporation. This makes managers, who have got to get out their billings, often say, "How am I going to get my designs out if I give up my best engineers and program managers?"

The simple answer is that you need to make sure the projects selected are of highest priority to the organization and its customers. Then it's not a question of giving up anything, but rather devoting current resources to the highest priorities based on their potential to contribute to shareholder value. Those projects always get a lot more effort than is currently the case, whereas lower-value projects may be delayed. Ultimately, the champion will present the opportunities to his P&L manager for approval.

One of the benefits of selecting the future leaders as black belts and champions is that they will receive an exemplary experience in every facet of business management and effective use of resources. They will develop a customer-centric process, rather than departmental view of the business. Further, the potential for fast-track advancement based on a few years' success as a black belt works to retain this intellectual capital of the corporation.

Execution Infrastructure

Six Sigma possesses an infrastructure that effectively translates the CEO's agenda into a customer-centric set of projects chosen to maximize shareholder value and provides effective management and monitoring of results versus plan (see Figure 2-1).

Starting at the top ...

■ The corporate champions are armed with the CEO and P&L manager's agenda for financial performance and shareholder value increase.

■ These strategic goals are translated to an operational agenda by the business unit champions (sometimes called "deployment champions") who report to the P&L managers. These unit champions are

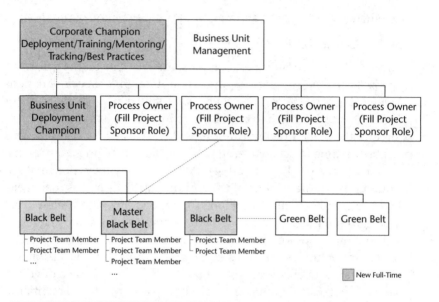

Figure 2-1. Six Sigma infrastructure

trained in the methods of identifying key value streams and prioritizing projects based on net present value (their potential contribution to shareholder value). The P&L manager has the ultimate authority for value stream identification and project selection, since his or her commitment to the process is essential for success.

- The customer critical-to-quality issues and the time traps within the key value stream are developed into projects and then prioritized. These projects (to execute cost reductions, quality improvements, etc.) are then executed by the black belts, who have been trained in the tools and team leadership skills of Lean Six Sigma.

- Project sponsors (who are or report to the P&L manager) own the process that is to be improved by a specific project. They have the specific authority to implement improvements and have ultimate long-term accountability for ensuring that the improvements and financial benefits stick.

- Implementation is accomplished by a mix of team members, including green belts (team members), black belts, and master black belts. Whereas the black belts and champions are assigned full time to improvement activities, the green belts who support black belt projects are generally part time and have received less training. (See Figure 2-2 for a comparison of these roles.)

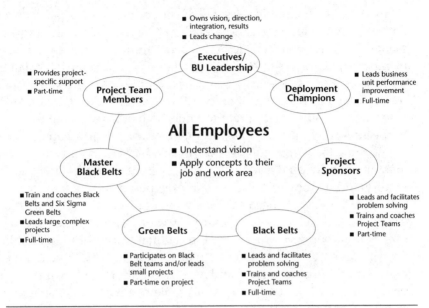

Figure 2-2. Performance improvement organization structure

You can also track the linkages in the reverse direction. Starting from the front line, the black belts and others can propose project ideas to their champion and business unit manager. These ideas are transmitted to the business unit champion (often via a Web-based tracking tool), who reports to the business unit GM. The business unit GM and controller review the projects with the champion and provide required financial data and verify savings potential. These projects are then ready to be prioritized against other known projects to ensure that those with the highest returns are executed next.

PREDICTING TEAM SUCCESS, PREVENTING TEAM FAILURE

The success of Six Sigma is ultimately dependent on the ability of teams to execute projects effectively. It might be thought that the assembly of many brilliant individuals would be a satisfactory approach, but that perspective has been proven false time and time again. Even the Six Sigma culture can't over come poor team composition. Although team design and leadership skills were not discussed in the early books on the subject, firms have been driven in this direction to attain results. We now have a number of different psychological models which point in the same direction and provide insight into the prediction of team success and failure. One area of common agreement is that it is possible to get much better results from a team if each member is playing his or her "preferred role," and if there is a balance of these essential roles on a team. Inexpensive software is available which facilitates relatively simple testing, which makes it possible to determine an individual's preferred role, both in his eyes and those of his peers. We will discuss this important topic again in Chapter 9.

To draw the best out of the team, master black belts and black belts must hone individual leadership skills, such as the ability to balance inquiry and advocacy in the pursuit of superior results from teams. Organizations experienced in the implementation of Six Sigma programs, such as ITT Industries, Starwood Hotels, and GE, have recognized the importance of team and individual leadership skills in the Six Sigma process and include training in this area as a basic requirement. In addition to understanding how to structure a team, black belts must learn the basics of team problem solving and facilitation skills so that they may be effective change agents.

THE SIX SIGMA PROCESS AND IMPROVEMENT TOOLS

You may be surprised that it's taken this long in the discussion of Six Sigma before the quality improvement tools were mentioned. That's because more organizations fail from a lack of creating the right culture and infrastructure than from using the wrong tools!

Some companies think Lean and Six Sigma is just a bag of tools and have attempted to implement Six Sigma by sending off people to black belt training and failing to make any of the substantive cultural changes described above. These programs end as just another "program of the month" failure. If you don't have the other elements discussed above—management engagement, a strong infrastructure, and so on—any effort put into improvement methods and tools will just be a waste of time.

So the key lesson as you're reading through this section is not to get lost in the statistical weeds or the improvement tools. Important as these are, the source of power is first and foremost in the *culture*.

Still, the improvement process and tools associated with Six Sigma are incredibly powerful. Motorola recognized that there was a pattern to improvement (and use of data and process tools) that could naturally be divided into the five phases of problem solving, usually referred by the acronym DMAIC (da-may-ick), which stands for

Define-Measure-Analyze-Improve-Control. The DMAIC steps are shown in Table 2-1 and described below. You will notice that at each of the DMAIC phases, tools associated with both Lean and Six Sigma are included:

- The purpose of the **Define** phase is to clarify the goals and value of a project. Teams and champions use those tools necessary to assess the magnitude of the value opportunity in a given value stream, the resources required, and a design of the problem-solving process.

- Assuming that the project is approved by the champion, the team proceeds to the **Measure** phase, in which the members gather data on the problem. Here, they primarily use data collection tools, process mapping, Pareto analysis, run charts, etc. (Teams working on non-manufacturing processes are often surprised at how much they gain by completing the Measure phase, because their processes have never been mapped or studied with data.)

- In the **Analyze** phase, the team examines its data and process maps to characterize the nature and extent of the defect. The tools help them pinpoint the time traps and define the tools in priority order. This detailed knowledge about the problem lays the groundwork for finding improvements (in the next phase) that will address the underlying causes of the problem.

- The **Improve** phase applies a powerful tool set to eliminate defects in both quality and process velocity (lead time and on-time delivery).

- When the process has achieved the required quality level, the tools of the **Control** phase are employed to lock in the benefits. Some of these Control tools, such as mistake proofing (known as *poka-yoke* in Japanese), create a monitoring, gauging, and feedback system to instantly detect and correct trends—and to shut down the process if necessary. Mistake proofing makes it impossible for the process to create defects.

Becoming familiar with the DMAIC process and knowing how and when to use data and process tools are critical for successful Six Sigma teams—and adding in the Lean tools makes the skill set even more robust. Do not assume that your employees have this knowledge; a brief glance at the tool set (Table 2-1) should convince you that this is a rich set of tools that could be very perplexing to a newly minted black belt. Most people will need training in the basic tools; in-depth comprehension of some of the complex tools (e.g., Design of

Process	Activity	Tools	
Define	1. Establish Team Charter 2. Identify Sponsor and Team Resources 3. Administer Pre-Work	Project ID Tools Project Definition Form NPV/IRR/DCF Analysis	PIP Management Process SSPI Toolkit
Measure	4. Confirm Team Goal 5. Define Current State 6. Collect and Display Data	SSPI Toolkit Process Mapping Value Analysis Brainstorming Voting Techniques Pareto Charts Affinity/ID	C&E/Fishbones FMEA Check Sheets Run Charts Control Charts Gage R&R
Analyze	7. Determine Process Capability and Speed 8. Determine Sources of Variation and Time Bottlenecks	C_p and C_{pk} Supply Chain Accelerator Time Trap Analysis Multi-Vari Box Plots Marginal Plots Interaction Plots	Regression ANOVA C&E Matrices FMEA Problem Definition Forms Opportunity Maps
Improve	9. Generate Ideas 10. Conduct Experiments 11. Create Straw Models 12. Conduct B's and C's 13. Develop Action Plans 14. Implement	Brainstorming Pull Systems Setup Reduction TPM Process Flow Benchmarking Affinity/ID DOE	Hypothesis Testing Process Mapping B's and C's/Force Field Tree Diagrams Pert/CPM PDPC/FMEA Gantt Charts
Control	15. Develop Control Plan 16. Monitor Performance 17. Mistake-Proof Process	Check Sheets Run Charts Histograms Scatter Diagrams	Control Charts Pareto Charts Interactive Reviews Poka-Yoke

Table 2-1. Lean Six Sigma tool set

Experiments, time trap determination of process delays, pull system design, etc.) can be obtained by enrichment courses for black belts or master black belts.

Design of Experiments: Secret Weapon of the Rapidly Improving

The complete tool set of Lean Six Sigma is vast; important parts of it are discussed in Chapters 10 and 11 in some detail. One Six Sigma tool that demands special attention is Design of Experiments (DOE), an entire body of knowledge around how to manipulate process and product design factors to discover the *combination* that is most effective, efficient, and/or robust in actual operating conditions. There are many variations of DOE (the Classical, Taguchi, and Evolutionary Operations models, to name just a few), but all address the issue of yield improvement through reduction of variation. I'd like to give you an example from our tier-one auto supplier.

If you look back at the list of Top 10 Time Traps (improvement opportunities) developed by the tier-one auto supplier (Figure 1-1), the fourth-highest priority was "DOE at Brazing." The company had already contained the customer critical-to-quality problem by mistake-proofing the tester. Now the internal time trap analysis indicated that the 1%-3% scrap rate at the braze operation was the next major time trap and cost opportunity. This problem had been with the company for years.

Very briefly, the machined and threaded coupling was brazed onto a pipe. Typically, 3%-5% of the output was rejected. If the viscosity of the solder was too low, the braze did not adequately cover the joint. If viscosity was too high, it did not provide a mechanically strong connection and might fail in a vibration test or in the field.

The challenge here arose because there were many major factors that could affect the quality of the brazing and that *interacted*. While viscosity is generally a function of temperature, many other factors affect adequate coverage and mechanical strength, including the chemical composition of the braze, the preparation method to ensure cleanliness of the coupling and pipe, the temperature of the braze material, and the preheat temperature of coupling and pipe.

No one really knew enough about the physics and chemistry of this process to compute the best combination of factors: this company needed a method for looking at the key factors simultaneously. And that's why they turned to Design of Experiments.

After making sure that the measurement system was precise enough to detect the effects being measured, the company conducted a designed experiment around what they believed were the four most important process factors, each tested at two levels:

- Temperature of the brazing material (high or low, denoted as + and – in Table 2-2).
- Whether the components were preheated (yes or no).
- Chemical composition of the braze (two mixtures, denoted with H and L).
- Preparation method (two methods, denoted as C and A).

Trial	1	2	3	4	5	6	7	8	9	10	11	12	13	14	15	16
Braze Temp	+	–	+	–	+	–	+	–	+	–	+	–	+	–	+	–
Preheat	+	+	–	–	+	+	–	–	+	+	–	–	+	+	–	–
Braze Chemistry	H	H	H	H	L	L	L	L	H	H	H	H	L	L	L	L
Prep Meth	C	C	C	C	C	C	C	C	A	A	A	A	A	A	A	A

Table 2-2. Trial experiment for brazing

Table 2-2 shows that this designed experiment would consist of 16 trials in which every possible combination of the four process factors would be tested. During each trial, the results were measured by using an index to gauge the spread of the resulting flow/coverage. (An index of 5 is ideal.) As a result of these trials, the company was able to define which combination of these factors produced the best result (highest quality with fewest defects), as shown in Figure 2-3.

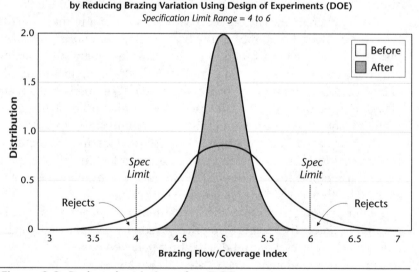

Figure 2-3. Reduced variation after DOE

As a result of their designed experiment, this company was able to:

- Quickly and simultaneously test key factors and interactions (rather than experimenting on one factor at a time) to understand how main events and interactions affect yield.

- Expand its knowledge of how key factors influenced the process.
- Identify the *combination* of factor settings that would optimize output quality.
- Understand how robust the optimum values were against environmental "noise."

This example also reinforces the links between Lean and Six Sigma—time *and* quality. Because Lean was implemented together with Six Sigma, the process velocity greatly increased. That meant the company could run smaller lots for each part number about *five times faster* than the initial process, with *no increase in cost*. In terms of learning, the company could even complete additional experiments for each major product five times faster than before the improvements and hopefully reduce variation five times as fast. (In the next chapter, you'll see additional reasons why this lead time gain is important.)

But does a busy CEO need to be aware of such an arcane quality tool? Let's hear from Lou Giuliano, the CEO of ITT Industries

> We have some divisions within our businesses that I know we could not operate today if we didn't have the practice of regularly using quality improvement tools—tools such as Taguchi methodologies [Design of Experiments]—on a regular and routine basis. The one that comes to mind specifically is our Night Vision business, where we make night vision goggles for the U.S. Army and allied militaries all over the world. Producing Night Vision goggles is a very complex process.... [T]en years ago there were four U.S. manufacturers in that business. Today there are two. The other two have gone out of business, and the other one that still is in business has been losing money for years. Over that ten-year period we've been making money consistently and earning in excess of our cost of capital—even though it's a very capital-intensive business. I credit continuous process improvement for this success."[1]

Design of Experiments is one of the most powerful tools in the Six Sigma repertoire, but similar gains can be made with many of the simpler tools as well—especially in organizations that have not yet applied Six Sigma methods to their processes. Tools such as flowcharts, run charts, and Pareto charts and help organizations pinpoint the true causes of a problem, which is the most important step on the road to finding effective solutions.

The e-Infrastructure

There is one more tool associated with Six Sigma that usually doesn't appear on any lists but which is proving to be vital.

E-tracking systems also allow people throughout the infrastructure to monitor the effectiveness of black belt projects. All projects can be viewed on the web, and rolled up by the company champion for easy comparison to the CEO's plan for increased ROIC and revenue growth. Plan versus actual outputs of each business unit are available, and can be drilled down to the project level detail if so desired. Some are even using software to evaluate team strengths and weaknesses.

In a Six Sigma organization, teams are not set adrift to wander through the DMAIC process on their own. Rather, the deployment champion and project sponsor conduct a gate review with the black belt at each phase of the DMAIC process, to make sure the project goals are attainable and still relevant to corporate needs. E-tracking tools allow the operating profit results of black belt teams to be audited by the controller at the P&L unit, then rolled up to the group and corporate level. This allows the CEO to track improvements in operating profit versus plan, as seen in the bar graph in Figure 2-4 (sources of Six Sigma conferences, consultants, and sources of tracking tools can be found at www.isixsigma.com).

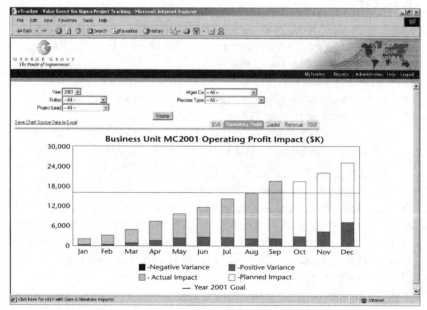

Figure 2-4. eTracker year-to-date impact chart

THE ROLE OF SIX SIGMA AS A METRIC

As a *process* metric, sigma level undoubtedly has value as an indicator of how often your organization's work fails to meet customer needs. Some advocates of Six Sigma have claimed that the concept also works at the corporate level. By some estimates, a manufacturer operating at 2 to 3 sigma guarantees that 15% of revenue is being wasted as cost of quality; by improving cost of quality to the 5 or 6 sigma level, that wasted 15% of revenue can be transformed into operating profit.

But other companies have been disappointed in trying to use the sigma level of the whole corporation as a valid metric. In service organizations, and even at the enterprise level of manufacturing firms, it's not always clear what should be counted as a "defect":

- From customers' perspective, long lead time and lead time variation are a defect that causes them to invest more capital in inventory (because they can't rely on getting the product when they need it from you, the supplier).
- Long lead time also causes excess internal costs, which is certainly a defect from the shareholders' perspective.

Attempts at calculating a meaningful enterprise sigma level opens a Pandora's box. Do you count long lead time as one defect? Or do you need to weight it by the thousands of products shipped late or by their cost to the client or by the lost revenue they entail in the future? Should excess inventory be counted as one defect? Or should each dollar, penny, or mil be a defect? Should we not count a new product that has excessive cost or poor performance as a defect? Is it one defect or many?

These non-manufacturing defects have enormous impact on operating profit and their removal can lead to huge improvements in operating profit and capital reduction. But is their importance related to the number of defects per million opportunities or rather to their value? These issues have not been addressed by many Six Sigma practitioners. Lean Six Sigma relates process improvement to specific income statement and balance sheet items rather than asserting that a company that achieves a higher sigma level will improve operating profit. I am sure it's true in a gross sense, but we prefer a more direct linkage.

The best approach is to use the sigma level as a *process* metric. Measure initial sigma capabilities for specific core processes as a baseline, then recalculate them once you have improved those processes. Defects—be they due to process quality or process velocity or any other source—should be weighted not on their *frequency*, but on their *importance* to customers and their *impact* on shareholder value at the enterprise level. This has the further merit that it ties the improvement process into metrics that the operating managers are trying to improve.

THE KEY IS IN THE CULTURE

We have talked a lot about the culture of Six Sigma, whereas most books put far more emphasis on the tools. It is my contention that the culture of Six Sigma is the reason for its success. It has been wisely stated that "culture eats strategy for breakfast." In Chapter 4, for example, we will provide data that indicates that most efforts succeed or fail based on *execution*; few fail for lack of a good strategy. Six Sigma provides the cultural framework to convert good strategy into good execution.

KEY MESSAGES OF SIX SIGMA

- Everything starts with the customer.
- The infrastructure for cultural change is the most powerful contribution of Six Sigma.
- Decisions about which projects to pursue must be based at least in part on the potential impact on net present value.
- Sustained improvement is possible only with management engagement.
- CEO goals are translated to frontline projects and coordinated through an organization of people and technical resources.
- A standard problem-solving process and associated tool set provides the means for basing decisions on data.

TO LEARN MORE

- Chapter 3 will explore Lean methods, then the two key elements of Six Sigma and Lean are brought together in Chapter 4.
- Implementation of the Six Sigma components is defined in Part Two.

Note

1. Lou Giuliano, Chairman, President and Chief Executive of ITT Industries, speaking at the Value-Based Six Sigma Executive Summit on June 26, 2000 in New York. Transcript available from George Group.

Lean Means Speed

Henry Ford was the first person to understand the impact of process speed on cost, the first to understand that inventory slowed down his process, and that slow processes are wasteful processes. He said:

> Ordinarily, money put into inventory is thought of as live money, ... but it is waste—which, like every other form of waste, turns up in high prices. We do not own or use a single warehouse! Time waste differs from material waste in that there can be no salvage.

This insight is counterintuitive; after all, isn't inventory an asset? In this chapter we will replace Ford's intuitive grasp with a logical description of why slow processes are expensive and how they can be accelerated. Ford's "process" was fabulously successful for a dozen years ... but ultimately failed because it could only produce one product.

The sovereignty of the customer and the profusion of products to satisfy every need require a process that can responsively deliver many different products with high velocity, high quality, low cost, and minimal invested capital. The goal of Lean is to quickly make to order a profusion of different products with the low cost first attained by Ford.

These seeming contradictions—low cost combined with high quality and high speed—were first overcome by Toyota. Their system was,
however, limited to the repetitive manufacture of a limited variety of
high-volume products. The Lean enterprise is a *generalization* of the
Toyota Production System (also known as just-in-time) to all processes.

As we mentioned before, Lean thinking is counterintuitive; hence a
sound understanding is necessary to build a roadmap to achieve these
goals. Lean remains a largely misunderstood improvement process.
One of my principal goals in writing this book is to equip the diligent
manager with a profound understanding of Lean, gained from more
than a hundred implementations during the last dozen years. The natural place to start is by looking at what most people think of as Lean.

IS THIS LEAN?

My friend Robert Martichenko of Transfreight, an expert in Lean logistics, likes to explain Lean by describing an idealized plant tour
inspired by actual experience. He "tours" a small company where
they believe they are practicing Lean manufacturing. This company
has one of the simplest product lines imaginable: they make widgets
in two colors, red and green. While he is there, he notices they are
making green widgets all day long. (When they don't have to change
the paint line, they can make 400 green widgets per day.)

In the middle of the day, the Logistics Manager, John, tells Robert,
"Watch this ... Lean at its best!" At that moment, the manufacturing
line is on its last box of green widget handles. Wouldn't you know it?
A truck shows up with a full load of green widget handles and the day
is saved because of the Lean system in place. John is very proud that
the truck showed up "just in time." After the day is over, Robert sits
down and asks John a few basic questions:

1. How many customer orders do you have confirmed for green
   widgets?
2. Why are you manufacturing only green widgets today?
3. On Tuesdays, do customers use only green widgets?
4. Why did you order a whole truckload of green widget handles?
5. Why will you still be making green widgets tomorrow when
   more than half of today's production is still in inventory?

John tells Robert that they had orders on the books for only 200
green widgets, but they make green ones all day because of the manufacturing economies of scale. As for the truckload of green widget

handles, well, the supplier gives such great volume discounts that John buys in truckload quantity. "But," John said, "the truck never shows up until we are just running out." (John didn't mention that a truckload of widget handles would last for two months!)

Is John really practicing Lean production? Unfortunately for his company, he is not enjoying the cost and process speed advantages of Lean.

The truth is that Lean is not just a raw material procurement strategy, but rather a process philosophy, with three purposes:

- To eliminate wasted time, effort, and material.
- to provide customers with make-to-order products.
- To reduce cost while improving quality.

THE ESSENTIALS OF LEAN

As in most factories, the material in the widget line spent more than 95% of its time waiting … waiting for value to be added … or waiting in finished goods inventory for a customer. In contrast, the goal of Lean is to virtually eliminate wait time. Instead, every operation becomes so flexible that the *actual* usage by the customer creates a demand on the factory to build *only* the amount consumed by the customer, whether external or internal. The Lean factory is flexible enough to efficiently build in small batches to keep up with consumption. When this goal is achieved, parts will move directly from one workstation to another at high velocity and reduce the waiting time, work in process, and finished goods inventory by 50%-80%.

Think of the factory as a water hose. If water is moving slowly, a larger-diameter pipe is needed to deliver a given volume per minute, so lots of water (work in process) is effectively trapped in the pipe. Lean can increase the velocity by a factor of five, so we can reduce the cross section and hence the WIP by a factor of five.

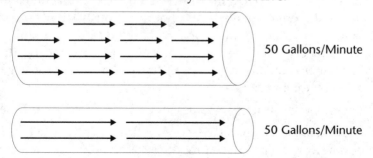

50 Gallons/Minute

50 Gallons/Minute

Figure 3-1. Velocity and WIP

As velocity increases, the cost of stockrooms, material movers and equipment, expediters, scrap, rework, obsolescence, excess capital expenditures—the *Hidden Factory*—will be removed. As a rule of thumb, if the waiting time is reduced by 80%, the manufacturing overhead and quality cost will drop by 20%. If the allocation of costs shown in Chapter 1 in Figure 1-3 is true, this will increase operating profit by roughly 5%.

The Keys to the Kingdom of Lean are founded on two principles that are observed in every factory or process we have ever encountered:

- Material usually spends 95% of its time waiting, which is due to the time delay injected by fewer than 20% of the workstations, which are known as *time traps*.
- Time traps can be prioritized using MRP data and the spreadsheet calculations or software and eliminated using the Lean Six Sigma improvement methods of Table 2-3.

Identifying and prioritizing time traps—at the most basic level, that's all you need to know about Lean! The rest of this chapter discusses how this process is implemented, with the details discussed in Chapter 13. You'll see that the basic principles and improvement opportunities apply to *any* process, not just manufacturing, and together they create a Lean enterprise.

THE LEAN METRIC: CYCLE EFFICIENCY

Since speed is a key goal of Lean, the natural questions are "How fast is fast?" and "How slow is slow?"

The answer comes by comparing the amount of *value-added time* (work that a *customer* would recognize as necessary to create the product or service) and the *total lead time* (how long the process takes from start to end). If the value-added time needed to manufacture a product down the critical path is 100 hours of touch labor (including machining, assembly, testing, etc.), to be world-class the total lead time should not exceed 400 hours. These two figures come together to produce a metric called *process cycle efficiency*[1] that we can use to gauge the potential for cost reduction:

Process Cycle Efficiency = Value-Added Time / Total Lead Time

A marketing executive at a major ERP firm recently asked me for a metric that would tell him if a process was lean or not. The answer is:

A Lean process is one in which the value-added time in the process is more than 25% of the total lead time of that process.

Let's look at one example. The tier-one auto supplier described earlier in this book knew that there was less than three hours of value-added time in their process (the time needed to machine, braze, assemble, and test a coupled hose fitting). However, the total lead time from release of raw material into the line to shipment was an average of 12 eight-hour days.

The ratio of these two measures gives us process cycle efficiency:

value-added time = 3 hours

total lead time = 12 * 8 = 96 hours

process cycle efficiency = 3 hours / 96 hours = 3%

In other words, it is taking 12 days to stick three hours of value into the product—the material is *waiting* for 11.6 days. You may think that a 3% cycle efficiency is low, but in fact it is fairly typical. Most processes—manufacturing, order entry, product development, accounting—run at a cycle efficiency of less than 10%. (Take some data on your own processes and calculate the cycle efficiency. I think you will be surprised.)

Process cycle efficiency varies by application, but an average of 25% is world-class (see Table 3-1). In the case of the coupled hose fitting, if the process lead time could be reduced to two days, for example, the wait time is reduced by 85%. The process cycle efficiency rises

Application	Typical Cycle Efficiency	World-Class Cycle Efficiency
Machining	1%	20%
Fabrication	10%	25%
Assembly	15%	35%
Continuous Manufacturing	30%	80%
Business Processes— Transactional	10%	50%
Business Processes— Creative/Cognitive	5%	25%

Table 3-1. Typical and world-class cycle efficiencies

to 19%—still below the Lean goal of 25% but much better than the current efficiency.

Any process with low cycle efficiency will have great opportunities for cost reduction. As we mentioned, increasing process cycle efficiency from 5% to 25% will allow the reduction of manufacturing overhead and quality cost by 20%. Since less than 20% of workstations are the time traps that inject 80% of the delay, focusing on these time traps gives the improvement process enormous leverage.

Where Do the Cost Reductions Come From?

The slowness of most processes—their low cycle efficiency—guarantees that there is a large amount of work in process (or projects in process) at any given time, either on the plant floor or finished goods in stock rooms. Much of the plant space is tied up with idle inventory, idle machines, stockrooms, rework labor, quality control, expeditors, schedulers, and related non-value-added activities. In other words, WIP generates hidden costs in overhead, rework, scrap, manufacturing overhead, invested capital, and unhappy customers ... and in consequence puts a company in constant jeopardy of losing existing business as well as revenue growth.

When process cycle efficiencies rise above 20%, much of these non-value-added activities can be eliminated. As a side benefit, the personnel associated with non-value-added work are often some of the most talented in the company, and sometimes the only people who really understand the whole process because they have had to cope with it. Thus, redeploying them into value-added assignments in manufacturing, engineering, marketing, or the Lean Six Sigma process allows them to be in a value creation role.

Figure 3-2 shows dramatic "before-and-after" photos of the tier-one auto supplier, reflecting the physical changes made possible by its speed and quality improvements. Since most factories do not produce such physically large parts, the effect of Lean improvements is generally not as visually dramatic, but the same types of improvements can be made.

The "after" outcome for this company was spectacular: If the volume of the company remained constant, they could have completed the needed work at two plants instead of three—saving most of the overhead for an entire plant (which would have amounted to about a 4% total operating margin improvement as a percent of revenue). This option was the one originally chosen but never executed because of the sales growth resulting from the dramatic reduction in lead time.

 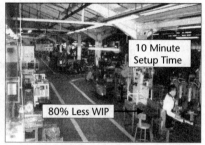

14 Day Lead Time— Low Velocity Supply Chain

Excess WIP / 2 Hour Setup Time

2 Day Lead Time— High Velocity Supply Chain

10 Minute Setup Time / 80% Less WIP

Before Lean Six Sigma
Metal Ware Flare running large batches with
large amounts of WIP at revenue of $145M

After Lean Six Sigma
Metal Ware Flare with pull system and
setup reduction: inventory reduced 85% at
revenue of $300M

Figure 3-2. Before and after photos of tier-one auto supplier

Sources of Cost Reduction

Let's again review the components of the Hidden Factory that can be eliminated through the application of Lean methods. The reduction of cost is *not* just from reduced scrap and rework or from having less money tied up in inventory. Shorter lead time and smaller inventory have a host of benefits that can be estimated in advance and tabulated (as you'll see later in this chapter):

- Shorter lead time, which can increase revenue growth dramatically.
- Less handling, which reduces the demand for people and equipment.
- Less cost for storage, floor, and stock room space.
- Fewer customer service activities.

When your inventory is small, you also *avoid* all the problems associated with large WIP, such as the following:

- Parts shortages caused by inflexible workstations.
- The need for extra operators, expeditors, supervision, and overtime.
- Shipping a disproportionate percentage of product at the end of the month though you have to pay for this peak capacity of property, plant, and equipment (PP&E), inspection, test, and overhead cost all month long.
- The increased likelihood that defects will be shipped to customers (who have been kept waiting for their parts), necessitating expensive field repair and loss of subsequent sales.

At ITT Avionics, a leading Defense electronics company, the lead time in printed circuit board production was cut from six weeks to four days. Several stockrooms were closed and 17 expeditor positions were eliminated. (The people were moved to value-added jobs, not fired!) A $200,000 expenditure for bar code tracking of the material was cancelled because, as the operations manager exclaimed, "If I release the kit on Monday and it enters test on Thursday, I don't care where it is in between!"

Shorter lead time for this Defense contractor also made a huge reduction in the cost of quality: reducing lead time by a factor of five reduces WIP inventory by the same factor. One supplier to this company shipped a product with a subtle dimensional change that caused an electrical short circuit in the customer's product. Because the process was operating "Lean," with shorter lead times, the problem was detected in just four days in test. Because there was also lower WIP, the changes caused only one-sixth the rework that would have been necessary with the higher WIP levels typical at this company before improvement. The Manager of Systems, Frank Colantuono, said: "It was the difference between making the month's shipments and disaster."

(Taking a process view of the business, we say that shorter lead times means there are more cycles of learning per month. Processes move more quickly, so you have more opportunities to learn what is and is not working and to see the effects of changes.)

By dramatically *reducing overhead cost*, managers are no longer tempted to overproduce to absorb overhead, a practice that merely clogs the factory with WIP and makes on-time delivery or lead time prediction impossible as well as irrelevant.

Eliminating time traps is just as dramatic as watching a river flow after beaver dams have been removed. It is one of those business experiences people never tire of recounting.

In 1987, Lean was first applied to a factory that produced Army radios. Eleven years later, in 1998, the former controller and then-president of an automotive unit recounted his amazement as he had watched lead times drop from a chaotic eight weeks to a stable two weeks in just a few months. He implemented Lean in his $2 billion division, leading to its sale at a very attractive price.

Speed Applies to All Processes

We've said it earlier in this chapter, but it bears repeating: when people hear "Lean," they think "manufacturing," but the principle of speeding up processes applies to non-manufacturing (transactional) processes as well as manufacturing. In fact, even if you wished to improve only manufacturing cost, quality, and lead time, you would have to improve the velocity, responsiveness, and quality of the associated transactional processes as well.

One example of how you can't really separate manufacturing from non-manufacturing applications of Lean Six Sigma comes from an early Lean implementation effort. A division of an $8 billion company that produced aircraft test systems had already used Lean tools and reached a point where it built in batch sizes of one with short setup times. The short lead time reduced the releases of material into the line, cutting down the number of "things in process"—both of which are primary goals of Lean.

However, many of the printed circuit boards produced by this division required as many as 60 modifications (called "cut runs" and "jumpers") to meet the current revision level. Because of the need to make these modifications:

- The rework time approached and often exceeded the total build time of the board.
- The rework greatly increased test time.
- The reworked boards had a much higher field failure rate.

Most of the variation in the process time and quality was induced by these problems.

Since the factory ran each board type at least once a month, a team began work on implementing new printed circuit board artwork in hopes of making changes quickly so that the next month's production cycle could be free of cut runs and jumpers. All the boards were built in-house, so the team could achieve the desired production lead time for new boards … *if* it had the Engineering Change Notice (ECN) and new artwork release from Product Development in time for the next production round.

Unfortunately, no one person owned the ECN process. Rather, the Request For Engineering Change Notice required *eight* sign-offs before engineering would change the artwork—with the result that the ECN process normally took one to three months!

In creating a process map for the first time, the team found that *only three of the eight people* on the ECN review list *could add value* (that is, understand the technical purpose of the change enough to offer useful advice). The other five needed to be informed of the change so they could work effectively, but they should not have had sign-off authority. Most of these five were fairly high-level people with a lot on their plates, who frequently traveled. The ECN forms often were lying on their desks and nobody wanted to expedite them. So the major time traps in this process were all related to time the ECNs spent *waiting* in someone's in-box!

To solve this process problem, the five managers agreed to changing their role from consent to advise. The ECN cycle time dropped to less than two weeks and allowed a major improvement in manufacturing quality and cost.

This example is by no means atypical; in fact, just the reverse! I have seen that there is as much or more improvement opportunity in these business processes to improve speed, flexibility, and/or responsiveness and reduce cost. The point is that the manufacturing process could not have been improved if the non-manufacturing processes had not been leaned out.

Lean does not mean *manufacturing*. Lean means *speed*.

Specific Applications of Lean to the Service Industry

Remember Jack Welch's famous quote about the "awful *variation*" that some GE customers experienced in delivery time (it ranged from four days to 20 days)? Let's take an example of lean improvements in a service industry to illustrate the key points.

Hotel chain industry statistics indicate that guests who are "very satisfied" at one hotel will return to that hotel or stay at another in the chain anywhere from three to six times per year. Guests who are dissatisfied never return, but tell eight to 12 friends about the experience. There is thus enormous revenue growth potential by moving guests into the "very satisfied" category and reducing the numbers who are "dissatisfied." One of the biggest single factors in satisfaction is the speed of total check-in time.

For the sake of this discussion, let's say it takes a hotel clerk exactly five minutes to check in a guest. If a new guest arrives exactly every seven minutes *on the dot*, how long would you wait in line? *No time at all; there would never be a queue.*

Yet if I changed the word "exactly" to "on average," the situation changes greatly: many customers would end up waiting 10 minutes or more. How could this possibly happen? How would you feel if you were one of the people who had to stand in line 10 minutes rather than five minutes?

The root cause of the problem is *variation* in time. Many guests flash their preferred guest cards and register in three minutes or less.

But others have requests that take up more time. One customer might request a room that connects with another guest's. Another may claim to have a reservation that the clerk cannot locate. As a result, check-in time for most customers ranges between three and seven minutes, yet the *mean* is still five minutes.

To complicate things, there is variation in *arrivals* as well. Customers arrive in bunches—sometimes every four minutes, other times not for 10 minutes, but the mean time between arrivals is seven minutes.

If you plug this data into special supply chain accelerator software used to identify time traps, you get a diagram like Figure 3-3.

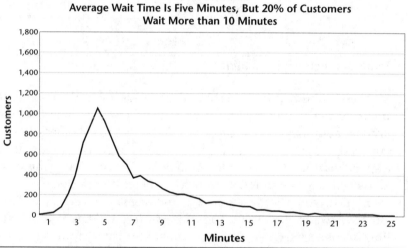

Figure 3-3. Variation in customer experience

As depicted in Figure 3-3, even though the average check-in time is five minutes and the average arrival time is seven minutes, some customers experience "heroic" three-minute check-ins while many others experience an "awful" 10 minutes or more. What is going on here? When guests arrive every 10 minutes, the clerks have nothing to do. But when a "difficult" guest happens to coincide with guests arriving every four minutes, the wait time can exceed 10 minutes for many guests. We say that these guests are caught in a time trap.

We can't do much about the variation in guest arrivals, but we can do a lot by just pooling our clerks and by training backups (from accounting and reservations) to cover peaks. We can test the solution with software to make sure it works. The result is shown in Figure 3-4.

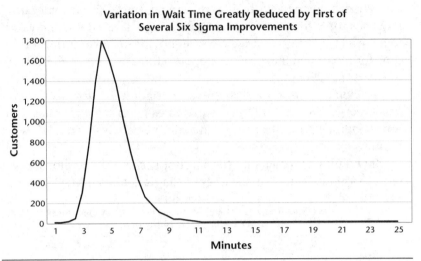

Figure 3-4. Reducing variation improves customer service

These gains can be achieved without adding any full-time personnel; just changing the queue design and cross-training personnel provide additional peak capacity. Thus the mean check-in time remained nearly the same but the variation in service was reduced, despite great variation in customer arrivals. Now the same number of guests wait seven minutes as formerly waited 11 minutes.

Even here, you can't ignore the key message of Lean Six Sigma: you have to focus your energies on *priority* problems that are most directly connected to significant shareholder value. In this example, we assumed that it was the check-in process itself that was the highest priority, to illustrate the impact of variation on delay time. But often in situations like these it is upstream processes—such as information flows on the availability of clean rooms, the room cleaning process, the availability of maids and linen, queues in the laundry room—that in fact affect the check-in time. That's why you need to use the tools described earlier in this chapter—value stream mapping and net present value analysis—to identify where you will have the greatest leverage.

This hotel check-in example shows how variation in arrivals and processing time *intrinsically* causes delay, even in a process much simpler than most manufacturing processes. The work was done at a single "workstation" (the clerk). It had no setup time, no scrap, no downtime—each of which creates delay and is a source of variation. There, it was absolutely clear where the delay occurred, why it caused the time trap, and where the company needed to apply DMAIC improvement activities to reduce variation. The obvious question is whether these same principles apply to processes that are more complex—and whether you find time traps by intuition or by looking at the plant, as some claim they can?

Pop Quiz: Where Are Your Manufacturing Time Traps?

If 80% of the delay is caused by 20% of the workstations, it is essential that we find those 20% and eliminate them using the Lean Six Sigma tools. So, how would you identify the time traps in your processes? The intuitive answer is "Look for where the work in process (materials, hotel guests, mortgage applications ...) is piled up." But is that really true?

Take a look at Figure 3-5. In this process, the value-added time per part is a few minutes, yet the total lead time of the process, including queue time, is 28 hours. The low process cycle efficiency is a tip-off that this process has a lot of waste in it. You will notice a pileup of inventory in front of the assembly station and some would say that it is a "bottleneck" or time trap. Do you agree?

Most people would intuitively guess that assembly is the time trap. But here's a radical idea supported by Lean principles: the assembly station is *not* the real time trap. How do we know? Like all Lean Six Sigma efforts, we replace intuition with data and calculation. Here's the data. The assembly operation is the last of a five-step process:

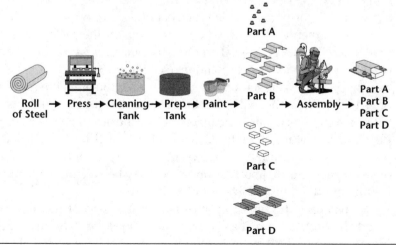

Figure 3-5. Where are the time traps? Where the inventory stacks up?

1. The press molds four parts (A, B, C, and D), by cutting and stamping a roll of steel. It first performs a setup that takes four hours, then presses out a batch of 1000 of part A at the rate of 100 per hour (36 seconds per part). It then performs a setup and stamps a batch of part B, and so forth.
2. After a part is pressed out, it drops into a cleaning tank for about 30 seconds.
3. The part is moved to a prep station, where it spends 30 seconds being prepared for paint.
4. It is painted in 40 seconds.
5. It finally moves to assembly, where one part A is bolted to one part B, to one part C, and one part D in 2.5 minutes. That completes the product that we will call ABCD.

Using this process data, we quickly see that the value-added time is just four minutes and 45 seconds—but the process lead time is 28 hours. That sounds like less than a 1% cycle efficiency to me, which means there is money to be made!

The press operators perform a setup by changing the dies and making adjustments, all of which takes four hours. Because of the long setup time, these operators cannot just press one part A, perform another setup, and press part B—because then the production rate will be one part every four hours, while the demand is for 17 of ABCD per hour.

So instead, after a setup is complete, the operators press out a batch of 1000 of part A at the rate of 100 per hour, which takes 10 hours. They then perform another four-hour setup and press out a batch of 1000 of part B, which takes another 10 hours. They do the same for C, then D. They are then ready to start the cycle again. The time taken for this cycle—called the *workstation turnover time* (in analogy to inventory turns)—is 56 hours (see Figure 3-6).

The 56-hour workstation turnover time for the press is a reflection of its inflexibility. The WIP inventory of part A is nearly 1000 after the batch is complete; it falls to near zero before the next batch of A is completed. On average, therefore, there are about 500 of each part in process at any one time, consumed at the rate of 17 per hour. Similarly, on average, there are about 28 hours of delay between the time a part is built and the time it flows out of assembly.

So where is the time trap in this process? It's not the assembly, where the parts pile up; it's the press that's injecting 28 hours of delay into the process. That is, the assembly would not have such a big pile-up of inventory if the press could work in smaller batches! That means

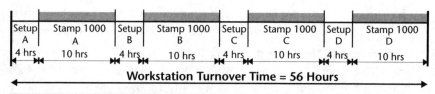

Figure 3-6. The inflexibility diagram

we'd get the most leverage by attacking the press workstation using the Lean Six Sigma tools.

Finding and Removing the Hidden Time Traps

Finding time traps is not a matter for guesswork. You have to use data to identify the sources of delays in a process. The key equation is captured in the First Law of Lean Six Sigma for Supply Chain Acceleration:[2]

$$\text{Customer Demand Rate} = \frac{\text{Batch Size}_{min}}{\text{Workstation Turnover Time}}$$

This can also be expressed with the following equation:

$$\text{Delay Time} \approx \frac{\text{Workstation Turnover Time}}{2}$$

$$= \frac{\text{Batch Size}_{min}}{2 \times \text{Customer Demand Rate}}$$

The key thing to remember is that you can use data that is fairly simple to collect on a process step or workstation and determine if this workstation is injecting long delay times into the process. These calculations can be performed easily with a spreadsheet or specialized "supply chain accelerator" software and the results tell you how much delay time each workstation is injecting and how much WIP and batch size are really needed to satisfy customer demand.

In this case, the company knows that the press is the time trap, so it then applies the appropriate Lean Six Sigma tool. The choice here is obvious: it's the long setup time between parts that's driving the operators to work in batches of 1000. To reduce setup time, they'd use the four-step rapid setup method (described in detail in Chapter 11).

- This method would allow them to reduce setup time by 90% with minor expenditure.
- A faster setup substantially reduces workstation turnover time. Using the First Law equation, the operators know they can then reduce batch size from 1000 to 100 and still meet the customer demand.

- The delay time for the process drops from 28 hours to 2.8 hours.
- Total WIP inventory drops from 2000 parts to 200 parts.

Naturally, this company wouldn't stop once this station is improved. They'd then move on to the next biggest time trap in some other part of the process, then the next largest one after than, and so on, until they achieve a cycle efficiency of 25% or more. As discussed above, achieving this level of efficiency means they can eliminate a lot of the non-value-added costs in manufacturing overhead and quality cost.

> **Conclusion:** *The cause of delay in a process is a time trap. You can't just look for where material piles up; rather, you must calculate how much time each workstation injects into a process using the First Law of Lean Six Sigma.*

> **Crucial Insight:** *Batch sizes must be calculated from process variables and the total number of parts produced at a given workstation.*

The press-to-assembly operations reduced the process lead time from 28 hours to 2.8 hours by following these three steps:

1. Find the time trap.
2. Apply the Lean Six Sigma improvement tool.
3. Reduce the batch size.

The last step is critical: if they had not reduced the batch size, the delay time would have been only slightly improved and the WIP inventory would be nearly unchanged.

As the discussion above illustrates, batch size is related to inflexibility: the more rapidly a workstation can switch to producing a new part, the smaller the batch size required and the quicker the flow velocity. The inflexibility of most manufacturing processes has guaranteed that factories have to produce in large batches to meet production demand.

There's more to the batch-size picture. Traditionally batch sizes have been determined using formulas such as the EOQ (economic order quantity) formula or those found in MRP systems. The problem is that these formulas do not consider how many different parts are produced at a workstation. Also, the batch sizes calculated from EOQ or most MRP systems are wrong because they do not consider the flow to the customer. They are fixed and are never reduced. *This prevents improvement in the lead time and is a key contributor to the slow progress most companies are making.*

Once you learn to appreciate the First Law of Lean Six Sigma, you understand that flow velocity, batch size, and workstation turnover time are all intricately connected. Anything that affects one of these factors affects the others. That means batch sizes should be determined based on process variables—setup time, the processing time per unit, and, most important, the number of different parts the process produces, etc.—and should be changed as a process improves. Fortunately, modern MRP/ERP/AP systems allow these batch sizes to be input externally. (You'll find more discussion of batch sizes in Chapter 13 and at www.profisight.com.)

VELOCITY OF ANY PROCESS

By reducing the WIP by 90%, we also reduced the overall delay time by 90%, yet still produced the same number of products per hour. This follows Little's Law, which states that

$$\text{Process Lead Time} = \frac{\text{Number of "Things" in Process}}{\text{Completions per Hour}}$$

This is really just common sense. If I have 10 things to do on my desk and it takes me an average of two hours to complete each one, then I have a 20-hour lead time for any new task (unless an expeditor interrupts me!).

In the assembly described above, the materials traverse five workstations. We can calculate the number of workstations per hour that the product moves through, which describes the *velocity* of the product through the process.

$$\text{Process Velocity} = \frac{\text{Number of Activities in the Process}}{\text{Process Lead Time}}$$

$$= \frac{(\text{Completions per Hour})(\text{Number of Activities})}{\text{Number of "Things" in Process}}$$

Why do I say "things" in process? Because it doesn't matter whether it is WIP in manufacturing or mortgage applications going down a chain of approvals; the velocity is inversely proportional to the number of things in process. This is of such importance it is referred to as the Third Law of Lean Six Sigma for Supply Chain Acceleration.

Figure 3-7 shows schematically how remarkably velocity increases as the number of things in process is reduced by improvement methods as in the example above.

It should be noted that the Third Law equation represents average process performance; it can tell you a lot about what is going on across

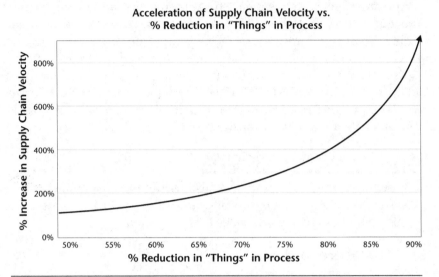

Figure 3-7. Velocity increases as work in process is reduced

a process consisting of several activities, but it can't tell you anything about a single activity and hence cannot show the location of a time trap. For example, in the press example, the Third Law gives tells you the overall process velocity for the five workstations, but if you apply it to just one workstation, it provides no information. As we've already determined, the assembly operates at a very slow velocity with lots of WIP backed up—but this slow velocity is caused by the press!

But that slow velocity is meaningless. Assembly is not the time trap. Improvements at the press are the only way to improve velocity. Nevertheless, the Third Law provides a guide to understanding average velocities of processes that consist of many activities. (Locating a time trap requires the detailed calculations of the First Law of Lean Six Sigma.)

Of course, instead of minimizing sources of delay, you could adopt Henry Ford's solution to a problem: have one press for each part. By having separate presses, Ford eliminated setup time and the resulting variation. Since he never performed a setup, his batch size was infinite! Unfortunately, that works only when you can produce vast quantities of a single product (like the Model T) to amortize the capital cost—which, as history has shown, eventually failed when consumers started demanding variety in the product. However, Ford accomplished so much in terms of showing the relationship between high process cycle efficiency (>50% at the Rouge Plant) and low cost that we must acknowledge his huge contribution.

KNOWING WHERE TO FOCUS: THE 80/20 RULE

The achievements possible with Lean Six Sigma principles will have little impact if you apply them to process steps that contribute little to delay time, costs, customer satisfaction, etc. As with other improvement strategies, to get the most out of Lean Six Sigma methods, you have to know where to focus your efforts and how to determine priority order.

In many improvement methodologies, "focus" is largely a matter of making judgment calls about what *seems* most important at the time. With Lean Six Sigma, focus jumps out at us because of the Pareto principle, which isn't just a theory but rather an empirical observation supported by years and years of data on actual factories: 80% percent of lead time delay is caused by less than 20% of the workstations (the time traps). We thus have to find and improve only 20% of the workstations to effect an 80% reduction in lead time and improve on-time delivery to better than 99%. This is always true of processes in which the value-added time is less than 5% of the total process lead time (i.e., have a 5% cycle efficiency).

The 80/20 rule is called the Second Law of Lean Six Sigma for Supply Chain Acceleration. It holds true whether the root cause of the delay is variation in times (arrival times, service times), non-value-added delays such as machine downtime or long setup times (as seen in the press example above), or quality problems (scrap, rework).

USING A VALUE STREAM MAP TO FIND THE 20% WASTE

In a Lean system, focus begins with a *value stream map*, which depicts all the process steps (including rework) associated with turning a customer need into a delivered product or service and indicates how much value each of the steps adds to the product. Any activity that creates a form, feature, or function of value to the customer is termed *value-added*; those that don't are called *non-value-added*.

Value stream mapping provides a clear understanding of the current process by:

- Visualizing multiple process levels.
- Highlighting waste and its sources.
- Making "hidden" decision points apparent.

With this knowledge, we can manage decision points, form a future roadmap for implementation, and identify opportunity areas. Value stream mapping also provides a communication tool to stimulate ideas by capturing critical organization knowledge and identifying locations for data gathering and process measurement.

We have given many examples of non-value-added activities (the largest contributors to non-value-added cost are manufacturing overhead and quality cost) and later in this book we will create classifications that are useful in determining what tools are needed to remove each type of waste so cycle efficiency can increase from less than 5% to over 20%.

The key insight is that a majority of non-value-added costs are in fact currently *required* to move the product through the "molasses" flow. You can't remove these costs until you remove the underlying causes; trying to do so will just create greater costs in the long run.

Creating a Value Stream Map

A value stream map starts with a pencil-and-paper sketch of the process to understand the flow of material and information needed to produce a product or service. (This sketch can be supplemented with many flowcharting software tools.) The diagram visually presents the flow of a product from customer to supplier and presents both the current-state map and future-state vision.

Value stream mapping typically classifies each activity/task type by asking a series of questions:

A. Customer Value-Added (CVA) Questions:

- Does the task add a form or feature to the product or service?
- Does the task enable a competitive advantage (reduced price, faster delivery, fewer defects)?
- Would the customer be willing to pay extra or prefer us over the competition if he or she knew we were doing this task?

B. Business Value-Added (BVA) Questions:

In addition to customer value-added activities, the business may require you to perform some functions that add no value from the customer's perspective.

- Is this task required by law or regulation?
- Does this task reduce the financial risk of the owner(s)?
- Does this task support financial reporting requirements?
- Would the process break down if this task were removed?

Recognize that these activities are really non-value-added but you are currently forced to perform them. You need to try to eliminate or at least reduce their cost.

C. Non-Value-Added (NVA) Questions:

- Does the task include any of the following activities: counting, handling, inspecting, transporting, moving, delaying, storing, all rework loops, expediting, multiple signatures?
- Taking a global view of the supply chain, having made these improvements, to how many factories do we really need to deliver projected volume? Will the faster lead time and lower costs fill up existing facilities?
- With faster lead times, how many distribution centers can be eliminated? (Experience shows that when three facilities are consolidated to two, you save half an overhead, about 17% of total overhead cost. This captures the operational value of higher cycle efficiency, but not the elimination of the cost of poor quality.)

In an improvement project, non-value-added tasks typically make up the majority of the time spent on any given task and are thus attacked first. Business value-added tasks are challenged next, followed by customer value-added tasks.

Traditional manufacturing engineering à la Frederick Taylor and Frank Gilbreath focused on the customer value-added processes, which are generally much smaller (less than half) than the non-value-added costs. Although improving customer value-added activities is important work, it is just a subset of the Lean Six Sigma DMAIC process.

Here is an overview of the creation of a value stream map:

1. Select a value stream (product family, etc.) whose improvement will create the greatest impact on operating profit.
2. Create a process map or download the MRP router information on that value stream. Because MRP routers generally have good data only on value-added steps, but not on the other 95% of the time used, you will initially start with a value stream that looks pretty clean (see Figure 3-8).
3. Have the black belt and his or her team "walk the process" to find out what really happens in the process and identify both value-added and non-value-added work, such as rework loops, quality inspections, moves in and out of stock (i.e., time that does not appear in MRP), and information flows. Most teams will be surprised to find more non-value-added steps in the process

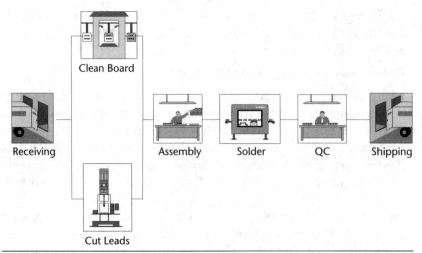

Figure 3-8. Value stream map downloaded from MRP router information

than value-added. (Compare Figure 3-9, which includes non-value-added work, with Figure 3-8.)

4. The team does a sanity check on MRP data, such as setup times, etc., by verifying the numbers with operators.

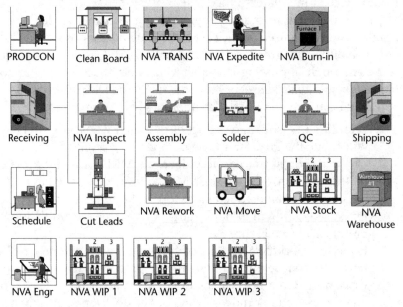

Figure 3-9. Value stream map highlighting the Hidden Factory

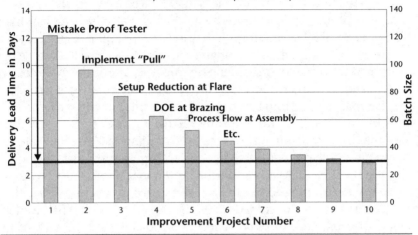

Output of Supply Chain Accelerator Software Tools
Reducing Cost and Lead Time Requires a Mix of Lean and Six Sigma
Selecting a 2-3 Day Customer Desired
Delivery Time Defines 10 Improvement Projects

Figure 3-10. Finding focus

5. Input the data into a spreadsheet or supply chain acceleration software. The time traps are then sorted on a spreadsheet or displayed in a bar graph. Figure 3-10 shows the bar graph discussed in Chapter 1 for the tier-one auto supplier, which was the output from this step.

6. The spreadsheet or software calculates delay time at each time trap and recommends application of Lean Six Sigma tools. The black belt can input how much improvement can be effected and the spreadsheet or software will recalculate the delay time.

7. Implement the improvement activities to address the time traps in priority order.

This process only works if the black belt and his or her team are trained to define and solve these problems:

- What are the non-value-added steps (rework, move, count, etc.) that can be eliminated?
- What are the time traps in priority order?
- What improvement methods are required at each time trap
- How much improvement is needed?
- What is the smaller batch size that can now be run?
- What is the shorter delay time at both the workstation and the whole process?

The Road Map of Lean Six Sigma

As a result of a value stream analysis, you'll be able to identify the "vital few" time traps (usually less than 20% of the workstations) that are disrupting a critical value stream. You will also have a prioritized list of Lean Six Sigma targets and a means of eliminating the causes of delay. When the time trap analysis is performed for the whole factory and prioritized improvements are executed, the total cost of manufacturing overhead and quality cost can be reduced by 20%, which makes a big impact on operating profit. Now that's *focus*!

In most cases, quality problems are usually near the top of the list, because of their *non-linear impact* on delay time—a 10% scrap rate can slow the whole process down by 40%! In other words, just a few quality problems can add an extraordinary amount of time to a process.

As noted, most people are amazed that the non-value-added steps outnumber the value-added steps! If they work with MRP routers, that's because they're used to seeing an idealized *future state* of the value stream map, at a point when all the waste has been driven out. The future-state map shows what can happen once the improvements are made to achieve a cycle efficiency of 30% and eliminate 20% of the manufacturing overhead and quality costs.

As an aside, experience shows that the people who work on non-value-added activities are in fact a vital resource that should be redeployed to value-added opportunities in manufacturing, engineering, or marketing and to staff the Lean Six Sigma effort. I have observed that rework is often performed by the most talented of workers and expediting is performed by people of the highest initiative. We generally suggest that the improvement process not cause any reductions of associated personnel, but that these highly talented people be reassigned. Any reductions should be to the company at large in response to inadequate shareholder returns, volume reductions, or lack of revenue growth.

THE MAJOR LEAN IMPROVEMENT TOOLS

While value stream mapping is the key measure tool of Lean, other methods and their associated tools are needed to achieve the full potential of improved speed. Details of these tools are in Chapter 11. Here are three of the most important:

Pull Systems: As discussed earlier in this chapter, process velocity and lead time are absolutely determined by the amount of the work in process. It therefore stands to reason that we must have a mechanical or electronic mechanism to keep the WIP ("things in process") below some maximum level or else the process lead time will grow uncontrollably. The Lean tool that achieves this goal is the pull system, which puts a cap on WIP and thus keeps process lead time below a maximum level. (This is sometimes called the Kanban system, after the Japanese word for "card" or, more literally, "visible record" or "sign." In Japan, WIP is released only when a card shows that consumption has occurred.)

Setup Reduction: The setup time is defined as the interval between the last good part of one run of part numbers and the first good part of the next part number. Chapter 11 shows how to use setup reduction techniques to reduce setup time by 80% with little if any increased capital expenditures.

Total Productive Maintenance: Data from scores of factories shows that machines are typically producing product only 60% of the time. About 20% of the downtime is scheduled for lunch, breaks, and maintenance. The other 20% is unscheduled, due to machine breakdown, setup time, parts shortages, absenteeism, etc. Total Productive Maintenance can virtually eliminate the *unscheduled* downtime; management initiatives can attack *scheduled* downtime. When a machine is running at near capacity, variation in the arrival of parts or machine processing times (similar to the hotel check-in example) can increase queue times by 10 to 20 times.

Just look at Figure 3-11. As the variation in demand increases, the actual wait time as a multiple of value-added time dramatically increases. (Notice that the "high variation" curve is much taller than the other curves.) In the hotel example, the process was running about 75% utilization with moderate variation, and a five-minute service time became an 11- to 13-minute wait for some guests. By providing some backup capacity they reduced the wait time to seven minutes.

In consumer product demand, we often see high variation and workstations operating at 90% utilization. Look at Figure 3-11. An activity that is at 90% of utilization of capacity and has high variation of arrivals or service times will introduce a delay time that is 15 times the actual service time. While hotel guests complain and get results, WIP just sits there silently soaking up costs. By increasing the uptime of any workstation (machine, clerk, etc.) by 20%, we can effectively run the workstation at less than 80% utilization of capacity. As Figure 3-11

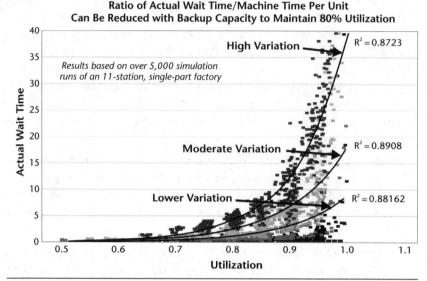

Figure 3-11. High variation contributes to longer wait times

shows, this eliminates most of the queue time caused by variation.

For those of you who like equations, the steep rise of the high variation curve can be predicted from the wait time equation:

$$\text{Process Delay} \approx \left[\frac{\text{Utilization\%}}{1-\text{Utilization\%}}\right] \times [\text{Variation in Supply or Demand}]$$

As utilization approaches 100%, the first term on the right gets very large. Any variation in supply or demand can drive the wait time to infinity.

The Hollywood Freeway

A lot of Lean was developed in manufacturing, principally because the data existed to examine process performance and a lot of clever people had the power to change things. In the service industry, the data often doesn't exist and the people don't understand what is causing delays.

Have you ever been driving at 70 miles an hour on a freeway and suddenly had to come to a complete stop? When you finally get moving, you expect to see a wreck up ahead, but often you see nothing at all! It is just that the freeway is operating so close to capacity that any fluctuation will drive the wait time up the curve in Figure 3-11 to infinity (i.e., a complete stop). But on the freeway, there isn't much data for the user and not much he or she can do about it. Lean Six Sigma gives you the tools to attack delay time in any application.

THE LEAN ENTERPRISE

It's difficult to overstate the opportunities represented by the slow processes found in nearly every organization. The problem that most firms have is in implementation. They perform training and conduct some isolated improvement efforts, but in the end make little measurable impact on overall lead time or cost (as we saw in the Preface).

Lean Six Sigma provides an unambiguous roadmap to implementation by prioritizing time traps and applying improvement methods, in that order. Eliminating the causes of wasted time allows a process to improve cost, quality, and responsiveness—characteristics that are critical to customers and shareholders. In most organizations, this can contribute 5% of revenue to operating margins. The speed and responsiveness of Lean can allow a company to increase revenue growth beyond its slower competitors. Finally, Lean methods apply to virtually all processes, from product development to order fulfillment. The increasing process speeds of Lean also enhance the power of Six Sigma tools such as Design of Experiments. But Lean alone, just like Six Sigma alone, isn't the complete answer. The next chapter will show how to bring Lean and Six Sigma together to create a powerful engine for value creation.

EPILOGUE ON FORD

I began this chapter with a quotation from Henry Ford. It may seem that this chapter is a complete refutation of his methods. But Lean "seeks not to destroy the Word, but to fulfill it." Ford certainly stood higher and saw farther than anyone else in 1908; in fact, I have often wondered why he, or his fabled team, failed to create Lean. I suspect the reason was hubris: he had a difficult time abandoning his fabulous creation to the changing realities of the market. Nevertheless, we must remember that when the president of Ford visited Toyota in 1982 and asked how they had developed their system, his Japanese hosts graciously replied: "We learned it at the River Rouge complex [a Ford plant]." While the Japanese are too modest in acknowledging their own contributions, there is no doubt that Ford pointed the way to the Promised Land, even though he could never enter it.

THE LAWS OF LEAN SIX SIGMA

- Lean means speed; it applies to *all* processes.
- Slow processes are expensive processes.
- The Lean metric is process cycle efficiency.
- Batch sizes must be calculated using flow variables.
- 95% of the lead times in most processes is *wait* time.
- To improve speed, you need to identify and eliminate the biggest time traps, which is possible using the *Three Laws of Lean Six Sigma:*

  Zeroeth Law: The Law of the Market. Customer critical-to-quality issues must be addressed first.

  First Law: The Law of Flexibility. Process velocity is directly proportional to flexibility. For example, in a manufacturing process, flexibility is proportional to workstation turnover time (Figure 3-6). Maximum flexibility is achieved by launching minimum batch sizes calculated per:

  $$\text{Batch Size}_{min} = \text{(Customer Demand Rate)} \times \text{(Workstation Turnover Time)}$$

  Second Law: The Law of Focus. 80% of the delay in any process is caused by 20% of the activities.

  Third Law: The Law of Velocity. The average velocity of flow through any process is inversely proportional to both the number of "things" in process and the average variation in supply and demand.

TO LEARN MORE

- Chapter 4 will show how Lean and Six Sigma blend together to create a powerful engine for improvement.
- Specific Lean methods and tools are described in Part Two.

Notes

1. The actual calculation only counts value-added down the longest router and subtracts process delays from heat treat, burn-in etc., from both numerator and denominator.
2. Used with permission from ProfiSight Technologies, www.profisight.com, protected by U.S. Patents 5,195,041 and 5,351,195.

Creating Competitive Advantage with Lean Six Sigma

Lean Six Sigma offers the CEO the means of creating and sustaining a significant competitive advantage. The value proposition discussed in Chapter 1 (pp. 9-13) is compelling: actual experience has shown that companies using *both* Lean and Six Sigma methods can reduce lead times by up to 80%, reduce manufacturing overhead and quality costs by 20%, and improve delivery times to above 99%. Applying Lean to the product development process can reduce time-to-market by 50% and enable the reduction of material cost by 5%-10%. The creation of the competitive advantage comes from developing a superior and sustained vehicle for transforming the CEO's strategy from vision to project execution and creating new operational capabilities that can expand the range of strategic choices.

The prime question is thus "How can we bring Lean and Six Sigma together into an effective strategy for creating shareholder value?"

Thanks to the work of many companies, the roadmap is fairly clear. Implementation of Lean Six Sigma revolves around three major phases, each of which will be discussed in greater detail in Part Two of this book. Here is a quick overview:

1. Initiation
   a. Obtain CEO engagement, develop financial and performance goals for the two- to five-year horizon, and gain P&L manager commitment.
   b. Create the future vision and organizational infrastructure.
   c. Train top leadership in Lean Six Sigma first.

2. Selection of Projects and Resources
   a. Select potential future leaders as champions and black belts.
   b. Create in champions an NPV mindset toward project selection.
   c. Train black belts in both team leadership and Lean Six Sigma tools.

3. Implementation, Sustainability, Evolution
   a. Provide expert coaching on initial projects.
   b. Track projects through the DMAIC process to final results.
   c. Build Lean Six Sigma into everything the company does and build the capability for Lean Six Sigma to remain an ongoing focus of the company.

This process wraps the best of Lean (value-based project selection, cycle time efficiency) around a Six Sigma infrastructure and sets the roadmap for the long term, which overcomes hesitation and creates a sense of initiative in the organization. But the most important element is something that neither method can promise: *executive support and engagement*. Fortunately, getting executives involved in implementation is relatively easy, since the Lean Six Sigma tool set includes ways for linking potential projects to *shareholder value creation*.

THE NEED FOR EXECUTIVE ENGAGEMENT

Lean Six Sigma has the potential to rapidly increase intrinsic value in less than a year. But this implicitly assumes that the criteria for success, defined by the Six Sigma *culture*, have been achieved:

- CEO and senior management engagement.
- Commitment of 1% to 3% of personnel full time to improvement projects.
- Infrastructure to prioritize, approve, and track project vs. plan.
- Focus on return on investment of Lean Six Sigma.

   Failure is just the reverse:

- CEO and top management not engaged.
- Commitment of part-time resources or significantly less than 1% of personnel full time.
- Black belts turned loose with no coaching or project prioritization.
- No infrastructure for project management or tracking vs. plan.
- Focus on cost of program, not returns or ROIC.

Securing CEO/Executive Commitment

Many people have looked for a holy grail of increasing share value and attributed it to leadership character, management vision, etc. Certainly the careers of Thomas J. Watson (IBM), Patrick E. Haggerty (Texas Instruments), Robert Noyce (Intel), and Jack Welch (GE), as well as Andrew Carnegie, Henry Ford, and Alfred P. Sloan, all confirm the importance of these leadership attributes.

A few years ago, however, a comparative study was made of 18 "visionary" companies that were considered far superior to "non-visionary" companies in the same industry. In examining this comparison (*Built to Last: Successful Habits of Visionary Companies*, by James C. Collins and Jerry I. Porras), we were struck by an interesting insight: to the extent that public information was available, superior performance was even better correlated to those firms that pursued a process of *management-led continuous improvement* than to those with visionary leadership. Some non-visionary companies actually outperformed their visionary counterparts when they focused on continuous improvement (known by various names—Operational Excellence at Colgate-Palmolive, Workout and then Six Sigma at GE, Value-Based Six Sigma at ITT Industries). In each case, *top management was engaged* and had committed substantial resources to continuous improvement.

When a CEO shows passion and support, *I have never seen Lean Six Sigma fail*. If, however, the CEO does not show this passion, *I have never seen it succeed*. If he or she leaves the initiative up to the divisions to decide to use Lean Six Sigma, it will generally fail to produce breakthrough results. If he or she fails to enforce the commitment of full-time champion and black belt resources, it will fail.

The CEO's engagement is necessary for another reason: to make sure the benefits of Lean Six Sigma impact the *whole* business. Isolated pockets of excellence cannot improve shareholder value. This point is best illustrated by an example.

We were once engaged to improve a factory that produced industrial hand tools. The company had a complicated product line of high-volume, low-volume, and ultra-low-volume spare parts. The products were shipped to a warehouse a hundred miles away and, from that point, sent to independent distributors upon demand.

The factory made a lot of progress in reducing quality defects, lead time, and inventory within the plant. For example, lead times of 80% of the high-volume products had been reduced from four months to less than three weeks. However, the production schedule was generated from annual plan budgets and field sales forecasts, not actual consumption by dealers, let alone ultimate customers. As much as 40% of production was not related to immediate consumption, but was used to fill the warehouse to meet a forecast. (This external scheduling process was really a historical response to a four-month lead time.) The result was that a chaotic demand in terms of total volume and by SKU prevented the plant from eliminating the Hidden Factory.

These problems can be solved only by Lean methods that reflect *real* consumption demand plus safety stock on the factory production schedule. This requires an engaged CEO or group president who has the whole supply chain process within his or her purview and who is leading the Lean Six Sigma initiative.

The problem, viewed from the shareholder's perspective, is that ROIC (profit after tax ÷ invested capital) principally equates to value. The profit numerator is depressed by extra plant cost, the lower gross profit due to lost sales, and the costs of maintaining a large warehouse. The denominator is increased by the large inventory and the property, plant, and equipment cost of the warehouse and the factory. The combination means that "pockets of excellence" in just a portion of the supply chain can gain only a small fraction of potential shareholder value.

This story has a happy ending. In the next implementation at that company, the entire billion-dollar construction equipment division was the client and the group president was very much engaged. We trained the president and his senior staff, obtained 25 full-time resources who were given four weeks of black belt training, and provided a few months of initial coaching. Cycle time reduction enabled a WIP turn increase of 92% and a labor productivity increase of 50%.

But of even greater importance was that the whole value stream was mapped, from supplier to end user, and true demand and dealer inventory were placed on line. Let's look at the performance of one division (Figure 4-1).

Just look at the impact on sales growth of on-time delivery. It would not have been possible to add $21 million dollars to a plant

Operational Improvements, Improved Availability and Reliability to Enhance Sales

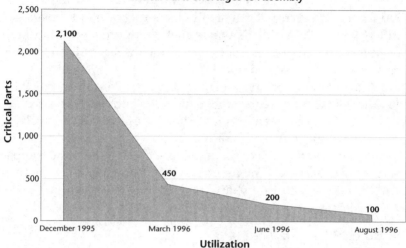

Critical Parts Shortages to Assembly

Before	After
■ Lost 160 machine sales (~$8M) due to lack of availability from January to June 1995	■ Lost 0 machine sales due to lack of availability from January to August 1996
■ Had 424 machine orders cancelled (~$21M) from January to August 1995	

Estimated Impact

- Revenue: 424 units @ $50,000 = $21,200,000
- Operating Income: $21,200,000 * 29% = $6,148,000

Record Divisional Performance in 1996 and 1997!

Realized Performance on Key Operating Measures

| Initiatives | Improvements | |
	Labor Productivity	**Inventory Reduction**
Product A	$5,468,000	($560,000)
Product B	$2,058,000	$3,530,000
Total	$7,526,000	$2,970,000
Improvement	275%	35%

"Within a 6-month period we had 20% more sales and we were using 30% less inventory and 15% less receivables."

—Group President

Figure 4-1. Results from division of example company

whose revenue had been $140 million without the president's engagement through the whole value stream. The ROIC was nearly doubled when the incremental operating profit was added to the $7 million in labor productivity and the invested capital reduced by the inventory reduction. This occurred in a highly custom, low-volume business, far different from the highly repetitive, high-volume tier-one auto supplier. This is just the first testimony to the universality of Lean Six Sigma as a process improvement tool.

After working on the initial projects, the 25 trained black belts fanned out across the corporation and were permanently assigned to continuous improvement projects. They were also actively involved in operational due diligence for acquisitions.

Remember: these two examples happened in the same company, under the same CEO. The difference is that learning had taken place and the need to address quality and lead time issues across the whole value chain became manifestly evident.

The Role of the CEO

The best way for me to describe the critical role of the CEO is to discuss what I have observed to be highly successful. I will give you two examples of what works, in the words of the CEOs:

Glen Barton, CEO of Caterpillar

I'm delighted to be able to kick off your 6 Sigma Champions meeting today. I'm sure you share my passion for quality or you would not have been given these important jobs. To help set the level for today's meeting, I want to make sure this is very clear—6 Sigma is the enabler for our new corporate strategy. Just like we reinvented the company in the early '90s, we're going to do it again. It's a new world order for value creation, one that rewards growth and is very fickle. We've been punished in the capital markets recently, and 6 Sigma is the vehicle to provide the returns that we deserve. I'm counting on you to help deliver that.

It's your job to launch this initiative with clarity, consistency, and commitment throughout the extended Caterpillar enterprise, as this impacts everyone—each and every continent, each and every employee, each and every supplier, and each and every dealer throughout the entire value chain. Everyone will be deeply impacted by this new way of working, an undertaking that will transform all that we do to achieve our quality and cost-reduction goals and help us deliver the $30 billion company we have promised by 2006.

So be clear. Yes, 6 Sigma is a continuous improvement strategy and discipline that provides specific methods to re-create our business processes so that defects never appear in the first place. But even more important than that, it is a cultural change to enable all of us to achieve the highest-quality products and services for our customers, investors, and employees.

And be consistent. You're dispersed in many different business units with different languages and cultures. For 6 Sigma you must operate as a team to ensure we get the global cultural change required. You must work together as a team with the same voice, the same methodology, and the same metrics. We have the 6 Sigma recipe. You adapt that recipe to the local taste of your business unit. We work together or fail apart.

And finally, you must be committed. Quality is my passion. I'm leading 6 Sigma, and I fully expect you to energize this organization to breakthrough performance levels. Some companies have failed at 6 Sigma, but when they have failed, it's not because of the process. The process is proven. They failed for lack of will. I can assure you that will not happen at Caterpillar. I am committed. I have placed myself as the owner of the 6 Sigma critical success factor and have listed it as corporate critical success factor number one. I fully expect your undying enthusiasm and commitment. Together, we'll achieve our bold goals. So listen intently to the messages you'll hear from Dave Burritt (6 Sigma Corporate Deployment Champion) today and get organized for the formal launch in January.

Good luck, and thanks in advance for the leadership you will provide the enterprise. We're counting on you to pave the 6 Sigma path.

Lou Giuliano, CEO of ITT

Value-Based Six Sigma is a subject that has become near and dear to my heart. The continuous improvement process is something that I've been involved in for a good number of years, something I believe in deeply, something that I have seen work. I know that it works. I know that it makes a difference in the organizations, and I know that it will continue to make a difference in our performance. … Our best bet to create shareholder value was to become a premier multi-industry company. One of the things we had noticed in our analysis was that while some people get a conglomerate discount, there are others like GE who get a conglomerate premium. And guess what? It all depends on performance, and if we could get our performance up sig-

nificantly from where it was back then, we felt we'd be able to earn those types of premiums as well. So that's become our strategy. We've been making acquisitions. We went out and told the world that this is what we wanted to do. We set what we considered to be significant, aggressive targets for ourselves.

The first thing that had to be done was to convince the management team that even though they were doing well in their industries and some of these businesses were doing better than others on a comparative basis, when you measured them to the multi-industry, premier peers—the GE's, the Tyco's, the Danaher's, the ITW's—we were a mediocre performer, even at 10 percent. That just wasn't going to get us where we wanted to go. Even though we had set high targets, we also recognized that those were just interim targets. We had to do a lot better.

That's how we started what eventually became for us Value-Based Six Sigma, or VBSS. Based upon my experience, I knew that the continuous improvement process would be important. It was the best way I knew of to change the way we did business. We were doing a lot of it in different parts of the company. We left it up to each company manager, each company president, to figure out how much effort and energy they put into this. There were a lot of different things being done, a lot of good work being done, but the results were spotty. They weren't getting us moving at the rate that we needed to move to reach our targets. So we decided that something else needed to be done, and I brought everybody together and asked how are we going to do this? Should we have a corporate-wide program? Do we know enough to do it ourselves? We've got a lot of people who have experience in problem-solving methodologies and quality tools. Should I leave it up to each management company to go out and figure out what to do? I knew if that happened everybody would pick some different solution that they liked. We went around and got everybody involved, and we said, "Let's go find out what's going on outside."

We wanted to be able to track what we were going to do, and that winds up in the software support tools. We wanted to have Six Sigma tools. That was clear. That was a capability that would supplement the tools of quality that we'd been using around the corporation. Here again, based on our experience over the years, you can clean up a lot of processes, but what really makes change in a factory are some of the Lean tools—putting in a pull system, reducing batch sizes, significantly changing setup times. All of a sudden everything starts to flow. Those are the types of things that we saw over time that really made a difference in our factories, and so we said that has to be a part of this training. That's where the Lean manufacturing comes in.

We've got a lot of people out there working hard at it. We're looking at saving roughly $400 million in operating income over four years. For us, that's a significant number. It's something that will make a difference to the corporation. It'll make a difference in our stock price. That's based upon a rather rough algorithm that I put together that takes a conservative look at what I think we can do with our black belts. That's where we want to go.

Black belt training began in April of 2000. The January 24, 2002 earnings release contained this comment:

Going forward, we are focused on maintaining our momentum, continuing to grow earnings and cash flow, investing in research and development, and constantly improving our processes. We're energized by the $100 million savings resulting to date from our Value-Based Six Sigma (VBSS) initiative, and intend to continue to expand the use of this strategy. With the continued deployment of the VBSS improvement tools and our new Value-Based Product Development initiative, I believe ITT has the potential over time to deliver performance consistent with a premier multi-industry company.

These are just two examples of many that share a common theme: the CEO makes it clear that she or he links the corporate strategy to the continuous improvement initiative, on which she or he is betting success. He or she is providing the resources and infrastructure and the personal leadership. This communication kickoff is supplemented with articles in the company newspapers, the annual report, "town meetings," and sometimes discussions with analysts. Everybody in the corporation knows that "this is it" and everyone had better get on board and support it.

The subsequent engagement of the CEO also takes the form of actively building Lean Six Sigma into the everyday management of the company by leading an executive overview class (typically one-two days) and conducting review sessions with the corporate deployment champion and his or her P&L managers so they know that their support via resources and engagement is being monitored. In some companies, this has taken the form of reporting an organization's or unit's performance in terms of a "traffic light" metric (green/yellow/red). A "red light" is given to any part of the business that has not provided the required number of black belt and champion resources. "Nobody likes to have a review with the Chairman and have a red light by their name," says Dave Burritt of Caterpillar.

CEOs are busy people, but Lou Giuliano made it a point to visit the kickoff of nearly every black belt and champion training class around the world. He visited China and commented on their Design of Experiments projects. He lives the process and is passionate about the process because it is congruent with his goals.

Part Two of this book will go into much more detail about CEO/executive involvement in designing and launching a Lean Six Sigma initiative. The major milestone event in getting the P&L managers on board with Lean Six Sigma is a one- to two-day meeting referred to as "The Transforming Event." At these events, everybody listens to the CEOs carefully. They should deliver presentations that show that Lean Six Sigma is integral to meeting their business plan objectives. Through this one- to two-day session, the top executives of the company learn what Lean Six Sigma is and how it meshes with the other initiatives to support execution of the CEO's agenda. The inclusiveness of "The Transforming Event" has proven to be a critical lever in obtaining the managers' commitment—not just compliance—in assigning the top 1% of their resources as black belts and champions.

Clearly a CEO who is unacquainted with Lean Six Sigma will be wary of making such a commitment of his or her executive resources. This step should not be taken for light or transient causes. One of the goals of this executive overview is to provide adequate depth in 100 pages such that a rational CEO could judge whether this initiative is worthy of further study in the full knowledge of the magnitude of his or her and the team's personal engagement.

Winston Churchill once wrote that people who wish to initiate great projects are very ill-advised to do so without the commitment of their chief. He was referring to his efforts as First Lord of the Admiralty to force the Straits of Gallipoli in World War I. His prime minister was a very hands-off manager and was too weak to order the Army to coordinate his attack with the initial naval barrage. The Army finally did attack six months after the naval bombardment. During the interval, the Turks had been prepared by their German allies and a slaughter ensued. Churchill was blamed, losing his great office in 1916 and apparently ending his career forever.

I ask you to remember that "politics is the science of the possible" and that a campaign of first enlisting the CEO is far better than launching an effort without his or her engagement. Part Two of this book, "The Lean Six Sigma Implementation Process," includes an entire chapter describing preparation for "The Transforming Event" and another for creating the infrastructure for change. This may seem an inordinate amount of detail, but I assure you that it is *the prerequisite* for shareholder value creation—and the difference between success and failure.

VALUE STREAM SELECTION À LA WARREN BUFFETT

The element of Lean Six Sigma that resonates most with executives is selecting the value streams that will be targeted for improvement, because that's the juncture *where the CEO's strategic goals are linked to frontline implementation.* Here is Lou Giuliano's linkage:

> We think about value-based management as a strategy made up of a series of processes and principles, that creating shareholder value is the number-one, overarching goal for the organization. We want to measure ourselves based upon value creation. We use Economic Value Added (ROIC% less the WACC% [weighted average cost of capital]) as one of our primary measures.

As we have discussed earlier, this linkage between economic value and project selection was missed in most TQM implementations. In contrast, Lean Six Sigma begins and ends with a simple proposition: improving value streams so that they have a high return on invested capital (ROIC) creates value.

The majority of champions, black belts, and quality professionals do not have an MBA degree; even those who do often do not connect their learning with project selection. Prioritizing based on shareholder value in particular is an area of their knowledge that cannot be left to chance.

We have found that we can drive home all the necessary concepts with just two graphs.

Graph 1: The Drivers of Shareholder Value

Project selection in Lean Six Sigma starts by identifying the *value streams with the highest potential increase in shareholder value per investment of resource*—that is, finding the sets of activities (value streams) that contribute directly to customer satisfaction and are likely to have the biggest impact on revenues and/or costs.

To identify these value streams, Lean Six Sigma has borrowed a method developed by investors such as Warren Buffett and Phil Fisher:

Businesses logically are worth far more than net tangible assets when they can be expected to produce earnings on such assets considerably in excess of market rates of return.
—Warren Buffett, Berkshire Hathaway
letter to shareholders, 1983

Buffet applies this wisdom to selecting investments. Lean Six Sigma applies it to prioritizing the investment of people and capital resources in projects that will create the highest ROIC and growth rates.

But can we really adapt Buffett's philosophy? Can we quantify potential gains in shareholder value based on ROIC and growth? Remember the stock price multiples chart from Chapter 1 (Figure 1-4, reproduced in Figure 4-2)? This chart was based on empirical stock market data gleaned from hundreds of financial reports.

As you can see, companies whose ROIC is much greater than their cost of capital ("market rates") trade at five to seven times book value, which confirms Buffett's thesis.

Let's focus first on companies with no or little revenue growth (the left side of the chart). Such companies that just earn their cost of capital—economic profit (EP%) of about 0, at the lower left corner—trade at about book value. These companies can increase their market value to *five times* their book value if ROIC exceeds cost of capital by 6% (upper left corner). And that's lesson #1: even if you don't anticipate revenue growth, you can still substantially improve shareholder value if your Lean Six Sigma efforts increase ROIC.

Even greater potential lies in the upper *right* side of the chart—with companies that are increasing revenue. Growth is important because it allows profits to be reinvested at above "market rates of return." When revenue growth of more than 10% is combined with improvements in ROIC, shareholder value (market-to-book ratio) improves by a factor of seven!

What does this mean for Lean Six Sigma? You can answer this for yourself by determining where on this graph you'd want *your* company to be. The obvious answer is wherever market-to-book value is high—i.e., toward the back of the chart ... and "back of the chart" translates to high ROIC relative to the cost of capital (weighted average cost of capital, or WACC%).

And there's the premise for all of Lean Six Sigma: we want to make sure that the sum of your improvement efforts drives your company's ROIC far above its cost of capital.

Though revenue growth, per se, is not often a direct goal of Lean

Six Sigma, in many cases it results from the other improvements made. Look at the dark arrow in Figure 4-2: this shows the impact of Lean Six Sigma on the tier-one auto supplier we've discussed several times. They went into Lean Six Sigma hoping to just retain the business they already had. But once they achieved Six Sigma capability and achieved fast, reliable delivery of a wide range of products, they attracted additional market share (= revenue growth).

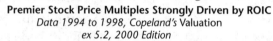

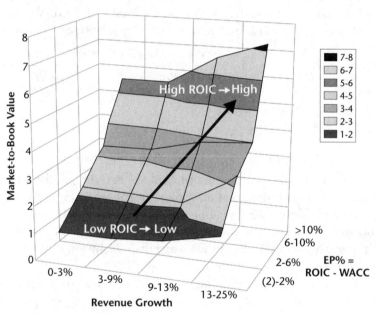

Figure 4-2. Stock price multiples and ROIC

Using Net Present Value

While Figure 4-2 clearly makes the point that we need to select projects with high ROIC, its practical use is limited in terms of project selection—no one has a lot of empirical stock market data lying around that relates to their own value streams! It would be much simpler if we had a formula we could plug into an Excel spreadsheet that would allow us to evaluate the potential impact of ROIC improvement *in our specific value streams* on shareholder value.

Once again, Buffett shows us the way:

In The Theory of Investment Value, *written over 50 years ago,*

*John Burr Williams set forth the equation for value, which we con-
dense here:* The value of any stock, bond or business today is
determined by the cash inflows and outflows—discounted at
an appropriate interest rate—that can be expected to occur
during the remaining life of the asset.

—Warren Buffet, Berkshire Hathaway,
Letter to Shareholders, 1992

In other words, what we need is a formula that relates the net
present value of discounted cash flows to ROIC and revenue growth.
Fortunately, there is such an equation, derived by J. Fred Weston in his
financial management textbook. For you "math-philes," here it is:

$$\text{Value} = \frac{No\,(1 - G/R)}{(1 + W)} + \frac{No\,(1 - G/R)(1 + G)}{(1 + W)^2} + \frac{No\,(1 - G/R)(1 + G)^2}{(1 + W)^3} + \ldots$$

$$= \sum_{n=1}^{N} \frac{No\,(1 - G/R)(1 + G)^{n-1}}{(1 + W)^n}$$

where G = growth rate%, R = ROIC%, W = cost of capital%

"Value" is what we call net present value (NPV) in this book and
it substitutes for the market-to-book ratio shown in Figure 4-2.

As with Figure 4-2, the slope toward the upper right shows that as
you increase economic profit by increasing ROIC, the value of the
company increases. So again we reach the conclusion that we need to
select projects that will have a very high ROIC.

But wait! A project that has a high ROIC today may turn around
tomorrow—and we don't want to invest in buggy whips that are
going obsolete! So how do we identify value streams that will have a
high ROIC *into the future*? Look again at the equation shown above.
Because NPV is calculated based on the "discounted value of future
cash flows," it captures both the present *and projected future* performance. (An implicit link here is that performance is determined by customers' reaction to the product or service—therefore NPV also
embodies the Voice of the Customer.)

Graph 2: The Destruction of Shareholder Value

Another benefit of using graphs based on NPV is that they clearly disclose information about value *destruction* that is not evident from
empirical stock market graphs.

Figure 4-3 is a graph of the value equation rotated to highlight

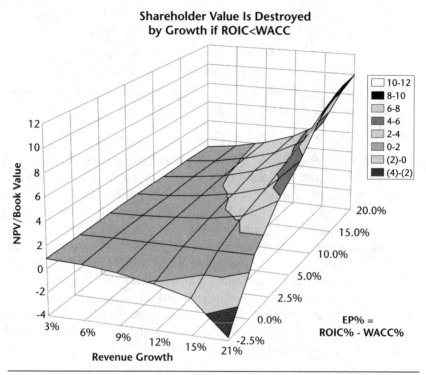

Figure 4-3. Destruction of shareholder value

areas of the graph where ROIC is low. Notice the plunge in shareholder value (as reflected by NPV/book) in the lower right corner. In
fact, NPV is less than book value if the ROIC is less than the cost of
capital—in which case, the faster you grow, the more value you
destroy! Of course this makes logical sense: shareholders would be
much better off with their money invested at market rates rather than
at lower rates of return inside a business.

When ROIC is less than cost of capital, the NPV formula is telling
you that the assets actually are worth less than book value. How can
this be? When Buffett sold Berkshire Hathaway's spinning equipment, he provided us a graphic example:

> *Some investors might weight book value heavily in their stock buy-*
> *ing decisions. Some economists and academicians believe replace-*
> *ment values are of considerable importance in calculating an appro-*
> *priate price level for the stock market as a whole. Those of both per-*
> *suasions would have received an education at the auction we held in*
> *early 1986 to dispose of our textile machinery... the equipment could*

have been replaced new for perhaps $30-$50 million. Gross proceeds from our sale of this equipment came to $163,122.

—Warren Buffett, Berkshire Hathaway,
Letter to Shareholders, 1985

The lesson: it is critical to pick value streams and projects where you can drive ROIC at least 5% above the cost of capital.

Lessons of the Two Graphs

Taken together, the graphs shown in Figures 4-2 and 4-3 lead back to the basic value proposition of Lean Six Sigma. You need to focus your efforts on value streams and projects that have the highest potential for the greatest increase in NPV. This will create the fastest rate of increase in shareholder value.

Seeing these charts often has a real impact on champions and causes them to "get it." We recommend the NPV approach because it allows us to apply analytical tools that are widely known and easy to teach. When champions start using the language of net present value, we know the company is headed for success. A clear linkage is established from the CEO's strategy all the way to the shop floor initiatives, with tracking and reporting on the process.

COMPETING WITH LEAN SIX SIGMA

With every executive under the gun to improve profit sooner rather than later, Lean Six Sigma offers advantages that are critical in today's marketplace. The acceleration of cost reduction in particular and of process speed in general allows a firm to respond to market conditions and opportunities faster than the competition. In the June 2001 issue of *Wired*, Andy Grove of Intel stated:

The most direct way of increasing productivity is doing the same thing in a lesser period of time—turning things faster. And productivity is the key to everything—greater productivity increases economic growth.

If every company suddenly made these cost improvements, competitive pressures would no doubt pass the savings on to the customers in terms of lower prices. Yet so far, it seems that comparatively few companies are in fact improving lead time, and we can infer that continuous improvement in general is very slow (see the survey results described in the Preface). Thus, the company that aggressively pursues Lean Six Sigma will have a sustainable advantage over the competition.

One of the most critical factors in Lean Six Sigma is creating a culture is that incorporates *learning* and provides a well-defined infrastructure for CEO engagement, training, coaching, results tracking, and regeneration via internal training capabilities (i.e., master black belts). Because of this infrastructure, Six Sigma has been able to deliver operating profit improvements of $250,000 to more than $1,000,000 per black belt.

Combining the capability for those kinds of achievements with the gains provided by Lean methods—including reduced costs and improved speed—provides the key link of an improvement methodology with the everyday business of the organization. The ability to equate *output value* to *input cost* makes it possible for a CEO to view Lean Six Sigma not as a quality cross to bear (as was true of TQM), but as a means of translating strategic goals for shareholder value creation into an implementable set of initiatives.

The payoffs of Lean Six Sigma have an interesting phasing. Projects that are primarily Lean (concerned with process velocity and efficiency) pay off very quickly in inventory and manufacturing cost reductions. Then Six Sigma projects that are working to improve quality (reduce defects) provide a mid-range addition, aided by the faster process cycle times achieved from the Lean efforts. Design for Lean Six Sigma efforts (which can require a year or more) have much larger payoffs, as they impact the 50% of the product or service cost determined by design.

The present value of all these payoffs is strongly positive. Lean Six Sigma will convey competitive advantage and better shareholder returns at a faster rate than any other currently known process.

Is Lean Six Sigma the last word on continuous improvement? It's an old joke that each generation thinks it invented sex. The same is probably true of improvement methods. Starting with Zero Defects in the 1960s, over a score of fads have come and gone, most of them making some advance on the predecessor. Six Sigma has performed better, due to its cultural strength, and the addition of Lean speed gives it legs. To my knowledge, no other continuous improvement process has ever encapsulated so much wisdom in such an effective and sustainable form.

I don't claim that Lean Six Sigma is the last word; I just say it is the best current practice to create shareholder value. Given the rapid state of advance, it is best to remain humble about Lean Six Sigma, as the next generation will no doubt be even better equipped. What then do we say to this next generation?

Look not proudly down upon us, should you stand higher or see farther than we, but rather recognize how, with courage and strength , we raised and supported your standard. Do the same for those who come after you and rejoice.[1]

Lean Six Sigma is part of a large work-in-process that continues to increase the wealth and opportunities of society despite the resistance to progress and intellect in many parts of the world.

Note

1. J. Robert Oppenheimer, *Science and the Common Understanding* (New York: Simon & Schuster, 1954).

Part Two

The Lean Six Sigma Implementation Process

"Knowledge creates understanding, but only practice creates belief"

The purpose of Lean Six Sigma is twofold:

- To transform the CEO's overall business strategy from vision to reality by the execution of appropriate projects.
- To create new operational capabilities that will expand the CEO's range of strategic choices going forward.

Developing a corporate strategy is beyond the scope of this book. Fortunately, it appears that most organizations already know how to do it well. For over 20 years a number of securities analysts have been studying corporate performance from the perspective of tactical effectiveness. Here are a few insights:

- 275 portfolio managers reported that the ability to execute strategy was more important than the quality of the strategy itself. [Source: *Measures that Matter* (Boston: Ernst & Young, Boston 1998), p. 9.]

- A 1980 survey of management consultants reported that fewer than 10% of effectively formulated strategies were successfully implemented. (Source: Walter Kiechel, "Corporate Strategies Under Fire," *Fortune*, 27 December 1982, p.38)
- A 1999 *Fortune* cover story of prominent CEO failures concluded that the emphasis placed on strategy and vision created the mistaken belief that the right strategy was all that was needed to succeed. "In the majority of cases—we estimate 70 percent—the real problem isn't [bad strategy but] … bad execution…." (Source: "Why CEOs Fail," *Fortune*, June 21 1999.)

The consistency of the inference over so many years is clear: CEOs generally have well-thought out strategies; the failure comes in execution. The corollary is that success requires good strategy and good execution.

EXECUTION OF LEAN SIX SIGMA

Part Two of this book describes the Lean Six Sigma Implementation Process, which encompasses three streams of activities:

1. Initiation. Critical steps needed to get off to a good start. Almost all of the work in this stream involves the company's top leaders: the CEO and his/her direct reports become engaged in supporting the initiative, and managers with P&L responsibility are exposed to the benefits of Lean Six Sigma implementation.

2. Resource and project selection. Selecting people with leadership potential to provide the muscle for implementing projects that have the most direct links to customers' critical-to-quality issues and the creation of shareholder value.

3. Implementation, sustainability, evolution. Converting Lean Six Sigma from an initiative to a way of life that serves to constantly improve a company's performance and financial position.

For the purposes of this book, these streams are presented in a linear order, but in practice, the work within these streams overlaps, as shown in the chart on the next page.

The steps of Lean Six Sigma implementation are focused on translating sound strategy into effective operational execution by creating giving you the practical tools to answer three questions:

- *Where* do I focus?
- *How* do I execute the change?
- *Who* is going to lead the way to success?

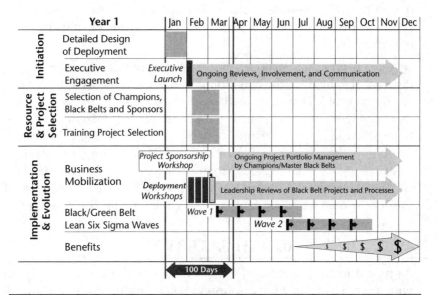

Lean Six Sigma implementation streams

You'll find much more detail on answering those questions as you read through the following chapters. As you do, look for the following themes that create a strong Lean Six Sigma architecture:

Driven from Strategy. Performance improvement derives from a system of tools you can use to link strategy to tactics, to set priorities, to select high-potential projects, to allocate resources, and to monitor performance. The link of these elements effectively answers the *"where"* question at a level of detail that can be acted upon—that is, you will move from your business goals to identifying and selecting specific projects that contribute to those goals. Providing this level of strategic focus is a critical ingredient to ensuring that your Lean Six Sigma process is relevant to the business and creates significant shareholder value. All CEOs face the challenge of rational capital allocation to create the greatest net present value (NPV) and hence shareholder value; Lean Six Sigma takes this a step further by enabling the rational allocation of *human* capital to process improvements.

Execution of Improvements. Once the highest-value projects have been selected, Lean Six Sigma provides specific tools for process improvement and methodologies for process design/redesign. Future chapters describe the Lean Six Sigma improvement process of DMAIC (Define-Measure-Analyze-Improve-Control) as well as the interplay of traditional Six Sigma and Lean tools that support each phase of that process. This set of tools comprises the "how" to execute the identified opportunities.

Organizational Acceleration. One definition of insanity is "expecting different results tomorrow by doing things the same as today." Lean Six Sigma provides specific methods and processes—such as management engagement, team effectiveness, and role/organizational definition—that can help you change how things are done today so you can get different and better results tomorrow. Likewise, providing the necessary "human dynamic "skills to the designated leaders is critical for success. These skills provide for effective and efficient execution of projects by teams that are often working together for the first time.

NAVIGATING THROUGH PART TWO

As an aid to navigating Part Two, consider where you are today on your own Lean Six Sigma journey. Some companies have started down the road on Lean or Six Sigma (or both); others may truly be at the beginning of the journey. The material in each chapter in Part Two will likely have different levels of importance based on your situation.

Chapter 5 (leadership engagement), **Chapter 6** (deployment/infrastructure planning), and **Chapter 7** (kickoff event) describe the key steps in the process for **initiation** of a corporate-wide Lean Six Sigma effort. They draw on the many lessons learned from previous efforts. Chapters 5 and 7 are most appropriate for those who are just beginning the journey. If you have successfully launched a large-scale effort within your company, you may want to skim that material. Chapter 6, however, covers important elements of planning for Lean Six Sigma and therefore is relevant to anyone reading this book.

Chapter 8 (resource/project selection) discusses how to select the people to fill the positions defined in your deployment planning and the projects that will be used to execute your plans. The sequence of these two activities is important: individual projects will come and go, but your infrastructure should last for a long time. So you need to carefully select the people who will fill champion and black belt roles; then determine where to assign them to project work. In working with companies that are already on a Six Sigma or Lean journey, these selection issues are common areas of concern and would be of value to all readers—particularly those who have experienced the pain of shortfalls in these areas.

Chapter 9 (teams), **Chapter 10** (DMAIC improvement process), and **Chapter 11** (DMAIC tools) cover essential Lean Six Sigma content (tools and methods) in the context of how they will be used in practice. The chapters also describe the keys to creating effective teams and provide guidelines for developing black belt training programs around this content. If you are just embarking on a Lean Six Sigma initiative, these chapters describe the basic content you should incorporate into any Lean Six Sigma training program; if you already have training programs under way, use the content here as a checklist for evaluating your content and focus.

Chapter 12 (sustainability and evolution) describes the all-important work of transitioning Lean Six Sigma to "business as usual." As with all performance improvement efforts, there is often the risk of creating just another "program of the month." While the significant infrastructure, processes, and results associated with Lean Six Sigma reduce this risk, there still needs to be a solid strategy for the transition and an ability to recognize the "red flags" of rejection. One of my colleagues, who focuses on Lean Six Sigma in healthcare, likens the effort to an organ transplant where the patient transitions through periods of intense support followed by intermittent assistance into self-sustaining status.

THE INDICATORS OF COMMITMENT

My associates and I have observed Six Sigma, Lean, and Lean Six Sigma implementation in dozens of organizations. One thing we learned early on is that employees will be scrutinizing every action that executives and managers take in the early stages of deployment to gauge the seriousness of the commitment. Specifically, they'll be looking at three indicators:

- *Are the company's leaders personally demonstrating a commitment to Lean Six Sigma? Is Lean Six Sigma becoming part of the fabric of the organization?*
  Do they use the talk? Do they walk the talk? Are discussions of net present value and cycle efficiency a standard component of staff meetings? Are people working on Lean Six Sigma efforts reinforced for their efforts? Or does Lean Six Sigma quickly become relegated to the sidelines?
- *Are the **best people** selected to become devoted Lean Six Sigma resources?* Are black belt and champion candidates screened care-

fully for their leadership potential and ability to lead projects to completion? Or does assignment come to people who generally have nothing better to do?

■ *Are the **most important** projects being worked on?*
Most people working in your company will either already have a sense of where the important problems lie or be able to recognize them when they see them! So everyone will be watching to see if resources are devoted to the important projects or if time is wasted on non-critical issues that do little to improve overall performance.

The content of the following chapters provides knowledge and tools that will help you answer "yes" to each of these questions. If the answer to any of them is "no," then no one in your company will believe that you're really serious about implementing Lean Six Sigma and you may as well save yourself a lot of time and effort.

Chapter 5

Initiation: Getting Commitment from Top Management

O ver the past dozen years in working with both successful and failed continuous improvement initiatives, my colleagues and I have learned one hard-and-fast lesson: the Lean Six Sigma effort will succeed or fail based on the *engagement and buy-in* of the CEO and executives with P&L responsibility. If these people are engaged in the process, Lean Six Sigma will allow the whole organization to bring its enormous latent energy to bear on value creation. If they are not engaged, Lean Six Sigma will be just another failed effort in the company's history.

Evidence abounds in support of this proposition. In the past, a traditional approach to deployment would have been for the CEO to set corporate goals and let the P&L centers decide what is best, each going their own way.

Here's a real example of why that approach doesn't work. A highly decentralized manufacturing company decided to launch a program in which improvements were mandated by corporate, but the program was to be designed, and the cost borne, by the P&L centers. In a Darwinian world, one would expect that the managers would evolve to the best solution on their own. But evolution is an extremely slow process. Most of the managers had neither the time nor the knowledge to design a Lean Six Sigma program and were rightly focused on how to make that quarter's or that year's numbers. A manager at this company explained his lack of significant effort this way:

> *Corporate has set goals for me to improve quality, reduce working capital and lead time. If I fail to do this, but make my profit numbers, I might get my wrist slapped. If I don't make my profit numbers, I get fired!*

This comment is typical of P&L executives, a tough crowd of hardheaded practitioners. They will support an initiative with their complete *engagement* only if it helps them meet the profit and growth plans they have agreed to with the CEO or group president. Out of necessity, therefore, P&L centers are primarily *tactically* focused. Budgetary constraints and bonus compensation make it very difficult for P&L managers to make *strategic* investments in process or people development. To the extent that managers make such investments, they rarely allocate the critical mass (e.g., 1% of their personnel) needed to achieve breakthrough performance.

At the unit level, it is also common that the focus of implementation can degrade to managing the cost of implementation to budget. While I do not recommend ignoring implementation cost, worrying solely about what a program investment *costs* without any reference to what the investment *pays* is a problem.

It is reminiscent of what Buffett calls the *cigar butt theory of investing:*

> *A cigar butt found on the street that has only one puff left in it may not offer much of a smoke...*
>
> —Warren Buffett, Berkshire Hathaway,
> Letter to Shareholders, 1989

Buffet also says, "Practice doesn't make perfect, it makes permanent. And thereafter I revised my strategy and tried to buy good businesses at fair prices rather than fair businesses at good prices" (Letter to Shareholders, 1992).

Therefore, the most important factor with this or any other major investment decision is the *net present value* (NPV) represented by the opportunity. NPV, discussed back in Chapter 4, reflects the discounted value of *what something pays* less the discounted value of *what it costs to improve shareholder value.* This is the charge given to a CEO by the Board and, in our experience, he or she alone has the value perspective necessary to initiate and drive the Lean Six Sigma process and ensure that it is properly funded so that it will meet strategic earnings and capital investment goals. On the cost side, it is important to design the program so that the profit benefits offset the cost in the first year.

Therefore, the purpose of the first phase of the Lean Six Sigma process is to secure engagement by the CEO and other top executives. If you are considering Lean Six Sigma, and there is *no "C" level executive engagement yet*, remember Churchill's admonition: get your chief on board first if you want to avoid a bloody Gallipoli.

LAYING THE GROUNDWORK

The most important outcomes of the first phase of Lean Six Sigma are to have:

- Executive commitment and involvement in the process (discussed in this chapter).
- A clear definition of the "burning platform" issue (discussed in this chapter).
- An estimate of the cost versus the benefit (discussed in this chapter).
- A plan for rollout during the first 100 days (discussed in Chapter 6).
- P&L manager awareness and buy-in (discussed in Chapter 7).

These elements lay the groundwork for a successful Lean Six Sigma effort by making sure that leaders agree on what Lean Six Sigma means to your organization. You should approach these tasks as you would consensus: striving for something that people will support both *publicly* and *privately*. It does no good to have your leaders nod their heads in an executive committee meeting, but then badmouth Lean Six Sigma to their own troops.

LEADERSHIP ENGAGEMENT

The leadership component of Lean Six Sigma initiation encompasses three specific activities:

A. **CEO/executive engagement,** as demonstrated initially by his or her active involvement in the upfront decisions about "where," "how," and "who" of Lean Six Sigma.

B. **Setting long-term (two- to five-year) fiscal and performance goals** for the organization that reflect Lean Six Sigma gains in operating profit, ROIC, revenue growth, and intrinsic shareholder value consistent with the overall business strategy.

C. **Commissioning a design/deployment team** to champion the design of the Lean Six Sigma policies and architecture for the company.

CEO Commitment and Engagement

In truth, actual *engagement* is something that executives and managers will demonstrate during the months and years that Lean Six Sigma is being implemented at your organization. However, engagement begins with *commitment*, which will happen when a CEO and other executives are convinced that Lean Six Sigma should become a major strategic effort for their organizations. This commitment typically comes when they realize that:

- There is a truly compelling need to run the business in a new way.
- Lean Six Sigma is the best choice.

Finding a "compelling need" is very company-specific and depends very much on where the company is currently positioned relative to customer requirements, shareholder expectations, competitive position, and/or financial performance. Here are a few examples I know from personal experience:

- A company with a long, proud history whose financial performance had suffered saw Lean Six Sigma as the method to "return to greatness."
- A company that was rated "mediocre" by Wall Street, relative to its peers, saw Lean Six Sigma as the way to achieve "premier" valuation status.
- A company reached a $20-billion sales plateau and saw Lean Six Sigma as a means to effect a breakthrough.
- One CEO provided his team with illuminating market data that established the fact that customers saw the company as very poor in performance.

These types of business-critical needs are often referred to as the *burning platform* for change. The term comes from the story told by Daryl R. Conner in *Managing at the Speed of Change* of a North Sea oil rig worker who once faced a truly life-threatening situation. The oil rig caught fire and he had to decide whether to stay where he was (and almost certainly be burned to death) or to jump off the platform, falling 150 feet into the cold sea. It turns out that he had the courage to jump and lived to tell the story.

The question, then, is whether there is a burning platform in your own company today that will provide the compelling need for the CEO and the rest of the company to embark on a difficult journey like Lean Six Sigma. Whatever it is, a burning platform must be rooted in fact and compelling enough at an organizational and personal level to inspire the troops to take on a new direction. Without it, the organization is unlikely to take the critical first steps.

Once a compelling need is established, the CEO must be certain that Lean Six Sigma is the best strategy to address the need. For example, CEO interest is often generated by talking to a peer, by arranging for a one-day seminar on the subject, or by reading compelling case studies. By whatever means, it must be an appropriate "C" level person who decides to move forward and to give a substantial part of his or her calendar to Lean Six Sigma. John Patterson, the founder of NCR, wisely said:

> *The executive must decide. He may decide right. He may decide wrong. But he must decide.*

In short, Lean Six Sigma is a *choice*, not a mandate. That means the CEO's choice may sometimes be to not execute Lean Six Sigma. Perhaps other priorities supervene, such as being acquired or acquiring a comparably sized company. In some cases, a firm already occupies the heights of entrenched market, brand, and distribution position; its earnings are protected by a franchise. (F. Ross Johnson, the former CEO of RJR Nabisco, once sagely observed, "Some genius invented the Oreo. We're just living off the inheritance.")

If, for whatever reason, your CEO does not have an intense interest in improving competitiveness and financial performance through operational improvement, then Lean Six Sigma is not appropriate for your firm at this time.

If the CEO and other executives decide to support Lean Six Sigma, the next step is to establish goals for the organization, which will in turn drive the choices of how to allocate Lean Six Sigma resources.

Setting Two- to Five- Year Goals: The CEO's Vision for What Lean Six Sigma Will Contribute

Part I of this book devoted a lot of attention to one aspect of Lean Six Sigma that sets it apart from other corporate improvement strategies: the direct linkage of a CEO's goals to frontline efforts. That linkage begins here, as executives determine just what those goals will be.

These goals must be specific to your company and should be driven by your corporate strategy. The issue here is to make sure that goals reflect the types of gains you need to get from your Lean Six Sigma effort—not what you can safely achieve using the same systems you have in place today. Here are some examples of typical multi-year stretch goals and financial performance:

- Improve gross margin 5%-10%.
- Increase ROIC 5%-15%.
- Increase revenue growth to 10% per year.
- Eliminate 20% of manufacturing overhead and quality costs.
- Gain 4% in market share each year.
- Increase capacity 12%-18%.
- Reduce the number of overhead employees 12%.
- Cut time-to-market and redesign in half.
- Generate an average return of $250,000 to $500,000 per black belt per year (judged in operating profit).

These goals are simple, but would establish a "mountainous" challenge in nearly any company. As you may recall from Chapter 4, the primary driver of Lean Six Sigma is to put your organization near the top of the "value mountain" (see Figure 4-2, p. 72). The intent is to clearly stretch the organization's thinking and to keep the goals clearly linked to a key driver of financial performance.

Once the CEO and P&L executives understand the power of Lean Six Sigma, they will be in position to select a set of goals appropriate to the business and market conditions. The actual process of refining and achieving these goals will require the contribution of many minds, which are usually formed into a design/deployment team, described below.

Commissioning the Design/Deployment Team

The launch of Lean Six Sigma represents a major directional change for most companies, and will affect every corner of the business. Part of leadership engagement in Lean Six Sigma is to undertake the responsibility to define and oversee what Lean Six Sigma will look like in the organization and how the need and benefits of this effort should be communicated to others. In most cases, the CEO assigns these responsibilities to a *design/deployment team* responsible for developing the business case and detailed plan for the first 100 days of implementation.

The overall charter of the design/deployment team is to create the vision, establish the goals and budgets, and make policy and infrastructure decisions that ensure linkage to the CEO's strategy.

Depending on the size of the company, the need for tailoring the initiative, and the complexity of the overall organization, this initial design team may be able to develop a preliminary design and business case in anywhere from two weeks to three months.

In fact, in one recent client engagement, the client was so committed that they began rolling out the process the *very first week* after they made the decision to go forward. They based their design on a template we provided and they created a concurrent process to modify and adapt it if needed as they went along. This accelerated approach is made possible because of lessons learned from the large number of companies that have already trod the path. This process is not for every company, but we can certainly say that it accelerated the time to results for the company by at least two months.

Documenting the Business Case and Developing the Preliminary Proposal

The design team is initially charged by the CEO and his/her operating committee to:

- Determine the gaps between current and desired performance.
- Determine how Lean Six Sigma can close the gap.
- Develop a preliminary design for the implementation of Lean Six Sigma.

You can make the initial gap analysis as complex or simple as you want. You should have some data on your current performance, though it may take some effort to get reliable figures. "Desired performance" will derive from long-term goals, though you may want to reframe some of them in customer-focused terms. For example, how much better would you have to get at delighting your customers in order to grow revenues by 5%? Establishing the difference between current and desired performance is important in giving your leadership a gut-level feeling about the magnitude of change required.

Once your design team has completed the gap analysis (which establishes the business case for change), it needs to develop a preliminary design of the program, analyze the costs and benefits, and outline its implementation. Detailed plans around infrastructure and launch will happen in the next phase; the purpose here is to sketch out the implementation framework.

The proposal should include:

- The general organizational structure and staffing needed to support a Lean Six Sigma effort.

- Implementation targets and plans (general timelines for launch, numbers of people who will be dedicated, types of training, etc.).
- Financial metrics and their targets (both costs and benefits). The benefits were most likely defined in your long-term goals; by far the largest investment is the salary cost of the black belts and champions, followed by the cost of green belts and external consultants.

This initial plan for the program will ensure that the management team understands Lean Six Sigma and its operational and financial benefits to the business. Sufficient depth of analysis is required such that the management team and, if necessary, the Board of Directors will understand the investment necessary and any risks involved.

At the end of these efforts, the design team will report its findings about the applicability of Lean Six Sigma to your business, present a preliminary proposal for discussion, and recommend any needed outside assistance.

THE NEXT MOVES

Once you are assured of commitment and know that executive leaders are on board and that they have a common understanding of what it will take to implement Lean Six Sigma, then you can confidently devote serious effort to planning the launch and deployment of your initiative (Chapter 6) and kick off the effort among all P&L managers (Chapter 7).

Infrastructure and Deployment Planning

Approval of the business case and preliminary proposal (described in Chapter 5) sets off a flurry of activity that should be led by the design/deployment team. The development of a detailed deployment plan can take from days to weeks, depending on company size. This is one place where empirical observations support the hiring of external consultants: people who have worked on many of these types of efforts should be able to provide you with planning and structural templates that can save you from having to reinvent the wheel. Starting with an existing template speeds up the planning process and allows you to begin implementation much earlier than if you operate entirely on your own—which in turn pays off in early results, which are key to making the process "accretive" in the first year. Meticulous planning for the first 100 days of implementation is a prime determinant of the ultimate success of a Lean Six Sigma launch and of your organization's ability to achieve major cost and lead time reductions and quality improvements in one year.

A major component of this initial planning is developing an infrastructure—including the organizational structures, processes, measures, and tools—to support Lean Six Sigma. One of the biggest risks that new Lean Six Sigma initiatives face is to become "collateralized," not part of the ongoing methods of doing business but rather a "program" or something that we do with spare time or resources. A strong infrastructure moves Lean Six Sigma from collateral to "business as usual." The failures of previous programs to stick and deliver sustained benefits are a strong paradigm that must be broken. For example, at a recent meeting with one company, they explained that they only had four people to dedicate to become black belts—but they had 50 full-time engineers and scientists working on solving quality problems in their processes with little history of addressing root cause! What level of transformational change do you think these four black belts would be able to drive without integration into the company?

PLAN COMPONENTS AND TYPICAL TIMELINES

Before we get into the details of creating a deployment plan, let's look again at the overall process and timeline (see Figure 6-1).

As you can see,

- The first step is to finish the detailed design of the infrastructure and the deployment (which is the subject of this chapter).
- The executive launch (discussed in the next chapter) is the key event that begins the engagement of the rest of the organizational leaders.
- As a result of the executive launch, business leaders and P&L

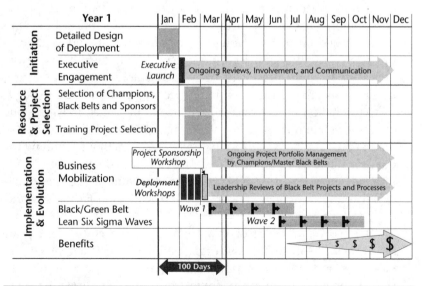

Figure 6-1. Example deployment timeline

managers select the champions and black belts—the key leaders of the implementation activities.

- The champions connect the business unit strategies and needs with the program through a project selection process (described in Chapter 8).
- Newly designated champions and black belts receive extensive training. This is usually conducted over a four- to six-month period, during which they attend classes one week per month and begin working on projects in between.
- Throughout the training and initial project implementation, leaders participate in training kickoffs, project "gate" reviews (discussed in Chapter 10), and ongoing communication.
- The rollout should be structured to drive benefits as you go. If it's done right, you will have an accretive program within your first year of effort!

This outline should be considered as a framework; you will need to customize this model to meet the unique needs of your own corporation. Actual timelines will vary greatly from organization to organization. A global rollout is more challenging, requiring among other things the training of hundreds of black belts in a single quarter. (To give you an idea of what it involves, know that Caterpillar called it the "Tsunami"—they trained 750 black belts in six months—and Starwood Hotels referred to theirs as the "Big Bang.")

One important aspect of this Gantt chart is to show how much has to happen within a short timeframe: finishing the plan, developing training, selecting and training dozens or even hundreds of belts, selecting projects … all of which occurs prior to the official launch! Dave Burritt of Caterpillar noted that one of the advantages of speed is that it creates a tension that gets everyone on board and eliminates opposition.

For the sake of clarity, each of the activities discussed below is presented as though everything was happening in sequence. But when creating your own timeline, do not wait for each element to be perfect before moving into implementation.

A good solution applied with vigor now is better than a perfect solution applied ten minutes later.
—General George S. Patton

Look for ways to work in parallel so you can speed up the process overall. You should also maintain a bias for action followed by continuous improvement.

THE DETAILED DEPLOYMENT PLAN

The major components of the detailed deployment plan are:

A. **Process**: Designing the critical Lean Six Sigma sustaining processes to be part of the normal business mode of operations.
B. **Organization**: Fleshing out the organizational structure by determining the roles, responsibilities, and reporting structures. Developing the criteria and selecting the champions and black belts. Identifying what training will be given to which groups of people.
C. **Measures**: Determining the measures of success.
D. **Rewards**: Establishing mechanisms for collection of information and methods for providing rewards and recognition.
E. **Tools**: Determining requirements for supporting software tools.

Typically, initial decisions about infrastructure will be reviewed by the operating committee or management team, along with a representative sample of P&L managers. This plan is evaluated by leadership at the initial kickoff (known as "The Transforming Event") and finalized shortly thereafter.

A. PROCESS FOCUS

Process focus applies to the proper implementation of Lean Six Sigma in a company. At the simplest level, you won't get different results if you keep doing things the old way. Most companies are currently organized around the so-called functional or silo view: departments and individuals have narrowly defined responsibilities related to specific functions (accounting, customer service, manufacturing product X). Countless examples have shown that a functional organization may optimize a given department's costs at the expense of high overhead costs, excess investment, long process cycle times, and poor customer satisfaction. It's not unusual for customers who need information to fall between the cracks because no one person owns the *process* for satisfying a customer. It is just up to the initiative of the individual to do the right thing, unsupported—and perhaps unappreciated and unrewarded—by the process. Product designs may be held up because no one is sure whether the final decisions rest with product engineering, marketing, manufacturing, or even finance! Again, the vital inputs of each of these functional organizations are not built into the development process.

Lean Six Sigma adopts the view that businesses are composed of processes that start with customer needs and should end with delighted customers using your product or benefiting from your service. Each major process is referred to as a *value stream* (the set of activities that turn a customer opportunity into delivered outcomes). All work should therefore be driven by an awareness of where it falls in the value stream's processes, what it needs from the preceding steps in order to be done well, and what it should deliver to later steps to meet customer needs.

This process viewpoint of the value stream has a profound impact on how the organization operates and how teams view their work. For example, many Lean Six Sigma projects will focus on accelerating flow through a *process* by eliminating time traps. To achieve that goal, these projects *cut across the departmental or silo boundaries* of each process step. In fact, champions and black belts will often map the process across current departmental boundaries, define interface problems, and propose cross-functional solutions. If the people working in the various departments aren't prepared for this approach or have not received Lean Six Sigma training, you're likely to encounter amazing resistance.

It is not necessary to "re-engineer" a company to reflect a process structure. Lean Six Sigma effectively creates a process mindset through the value stream mapping that drives project selection. A process-driven organization achieves greater quality and speed by reversing the paradigms that created functional organizations, as captured in Table 6-1 (developed by Caterpillar and reprinted here with their permission).

This process view helps shape decisions made here in the planning stage that will affect actions in the selection and implementation of Lean Six Sigma such as ...

- Selection of projects based on the customer needs, strategic direction, financial requirements, and process performance of the company. (See Chapter 8.)
- Prioritization and allocation of resources to produce fast results. (See Chapter 8.)
- An ongoing development of individual skills and team effectiveness. (See Chapter 9.)
- A system of rewards, recognition, and communication that is integrated into the company culture (not excluded from the rest of the organization) and that creates a virtual circle of momentum. (Discussed later in this chapter.)

Functional Organizations	Process Organizations
Quality is for QC Department	Leader drives for 6 sigma results
Focus on department optimization	Focus on process for customers
Defines problem and solution	Leaders set objectives with team involvement
Decisions by past experience	Decides based on data gathered by team
Focused on accounting measures	Also focused on customers, markets, speed
Delegates training to HR	HR engaged in training as a process driver
Overhead cost is a necessary evil	Overhead cost can be reduced by speed

Table 6-1. Comparing functional and process organizations

- A process of evaluation of the financial results of the individual projects to create accountability and address barriers expeditiously. (See Chapter 8.)
- A planned process of critical, multi-media communications that engage all leadership levels and penetrate the organization from top to bottom. (See Chapter 12.)

Defining these processes is the job of the design team, supported by the functional leaders in the company. Many organizations have existing processes that can be leveraged in the deployment of Lean Six Sigma. To avoid an early collateralization of the process, the design team must engage the organization in the development of these key infrastructure processes. A simple example of integration vs. collateralization is the choice of communications media: to properly integrate communications, the Lean Six Sigma initiative should leverage existing media (like company newsletters) to the extent possible rather than inventing new channels for communication.

B. ORGANIZATIONAL STRUCTURES

The Lean Six Sigma organizational structure has three specific purposes:

- Institutionalizing the Lean Six Sigma effort.
- Establishing clearly defined roles, responsibilities, and accountabilities.

- Establishing clear lines of communication that link organizational leadership to team members.

The natural question is how do you establish the organizational critical mass for gaining momentum and at the same time avoid the risk of collateralization? The answer is to create a structure that integrates Lean Six Sigma responsibilities into the traditional organizational structure and institutionalizes the processes described in the section above. One organizational model is shown in Figure 6-2.

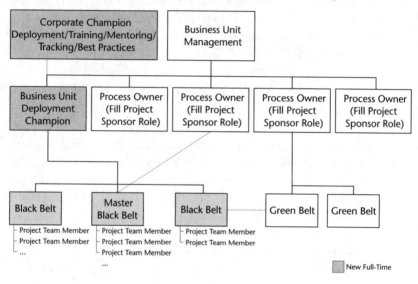

Figure 6-2. Lean Six Sigma implementation structure

As you can see, the Lean Six Sigma organization includes a mix of people whose primary job is the traditional line responsibilities (executives and managers) and a new set of people who work on Lean Six Sigma full- or part-time. Though the two interact, we'll look at them separately. The important thing is to ensure that their responsibilities support the key processes described above—they are not "occasional" tasks to be performed as time permits. Painting a value stream map of their involvement in key processes drives home the importance of their roles.

Infrastructure Positions with Line Responsibilities

Line managers in your organization are critical to achieving breakthrough performance. They are key players in conscientiously assigning champions and black belts and in achieving process owner support. To make sure that implementation goes smoothly and that the effort is used to drive shareholder value, various line positions must have specific Lean Six Sigma responsibilities and goals. And that dictum begins at the top of the organization.

CEO/President

The previous chapter described the need for CEO or COO engagement in the Lean Six Sigma process. By definition, a lesser person is *not responsible* for overall company performance and hence the company champion should report to the "C" level person. If, for example, adequate resources are not provided by a given business unit, it is the job of the engaged CEO or COO to make a resolution.

Besides being the person who must decide that adoption of these new methods is of strategic importance to the company, the CEO must also perform a role in infrastructure processes by ...

- Consistently communicating the strategic priorities to direct reports (both unit managers and the company champion, for example).
- Following up communication with action by constantly reinforcing the importance of Lean Six Sigma efforts to both direct reports (e.g., by monitoring detailed planning, informally inquiring about progress) and to the organization as a whole (e.g., through memos, presentations).
- Monitoring the rolled-up results vs. plan and taking corrective action.

Business Unit (P&L) Managers

The business unit managers work with the champion to clearly articulate the unit's strategy, which becomes the "specifications" or criteria for selection of the highest-potential NPV value streams and approval of their supporting black belt projects (a process that the champion typically facilitates with the business unit leaders).

The final decisions about which value streams to select, which projects to execute, and in which order belong to the business unit manager. This combination of infrastructure process and organization helps leaders meet operating and capital plans, thus moving Lean Six Sigma toward "business as usual." In some cases, it starts to restore the lost trust that many managers feel toward performance improvement initiatives.

This integration continues as the business unit manager works with the champion to:

- Identify black belt candidates.
- Develop and support black belts and other resources in their project work.
- Create a Lean Six Sigma deployment plan for their unit.
- Use Lean Six Sigma to actively solve the most pressing problems in the business.

During the roll-out of Lean Six Sigma, the greatest contribution that business unit managers can make is to inspire and drive the initiative. They must learn and use its tools and language in daily operations and make its success or failure their and their teams' responsibility, not a consultant's or anyone else's.

Line Manager

Line managers reporting to a business unit manager own the processes that will be improved by Lean Six Sigma. They are often referred to as *process owners* and are responsible for the largest number of people in the processes. While the black belt, green belts, and other specialists are responsible for developing solutions using the Lean Six Sigma tools, the timely implementation of those methods is the responsibility of line managers, who will typically fill the role of project sponsors.

The line managers' specific responsibilities include:

- Aid in project selection within the value stream by contributing their intimate knowledge of the process, its customers, and its suppliers.
- Help select black belts based on an intimate knowledge of their capabilities.
- Create an environment for project success.
- Work with the unit champion and black belts to help provide data and insight on the projects that the teams are working on.
- Monitor the progress of the project by conducting DMAIC stage gate reviews.
- Sustain the improvements and financial gains after the black belt has moved on to the next project.

New Infrastructure Positions with Specific Lean Six Sigma Responsibilities

To successfully implement an entirely new way of doing business, you can't rely solely on people for whom Lean Six Sigma must compete with other priorities. That's why Lean Six Sigma builds new, dedicated positions around the traditional infrastructure. These positions fall into two broad categories:

- **Champions**: Full-time managerial-level personnel responsible for coordinating and overseeing Lean Six Sigma implementation, champions are direct reports to either the CEO (or other "C" level person) or a unit P&L manager/president.
- **"Belts"**: Black belts and master black belts are full-time positions that report directly to the unit champion. Green belts and white belts are additional trained resources for Lean Six Sigma projects; these positions provide a development path to becoming a black belt.

The black belts and champions should be selected with the view that they are potentially the managers and executives of tomorrow. Being full-time, dedicated resources, they will receive extensive training, develop a process view of the organization, and gain experience in solving real business problems to create shareholder value. When a management position opens up, companies often have to scramble to find a successor, who may not have the balance of skills or experience. The Lean Six Sigma process naturally provides the requisite balance of skills and bench strength.

Does it work? I was a member of such a training program when I joined the Texas Instruments Semiconductor Division right out of college. The company recruited about 25 young people into the program every year. Each person spent one to two years in programmed assignments in marketing, manufacturing, engineering, etc., before receiving a permanent assignment. Due to a management change, the program was scuttled after about eight years of operation. I had already left the company, but for 20 years later I knew most of the senior executives ... they were all graduates of this programmed experience process ... but their ranks were not being replenished.

Company or Group Champion

The company champions report to the CEO or COO or president, as applicable. This direct reporting relationship is critical: if the company champion does not report to the CEO or COO, the "C" level officer's engagement will be suspect.

The champion leads the design team, helps develop the corporate Lean Six Sigma strategy, and ultimately monitors its execution. As such, his or her primary *responsibility* is to ensure that the rest of the company executes a consistent, rapid deployment. Because of this requirement and the need to be able to address major barriers that will arise, the company champion must be a very strong manager capable of making it happen. Another role is the monitoring and roll-up of Lean Six Sigma results as compared with the strategic stretch goals set forth by the CEO. This includes making intermediate determinations as to the deployment's effectiveness by monitoring the quality and quantity of training events, resources committed by the business units, and the ramp-up to accretive results.

Business Unit Champions

The champions within each business unit are the glue that holds Lean Six Sigma together by building the critical bridge between business unit strategies and black belt projects. Being a business unit champion is a full-time job and the role should be assigned to a person who the company thinks has the potential to become a business unit manager in three years. As such, being selected for a champion role is a "step to success" and *voluntary* acceptance of this role is a must.

The business unit champion responsibilities are to …

- Develop the Lean Six Sigma schedule and deployment plans for the unit (in conjunction with the unit manager and corporate design/deployment team).
- Oversee the deployment of Lean Six Sigma in their business unit.
- Identify and, with the business unit manager, remove barriers to deployment.
  - Lead the process for proper selection of high-value projects.
  - Provide mentorship, management, and performance review of five to 15 black belt teams.
- Provide communication (up and down).
  - Keep the unit manager informed of team progress.
  - Ensure that "best practices" are shared throughout the organization.
- Ensure business unit engagement, not compliance.
- Work with the unit's controller to validate the bottom-line impact of each improvement before the results are rolled up to the company champion.
- Track, validate, and upload business unit results to the corporate champion.
- Provide integration for cross-business unit processes.

Because these champions have such important responsibilities, they receive intensive training in the Lean Six Sigma tools related to value stream/project selection. Through this process, a champion understands what process flow really means and how Lean Six Sigma can find and create value.

Master Black Belt

Master black belts act as internal expert consultants to black belts and their teams. As such, the master black belts must be experienced in successfully managing improvement teams to reach goals using improvement tools and skilled leadership. In fact, a typical master black belt will have worked as a black belt and completed five to 10 projects with annualized benefits of $2 million per year.

Since master black belts train, mentor, and coach black belts, a candidate must also have proven teaching skills, often gained by teaching three or more sessions in a standard four-week black belt training course.

In addition, each master black belt is typically expected to become an expert resource in one or more specialty areas, such as the advanced Six Sigma or Lean tools. Master black belts provide the conduit to get best practices communicated with the unit champion and then out to the rest of the organization. For example, the master black belt would be the person who uploads examples of best practices onto an intranet or Web-based communication system. He or she would support internal meetings or symposia where teams share their results with others.

The education and grooming of master black belts is an important process in the organization. During early implementation, few organizations have people with the proper expertise, which is why external consultants initially fill this role. Eventually, as black belts get more hands-on experience with teams, they can be certified as master black belts once they gain training experience and additional education in their specialty area.

Black Belt

Black belts are full-time positions responsible for leading project teams. They are responsible for delivering the value and benefits that were determined for each of their projects during the project selection process.

Specific black belt responsibilities include:

- Working with the project sponsor (line manager) and unit champion to formulate and implement improvement projects.
- Training green belts in the DMAIC process.

Black belts need to have expertise in team leadership skills (see Chapter 9) so they can draw the best intellect, energy, and action from their teams. They will also work with their teams to identify best practices, which are then submitted to their master black belt (and then shared with the rest of the organization). Black belts often act as mentors to other black belts, specifically on the best practices they were involved in developing.

To become certified black belts, candidates receive extensive training, usually at least a five-week course built around the Lean Six Sigma improvement process, tools, and leadership skills. They must also have completed a training project and one or two additional projects with total annualized benefits of at least $400,000 per year and must have conducted green belt training.

Green Belts (Team Members)

A green belt works on a Lean Six Sigma project only part-time, on a specific process about which he or she generally possesses knowledge important to the success of the project. The green belt will typically receive two weeks of training from the black belt and will learn to apply the specific DMAIC skills that relate to the project at hand. In addition to assisting the black belt, the green belt may be assigned specific projects for independent execution.

Green belts have regular duties assigned by their line managers, but usually they regard the green belt position as an opportunity to excel and gain valuable tools and experience.

White Belts

White belts are another part-time resource that some organizations use to expand the pool of people who have some understanding of Lean Six Sigma goals and tools. (The term "white belt" is generic: this role may be designated by the company color.) White belts receive awareness training through classroom instruction, distance learning, books, and/or articles. This typically requires two to four hours of effort. The white belt may take the initiative to join a team as a potential green belt resource and make a contribution to the continuous improvement process.

Transition Tips

The management structure outlined above should be considered as a straw model to be modified to suit the needs and culture of your company. Most of the successful companies we have served and of which we have direct knowledge use a similar structure. The benefit of this structure is that it has been found highly effective in smoothly transforming a company from a functional to a process focus without disrupting existing managers or departments as did some implementations of "re-engineering." The structure respects the existing balances of power within the corporation and uses these strengths to assist the Lean Six Sigma process.

The career advancement opportunities inherent in being selected as a black belt or a champion are not lost on participants. It is not uncommon to have many more black belt candidates than positions. This enthusiasm helps creates a virtuous cycle and organizational momentum.

Yet, like all successful change initiatives, with Lean Six Sigma the new must grow out of the old. Before you make a lot of innovations, I suggest you speak to people at other companies who have Six Sigma implementation experience.

Black Belt Training

A well-rounded black belt training program uses diverse instructional techniques:

- Five to six weeks of classroom training, including one week of leadership training, four weeks of Lean Six Sigma, and an optional week to go into deeper detail on Lean or Six Sigma tools—training that should be rich in demonstration, simulation, student practice, and exercises.
- Expert coaching (opportunities for one-on-one or small group interactions centered around project needs) to increase the socialization process and accelerate internalization (typically five-10 days across the overall training cycle).
- Individual testing to provide feedback on the effectiveness of learning.
- Application of new methods on real projects so participants can internalize new skills.
- Access to training materials, case studies, and other resources through both printed and electronic means.

Champion Training

The role of the champion differs significantly from that of the black belt and is less standardized across companies adopting LSS. Their primary roles are LSS program governance, communicating LSS to the organization, and ensuring value creation through project selection and effective barrier removal. In essence, the champions are the liaison between the Six Sigma program and the P&L management of the company. They will receive between four and eight weeks of training in the first year of the program and may assist with the training of others beyond this. A typical roll-out of champion training is shown in Figure 6-3.

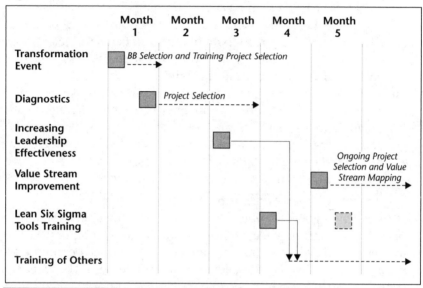

Figure 6-3. Champion training roll-out

As you can see, the content differs substantially from that of black belts:

- The champions must learn how to both manage the new Lean Six Sigma infrastructure and productively interact with traditional line management.
- There is a heavier emphasis on strategic issues rather than tactical. The champions focus on top-down analytical abilities in order to better direct black belts at key improvement needs. This typically means *thorough training and application of financial and NPV analysis* and an understanding of valuation theory. It also requires a tool set for decomposing the entire business cost into relevant value streams and being able to select the most critical ones for further effort. These are provided in the diagnostic courses and the value stream improvement courses.

- Champions need to be trained to comprehend the tools and techniques of Lean Six Sigma, but only to a depth sufficient to manage black belt teams and know what results to demand. Thus, the "tool" portion of champion training is an abbreviated version of that given to the black belts. In some cases, the champions will attend all the Six Sigma tools sessions along with the black belts, but in most cases they can be adequately prepared with one to two weeks of Lean Six Sigma DMAIC training.
- Because a key responsibility of the champions is to be able to remove barriers from the path of the black belt and LSS program, champions also attend the leadership effectiveness course to enhance their interpersonal capabilities.
- A key element of effective champion training is to ensure that they are capable of delivering of awareness training to the broader organization. This is the true test of how well they have absorbed and internalized their own training. They will often help train local management staffs, project sponsors, and possibly even green belts. This has the side benefit of reducing the overall cost of the initiative by minimizing reliance on external trainers.

The same general approach is taken with the champions as the black belts to ensure effective training and high retention rates. They are generally in a classroom environment for one week per month and the material covered is provided on a just-in-time basis. The tools, concepts, and methodology covered in the class will be applied within the coming weeks as they face their next set of deliverables in launching the Lean Six Sigma initiative.

It should be noted the training regime above represents the *minimum* and may need to be augmented with remedial or supplemental skills training for some champions. Remedial topics would address deficiencies in financial skills, basic math, or statistics. Supplemental topics may include lean production, product development or Design for Six Sigma (DFSS), more or deeper Lean Six Sigma tools, or intensive "train-the-trainer" programs.

Leveraging the Learning

For Lean Six Sigma to truly take hold, both formal "classroom" learning and knowledge gleaned from guided practice must be communicated and shared broadly across the company. There are several strategies for doing so:

- **Build a robust curriculum.** For the more formal learning, it is important to have a robust curriculum that can be modified or broken down into modules and shared electronically with various groups that need elements of the training. You will need to either license a curriculum or build one of your own. Most Six Sigma consultants will license a curriculum to you and this is usually a much better decision from a perspective of overall quality and effectiveness than taking on the challenge of building several weeks of engaging, exciting training with the limited time you will have to get the Lean Six Sigma process off the ground and earning a profit.

- **Provide means for people to interact.** Both research and experience have shown that some of the most effective learning happens when people interact. This can happen in a classroom setting, through one-on-one coaching with an experienced master black belt or other expert, or even through computer bulletin boards and chat rooms. In short, don't bring your black belts together one week a month and then leave them on their own the rest of the time to work in isolation. You can speed up the learning of *all* the black belts by providing forums for them to share challenges, frustrations, and lessons learned.

- **Exploit technology.** Yes, some human interaction is necessary for people to develop a deep, practical understanding of a topic. But technology-based education and communication can help speed the process. For one thing, software is infinitely more patient than most people! And e-based instructional materials, self-tests, and so on provide easy access to anyone in your organization, no matter where they are. Also, electronic materials are more easily customized than printed materials. There are even programs like Virtual Coach that people can access through CD-ROM or the Internet that allow them to practice skills and revisit material they learned in classroom.

- **Document and share best practices throughout the company.** A company with thousands of employees and hundreds of common processes is naturally going to have some problems that are shared by many operations and geographies. Whether it is a wave solder machine or response to a customer call, creating a process to do it well *once* gives you the opportunity to leverage this learning across the corporation and multiply the payback on your Lean Six Sigma investment. If you are managing a dealer network of hundreds of branch locations, developing a process that avoids long queues will be valuable at all branches. Leveraging this knowledge across the corporation—rather than creating "pockets of excellence"—is a critical strategy for achieving the primary

Lean Six Sigma goal of significantly improving shareholder value in under a year.

Leverage has an important impact on implementation strategies: you don't have to spread your improvement efforts across the entire organization in order to achieve organization-wide benefits. Instead of pursuing separate and unconnected initiatives at several sites, it makes a lot more sense to focus improvement resources on one site or one team, identify and refine process improvements there, and then share best practices with others. In fact, once you come up with a best practice, package an explanation of it into an hour or two of material with lots of supporting examples. These packages can help others understand how to implement the same or similar techniques in their processes. If you have a centralized computer project coordination tool, you might consider using it to transfer best practices and innovations.

C. MEASURES

The eventual success of your Lean Six Sigma program will be determined by the financial results that Lean Six Sigma adds to the bottom line. As you plan your deployment, you must think in terms of measuring things that will be indicators of the potential financial results to come.

I like to measure the program in terms of leading indicators that will tell me two things:

- How quickly will the program reach critical mass to pay for itself?
- Once the program is established, what is the ongoing return on investment?

On the first question, the leading indicators are tied to the initial actions that the deployment team business unit management must take to get the program off the ground. These are straightforward and easy to measure. For example:

- Number of executives trained.
- Number of full-time champions identified and trained.
- Number of full-time black belts selected, as % of target.
- Number of full-time black belts trained.
- Size and value of project "queue."
- Measure of organizational readiness for change (includes management communication and development of the business unit specific "burning platform").

On the second question, we can break the value equation down into its key drivers, some of which are quite straightforward to measure. As Figure 6-4 shows, overall value delivered can be broken down into two major factors:

number of projects completed × average value per project

The number of projects completed is a function of the number of black belts and the average project cycle time. The value per project is simply a function of the quality of projects selected (Are they valuable and strategically important?) and the quality of the solution delivered by the team (Were they able to get to root cause? Were they able to address the whole problem?).

At a minimum, you must measure project cycle time and project values on a regular basis and gain an understanding of the level of variation in these numbers (as shown in Table 6-2).

Some of the deeper drivers shown Figure 6-4 are the root causes of performance issues you may encounter and can also be measured with creativity. Surveys, project audits, team evaluations, and coach-

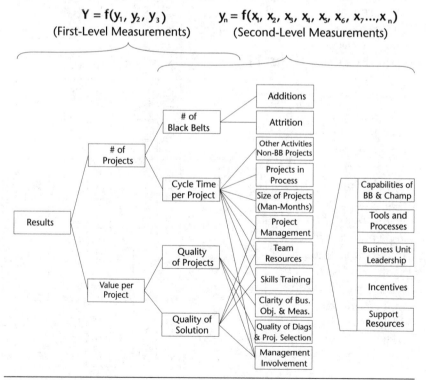

$$Y = f(y_1, y_2, y_3)$$
(First-Level Measurements)

$$y_n = f(x_1, x_2, x_3, x_4, x_5, x_6, x_7...,x_n)$$
(Second-Level Measurements)

Figure 6-4. Identify critical inputs to measure

ing/training evaluations can provide some of the right data.

In essence, the company deployment team should accept the same challenge that it has put forth for its black belts for project execution: to go get the data and to let the data speak on the performance of the program. I recommend that any organization that has a Six Sigma or Lean Six Sigma program under way that is performing below target results should pursue this type of program performance analysis to understand the root causes of underperformance in each major business unit.

| BB Project Data | Completed Projects | | | | | | | | Active Projects | | | | On-Hold/ Queue Projects | | |
| | 2000 | | | | 2001 (YTD) | | | | | | | | | | |
	Number of Projects	Average Duration per Project (weeks)	Average Savings per Project (annual $K)	Median Savings per Project (annual $K)	Number of Projects	Average Duration per Project (weeks)	Average Savings per Project (annual $K)	Median Savings per Project (annual $K)	Number of Projects	Average Duration per Project (weeks)	Average Savings per Project (annual $K)	Median Savings per Project (annual $K)	Number of Projects	Average Savings per Project (annual $K)	Median Savings per Project (annual $K)
Region A	6	12.0	$467	$390	4	11.0	$309	$216	7	14.6	$204	$200	20	$165	$122
Region B	8	16.0	$250	$255	8	16.0	$340	$280	11	14.0	$286	$250	21	$249	$240
Region C	4	18.0	$259	$188	1	31.0	$1,686	$1,686	7	20.0	$190	$109	7	$250	$250
Region D	7	19.0	$134	$120	7	21.6	$306	$108	9	21.3	$410	$250	8	$486	$294
Region E	4	23.6	$158	$128	4	14.0	$556	$511	5	15.0	$246	$250	12	$214	$250
Region F	2	20.0	$165	$165	2	15.0	$360	$360	3	12.0	$200	$200	9	$175	$175
Total	31	17.4	$250	$177	26	16.9	$413	$320	42	16.6	$272	$225	77	$238	$245

Table 6-2. Displaying project results

Quantitative measures of financial improvement should be linked to every initiative. This may seem obvious but is not always the case. For example, a champion once reported that they were going to embark on Lean training. I asked what the goal was and he replied: "To sensitize people to Lean." There was no defined goal for reduction of lead time, inventory, or manufacturing overhead cost. Lean Six Sigma methodology must be driven to measurable financial results, not activity traps.

D. REWARDS AND RECOGNITION

"Infrastructure" is more than just job responsibilities and reporting relationships. Everything that defines the organization's culture and employee practices affects whether people will be interested in and willing to drop their current career path in favor of accepting a new role.

In selecting black belts and master black belts, your company is selecting its future leaders. The company is providing extensive training that will leave these high-potential candidates a highly marketable skill. The last thing you want to have happen is to invest a lot of time and resources in these people, then have them leave for greener pastures. Two issues that will help you retain these resources are *compensation* and *recognition*.

Compensation

Clearly it is useful to know what other firms have done and what have been their results. My company looked at base salary, cash and stock bonuses, and key lessons learned. To collect this data, we personally interviewed over 100 black belts and master black belts, analyzed recruiting Web sites (e.g., HotJobs) and résumés, and discussed compensation plans with a dozen companies considered to be leaders in Six Sigma implementation. The conclusions?

- The base pay was very dependent on work experience, industry, and location.
- The bonus cash compensation amounted to an average of 20% of base per year for black belts and 25% for master black belts.
- When stock option compensation was used, it amounted to about 30% of base, but had a huge variance in valuation and vesting over time.

To the extent that bonuses are paid on project performance, it is more likely tied to hard savings rather than cost avoidance. But few firms (some notable exceptions) tied black belt compensation to project performance because, in their opinion:

- It was difficult to estimate who contributed what.
- It was prone to gamesmanship.
- It rewarded low-hanging fruit just as much as tougher mature projects.
- It only created resentment among other team members and hurt overall results.

Here are some recommendations based on the results of our investigation:

- Have a modest increase to base salary of 5%-10% when black belts complete their DMAIC training.
- To the extent that a bonus is tied to project performance, create a pool of money at the business unit level from savings generated, then share that pool out to all black belts, champions, and green belts.

This approach is non-competitive and non-divisive. Remember: you're trying to develop the future leaders of the company, not cowboys or free agents. The type of person needed for general management must be a team player who believes in team rewards. All evidence indicates that it is career growth that black belts crave and that they see participation in Six Sigma as a step along that path. It is more important for the company to generate career opportunities for black belts than cash compensation. If you want a more direct tie of rewards to results, we recommend a pilot project so that the impact on your company's culture can be understood and necessary corrections made.

Recognition

One piece of good news from the research we did was that the black belts we talked to who wanted to jump ship did so for reasons that are easily addressed: they felt they were not receiving adequate recognition or career development and were being "pigeonholed." The fear expressed by some managers that they will lose the black belts to the "market" is not borne out.

Recognition can come in many forms. One of the most meaningful is to have management involved at significant milestones in a black belt's development. As mentioned, Lou Giuliano, CEO of ITT Industries, attended the kickoff of every black belt and champion training wave around the world. An executive presence at a ceremony at the completion of the four weeks of black belt training and/or at the subsequent certification is also appropriate. Not every CEO can manage this time commitment, especially in very large companies that may have as many as 200 black belts, but some level of executive sponsorship will go a long way to both reinforcing corporate commitment to the Lean Six Sigma effort and demonstrating that the black belt team's work is important to the organization. At the green belt level, the business unit manager and champion should conduct the recognition ceremony, again showing the unity of Lean Six Sigma and line management.

Institutionalizing the Decisions

The decisions made about compensation, recognition, and even promoting people through each "belt" level need to be firmly established in corporate policy prior to selecting people to fill the new positions. The management teams that will interview candidates need to be able to speak with authority about how these systems work so that people will feel more comfortable moving over to this new, parallel infrastructure.

E. INFRASTRUCTURE TOOLS

As you're probably aware by now, Lean Six Sigma is a major initiative that needs to both reach down to the frontlines throughout your company *and* be easily viewed from a macro level to ensure that efforts are truly contributing to shareholder value.

Many clients that we have worked with have found tremendous value in the deployment of tools to support the deployment of programs. These fall into several categories:

- Project identification and selection software tools
  - identify time traps and opportunities in the value stream
  - support the prioritization of projects
- Program management software tools
  - track project progress and roll up financial results and financial results drivers
  - detailed project management tools
- Learning and leverage software
  - learning and reference tools (online and PC-Based)
  - best practice tracking and sharing
- Team assessment software

Several of these tools are discussed later in this book. For example, you'll find project selection tools discussed in Chapter 7 and team assessment software in Chapter 9. Each of these areas represents a special area of expertise that you will need to investigate on your own so you can develop tools that will work within your own company culture and computing environment.

COMPLETING THE DEPLOYMENT PLAN

This chapter covered most of the areas you need to address in a deployment plan, but here is one more ingredient that hasn't been addressed yet: plans for the official kickoff of the initiative, which will bring all your P&L managers on board. This issue is so important that we've devoted the entire next chapter to describing it!

Chapter 7

Kickoff: Establishing the Vision Company-Wide

The very first actions associated with Lean Six Sigma implementation—getting CEO engagement and deployment planning—are focused at the highest level of the company. That means only a small cadre of people have been involved: the CEO, executives, perhaps a few upper-level P&L managers, the corporate champion, and perhaps an external consultant.

Obviously you can't achieve Lean Six Sigma goals if only a handful of people are involved in the effort! Very soon, your P&L managers will have to come off the sidelines and actively join the initiative by selecting some of their key staff to become full-time Lean Six Sigma resources and by championing the translation of corporate goals into value-creating projects.

Remember that many P&L managers (and others in the organization) will likely approach Lean Six Sigma with some skepticism, especially if they have privately heard negative reviews of Six Sigma: that companies claimed benefits that Six Sigma did not actually produce, that it didn't work somewhere, etc. Yet in essence you're now asking these managers to use Lean Six Sigma as the *primary tool* to meet their business objectives, not just turn to it as an ad hoc addition to business-as-usual (as might have been the case with past initiatives).

It's impossible to convert skeptics to implementers in a one-hour presentation or with a memo signed by the CEO. You need to create an *experience* that gives people time to digest and analyze what they've learned and experience the benefits of Lean Six Sigma firsthand. The vehicle we've found most successful for this purpose is what we call a "Transforming Event," an intensive two- to three-day meeting, held off-site, designed to convince P&L managers that Lean Six Sigma …

- Is "something different."
- Addresses the "burning platform" need to increase shareholder value.
- Provides breakthrough profit potential.

As noted, P&L managers are the primary audience for the Transforming Event because they will soon be asked to dedicate their greatest asset, the *best people* in their unit, in support of Lean Six Sigma implementation *and* to ask them to attack the biggest problems in the business with a new process. Being exposed to the value proposition of Lean Six Sigma can begin to convince these managers that they are not giving up anything, but rather deploying their best personnel to most effectively execute projects that offer the highest value potential. Other attendees might include corporate or unit champion candidates (they are relatively few) and a selection of other organizational leaders.

No single event can be expected to make every attendee an instant Lean Six Sigma convert forevermore. But having a widely publicized, widely attended event will initiate the process with a healthy level of optimism. The plans for this event should be part of the larger deployment plans developed by your design/deployment team.

STRUCTURE OF THE TRANSFORMING EVENT

A Transforming Event typically includes five elements, each with a particular purpose:

A. **CEO presentation**, to demonstrate personal leadership commitment to the effort and to clearly establish the "burning platform" issue that affects shareholder value

B. **Design team presentation**, which presents a credible picture of how the company will look when process efficiency and quality improvements are rapidly increasing shareholder value

C. "**Testimonials**" from trusted outsiders from experienced companies, to show that these ideas work in actual situations

    D. **Lean Six Sigma simulation**, so participants can experience first-hand what it's like to improve quality, reduce cycle time, and understand their co-dependent interaction

    E. **Launch preparations**, discussions that pave the way for transition from this event to ongoing work in support of Lean Six Sigma

Here is more detail on each of these activities.

A. CEO PRESENTATION

The CEO should always kick off the Transforming Event with a concise, upbeat presentation that conveys his or her vision of the company's present and future and the resulting overall performance goals in terms of ROIC, revenue growth, and share valuation. The CEO generally makes the case for using Lean Six Sigma to achieve these goals by presenting facts and comparative data to show the "burning platform"—the business-critical issue that is facing the company. This includes linking Lean Six Sigma to issues such as the following:

- The breakthrough nature of results needed to achieve higher shareholder value or surpass the performance of a competitor.
- The need for improved responsiveness and flexibility in meeting customer needs.
- The need to develop and deliver a superior product or service in far less time.
- The major challenge of sustaining earnings growth (key to shareholder value).
- Achievements made by other firms that are adopting Lean Six Sigma.

In other words, the key message is that by implementing Lean Six Sigma, the company will have the highest level of customer retention, the lowest marketing cost per revenue dollar, and the ability to attract and retain personnel better than others in the marketplace. All of this success would be solidly based on the shortest lead times, best on-time delivery, highest quality, and fastest development in its industry.

In this presentation, the CEO must be real, honest, and personal with the group about the need for change. He or she must demonstrate a personal commitment to the process by explaining the actions he or she will personally take to lead the change.

B. DESIGN TEAM PRESENTATION

The CEO's presentation is followed up by a presentation by the design team in which they show how the organization is going to act on the CEO's strategy. In essence, they are previewing the major aspects of the detailed deployment plan:

- The new infrastructure, including targets, roles, and reporting relationships for champions, black belts, and master black belts.
- A preview of black belt and champion training material and how that material can be tailored to the processes of the individual business units.
- Communication strategies and tools (e.g., specs for Web-based project- and results-tracking tools, learning strategies, and best practice sharing).
- Targets for completion of detailed divisional and business unit roll-outs.

The purpose of this presentation is to develop a clear understanding of the goals, the approach, and the tools by delivering a consistent message across the corporation.

C. "TESTIMONIALS" FROM EXPERIENCED COMPANIES

To add a touch of reality, follow up the CEO's address and design team presentation with a case study or testimonial from an executive of a firm that has already implemented Lean Six Sigma. In the case of Caterpillar, for example, CEO Glen Barton's address was followed by Larry Bossidy, CEO of Honeywell, and Lou Giuliano, CEO of ITT. Ideally, this testimonial should come from a trusted customer or supplier who can generate belief with the audience.

D. SIMULATION

It's likely that the majority of your P&L managers will have little direct experience with Lean and/or Six Sigma. Listening to presentations may make them aware of Lean Six Sigma as an improvement strategy, but they will probably remain skeptical until they see for themselves that the methods and strategies work. The goal in this portion of the Transforming Event is for the P&L managers to internalize the message of the CEO and apply it to their own businesses.

What we've found most effective is holding a full- or half-day exercise in which the P&L managers apply Lean Six Sigma tools to a simulated process where they are asked to identify process changes, make them, and measure the benefits after multiple improvement cycles. This combination of minimum lecture and maximum application has proven extremely effective in gaining managers' commitment to Lean Six Sigma.

The goal in the simulation is to get the participants to focus on the power of Lean Six Sigma tools in accelerating process speed and reducing process defects, cost, and capital. The method is powerful because it provides a genuine learning opportunity (much like those that the black belts and champions will get in their training) and because it is engaging enough that the participants will momentarily forget their concerns and skepticism as they become completely focused on driving process improvement.

In our own consulting practice, we base the simulation on situations that will be familiar to participants, but do not duplicate the client's process or use actual client data. Why? Experience shows that people are too easily distracted by minute details when presented with their actual process; they spend their energy debating how their process works, which is not the point of the simulation.

Reaching the Great "Aha"

As the participants begin applying Lean Six Sigma principles to the simulated process, they find they can remove some of the non-value-added steps from the process map, dramatically reduce defects, and accelerate process speed—just as will happen in actual application. They run the process again and again collect data. Participants then discuss the improvement in sigma level, process speeds, cost, and customer satisfaction levels. This will be followed by teaching and applying the appropriate *Improve, Control,* and *Lean* improvement tools, then running the process and collecting data a third time.

With each stage in the simulation, participants see a dramatic acceleration in process speed, an improvement in quality and customer satisfaction, and a reduction in cost and capital. This creates a great moment of enthusiasm, a great "Aha" that is typically not achieved with presentation materials alone.

At the end of the simulation, the design team can revisit the company's Lean Six Sigma program because participants will now have more receptive, educated ears with which to hear the intended messages. They can cover the projected roll-out, resource requirements and roles and responsibilities, and the criteria for success. The P&L managers now understand that they are going to have to supply the black belt and green belt resources, generally without replacement, to make this process yield the results demanded by the CEO.

E. LAUNCH PREPARATIONS

The final agenda item at the Transforming Event is preparing participants for work they should be aware of and/or involved in once they return to their "regular work." The content of this agenda item varies greatly from company to company: the key is to set realistic goals based on how much time you can use at the event itself vs. how much will have to happen through other venues as a follow-up. Two issues that are typically covered are:

- **Project selection.** The high-level managers attending a Transforming Event rarely have the frontline knowledge needed to identify specific projects on their own, but they will almost certainly be involved in making the final selection within their business units. Therefore, rather than spend time at the event trying to brainstorm project ideas, the time is usually better spent introducing them to key aspects of the project selection process (described in Chapter 8) and perhaps brainstorming *criteria* for selecting appropriate projects.
- **Barriers to implementation.** Lean Six Sigma is never implemented on a clean slate; each of the managers attending the Transforming Event will have interests competing for their time and resources, organizational policies or procedures that might get in the way of implementation, etc. The event is a great forum to expose some of these concerns and have the managers work collectively to develop strategies for overcoming the barriers. The CEO and/or design team should lead this discussion; involving everyone in planning to address the barriers will help get them to commit to a set of actions to make it happen.

THE CASCADE OF TRANSFORMING EVENTS

The Transforming Event is now complete and a version, tailored to the specific business, will be repeated for the management of each P&L unit and will include presentations by the P&L manager.

Depending on the size of your organization, it may be that holding a single Transforming Event for all the P&L managers is impractical. In that case, you can adapt the Transforming Event model described above to various levels of the organization. The CEO and the design team can use this to launch Lean Six Sigma at the central corporate level; then, as the deployment plan work is going forward, each business unit manager can use it to deliver a similar event (typically three days) at the local P&L level, modified to address the local issues. (Remember: it is critical to obtain in-depth engagement from the business units because those managers will be asked to reassign high-quality personnel as champions and black belts.)

ACHIEVING A COMPANY-WIDE VISION

Transforming Events are an effective tool for promoting company-wide understanding of the CEO vision, but remember that they reach only a small fraction of the people who work in your company. Just as it was critical to transfer understanding and gain commitment to Lean Six Sigma on the part of the P&L managers, it is equally important to gain commitment from managers, employees, unions, and suppliers. Communication with these groups and, when appropriate, with customers and security analysts who follow the company is a critical element in a successful Lean Six Sigma process kickoff.

The first step we recommend is for the CEO to draft a memo that states the business case for Six Sigma. The memo should be followed up with a series of company-wide meetings to update the organization on progress and to provide a forum for questions and answers. So that the value of this effort can be retained, we suggest that the Frequently Asked Questions and their answers be posted on the intranet.

Many companies have effectively used an upbeat video featuring the CEO speaking on "Why Lean Six Sigma?" that can be shown to employees throughout the company. One benefit of this approach is that you can ensure that everyone will hear a consistent message. Be assured that the messages and actions of the top executives and P&L managers are closely observed by the whole organization; consistency within that group is a key element in securing employee buy-in.

ONLY THE BEGINNING ...

Remember that this kickoff process is intended only to gain the commitment from the organization to get the Lean Six Sigma process under way. As implementation follows, there will understandably be "bumps in the road" as people come to realize what they have gotten into. Once the honeymoon is over, true and lasting commitment will come only from generating results and believing that these results can be sustained.

Andy Grove appropriately titled his book *Only the Paranoid Survive:* I think that's a healthy state of mind for the design team that is charged by the CEO with implementation of a transforming event by their CEO.

I am reminded of an old story relished by Winston Churchill. A man received a telegram announcing that his mother-in-law had died and requesting burial instructions. He cabled back: "Embalm, cremate, bury at sea. Take no chances."

Experience tells me that it's hard to overestimate the importance of the Transforming Event and initial communication. A lot of mistakes in life are correctable, but an error at this stage due to lack of adequate preparation could have catastrophic effects. If you want to successfully launch Lean Six Sigma, take no chances.

Chapter 8

Selecting the Right People—and the Right Projects

I f you reflect back to the Preface, you'll recall we provided some astonishing data on how few companies are improving and provided a case study of what Lean Six Sigma can accomplish to deliver a significant increase in intrinsic shareholder value in a year or two. By this point in your Lean Six Sigma process, you should have two pieces in place that are critical to delivering on that claim: the engagement of senior executives and an infrastructure plan for widespread implementation.

The third and fourth pieces of the puzzle—the *people* who will be part of the new infrastructure and the high-potential *projects* they will work on—are the subject of this chapter. The order described here—people first, then projects—is deliberate. Remember that your black belts are being groomed to become leaders in your organization. They will hopefully hold their black belt positions through many projects and therefore represent a more significant investment than the projects themselves.

However, that's not to say that Lean Six Sigma advocates training a lot of black belts and turning them loose on the company. This was the approach of most TQM initiatives in the 1980s and 1990s and, with a few notable exceptions, these initiatives were not successful. To make sure your black belts and other resources are delivering value, you need to identify and select high-value-added projects and ensure that the training has been designed to enable the black belts to efficiently complete those projects.

SELECTING BLACK BELT RESOURCES

Knowing that you need to staff champion and "belt" positions is a long way from actually having appropriate, trained people in place. The general process for selecting and developing these resources is best modeled by looking at black belts, the largest group of people in an organization who are working on Lean Six Sigma full time.

The selection of the black belt candidates is a collaborative effort of the business unit management, the business unit champion, and the line managers who own the processes. This group:

- Develops position descriptions.
- Develops the criteria for selecting black belts.
- Screens, interviews, and selects candidates.
- Coordinates training of these resources.

Understand that black belt and champion selection is often the first major action that the organization will see management take in the implementation of Lean Six Sigma, so in that sense it is the first test of management commitment. Consequently, it is an important opportunity to communicate (through action) the importance of Lean Six Sigma. If the best people are chosen for these roles, the broader population of employees will know that management is serious and that Lean Six Sigma is not the latest flavor of the month.

Black Belt Selection Criteria

Some recommended criteria, in priority order, include:

- Team leadership skills.
- Project management experience.
- Problem-solving training and experience.
- Communication skills.
- Interest in a process view beyond his or her unit.
- Ability to learn financial analysis (ROIC, NPV, etc.).
- Computer and technical skills, ability to master tools.

The criteria need to be appropriately weighted—often, leadership and human skills have a higher weighting than do technical skills because *experience shows that tools don't solve problems, people do!*

The results are tallied for each candidate and that information is fed into the selection process. It is not possible to select black belts who can be predicted to meet all of these criteria, especially in the team leadership area. Shortcomings often emerge during training or the first few projects. You should plan for a 10%-20% fallout rate prior to certification. Being selected for black belt training is not an entitlement.

Being Realistic

After the opportunities for black belt or other positions are posted internally, interested candidates almost always have a lot of questions and concerns. The best candidates will already be high performers with a great career trajectory and may be worried about what happens if Six Sigma is a failure or gets dropped. That concern can be addressed only if there is active, visible support by every manager from the CEO on down.

In addition, the selection group needs to be able to clearly articulate the roles, responsibilities, interactions, and financial results expected of a black belt. They need to frankly discuss with their candidate his or her ratings on the criteria and have a plan to correct any weaknesses. Candidates must understand the personal investment they will be making in training, travel, and the usual "long hours" it takes to achieve results. Perhaps most important, the team also needs to be able to clearly describe how accepting the position will help candidates propel their careers upward within the business.

SELECTING PROJECTS

Effective project selection is a key factor in determining the effectiveness of your Lean Six Sigma effort. Why? Some Six Sigma programs have failed to deliver on their potential because black belts became elitist cowboys who competed for scarce resources for projects that were not necessarily *sanctioned by the P&L manager or process owner*.

The Lean Six Sigma infrastructure defined in Chapter 6 goes a long way toward preventing this problem, ensuring that black belts work on delivering results via the right projects in the right amount of time. However, it is still critical to ensure that the first projects are successful, so that the program grows of its own momentum to larger, very-high-NPV opportunities.

The projects must be selected based on a trade-off decision comparing *value delivered* with *effort expended*. One of the most powerful tools for this purpose is the benefit/effort graph (see Figure 8-1).

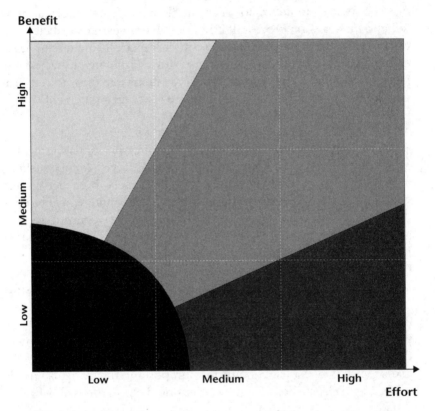

Highly Desirable Opportunities – Projects in upper left are the most desirable projects.

Potentially Desirable Opportunities – Projects in the upper right are potentially desirable, but usually require more analysis to ensure good decision making; "tie-breaking" variables include strategic fit, resource types available, project type, etc.

Less/Not Desirable Opportunities – Projects in the lower left are generally less desirable for applying a team, considering the smaller scope they encompass; this area often yields "quick hit" opportunities.

Least Desirable Opportunities – Projects in the lower right are the least desirable.

Benefits include:
- Strategic Fit
- Revenue Growth
- Cost Reduction
- Capital Avoidance
- Work Capital Reduction

Effort includes:
- Personnel Needs
- Length of Project
- Capital Cost
- Risk of Opportunities

Figure 8-1. Benefit/effort graphic

These graphs usually depict the increase in operating profit versus the effort required to deliver this benefit (including team resources plus any costs or capital). The projects in the high-benefit/low-effort square may become the focus of more data collection and analysis to determine NPV. Displaying potential projects in this way provides an easy way to make a first cut at deciding which projects have the greatest potential benefit.

Project selection can be viewed as having several evolutionary stages:

- At the outset of your Lean Six Sigma initiative, there may be some existing opportunities in the organization that must only be properly scoped and prioritized.
- During the kickoff Transforming Event (see p. 118), P&L managers, champions, and others will be asked to start thinking about criteria for project selection and brainstorming new ideas for projects.
- The method described in this chapter adds more rigor to the process, including specific ways to "prime the pump" of project selection by scouring your existing data sources and knowledge base to identify the initial wave of black belt projects.
- As you evolve through the first year of the Lean Six Sigma initiative, you'll start to rely more heavily on value stream mapping as a tool to identify the highest-impact projects.

While all of these approaches are valid and can contribute to the desired outcomes, only value stream mapping allows the *accurate* identification of time traps and the ultimate elimination of the biggest sources of waste. Realistically, therefore, your first few black belt projects are unlikely to bring the kind of impressive gains described in Part I, but they *will* prepare your organization to become increasingly effective in the second and third waves of projects that generate significant gains in shareholder value.

THE LANGUAGE OF PROJECT SELECTION

As you work through this chapter, there are several terms whose meanings you need to keep clear.

Value stream: The set of activities that convert customer needs into delivered products and services. Improving an entire value stream requires multiple projects.

High-potential-NPV value stream: A value stream that, once improved, can significantly contribute to shareholder value and be a key success factor for the company. *Example: improved cost position in product X.*

Opportunity: A bounded idea potentially composed of multiple projects. *Example: reduce assembly costs in Duluth for product X.*

Project: An idea that can be addressed by a Lean Six Sigma project team and largely meets established screening criteria. *Example: reduce scrap in product X assembly in Duluth.*

Quick hit: An idea that can be addressed by the line organization without the dedicated assistance of a black belt (but may require a Lean "kaizen blitz" team). *Example: sell scrap components from product X assembly, reduce travel cost by outsourcing, etc.*

Process cycle efficiency: A key Lean Six Sigma metric, measured as the amount of value-added time in a process divided by the total lead time (see p. 36).

Diagnostics: A series of observations, data collection, and tests used by champions to generate project opportunities.

WHO DOES WHAT

Project selection is first and foremost the responsibility of the management team within a company, division, or business unit. The role of the Lean Six Sigma champion is to help guide them through the selection process and its decision-making criteria and to educate them on the types of projects that lend themselves to Lean Six Sigma solutions. The management team of the business unit must provide initial guidance on strategy and criteria for project selection, provide input on opportunities throughout the process, and finally agree on which projects will be launched with scarce resources on a periodic basis.

A natural human tendency is to advocate one's own beliefs and managers typically have strong beliefs about the types of issues to deal with first ("pet projects"). The rigor of the entire process we will describe is designed to allow the champion to facilitate a meaningful discussion among upper managers that hinges on data that represents the future direction, rather than opinions and tacit knowledge that is the embodiment of the status quo. The champion will propose the value streams to work on and recommend specific projects for improving those value streams.

We have learned that low process cycle efficiency causes high cost and that 80% of the process delay is caused by fewer than 20% of the nodes (e.g., workstations or transactional steps) in any process. The champion will be aided in his or her endeavors by many new software tools, such as Supply Chain Accelerator, that disclose the time traps, each of which can be addressed by one or more Lean Six Sigma projects. The ultimate project selection decisions are in the hands of the P&L manager, group president, or CEO.

The key to the overall approach lies within your business strategy, which is the crucible through which all ideas must be refined and evaluated. Projects that do not align with the business strategy will not receive adequate management attention or support to succeed. This fact has been borne out time and again in our experience assisting clients, which has led directly to the approach described hereafter. Successful projects will close our performance gaps and reward us with better margins and increased revenue, letting us "climb the value mountain."

Project identification and selection is a process by which champions identify the key value streams and develop projects within those value streams, selecting those projects that can create the most value for the amount of resources applied.

DIAGNOSTIC PROCESSES FOR PROJECT IDENTIFICATION

A Lean Six Sigma program's *ultimate* success is highly correlated to its *initial* success. The stakes are high, given the opportunities for shareholder value and cultural change, so you cannot afford to fail early. So one goal in the process described below is to make sure you've sought out the best ideas in the organization. In fact, the first lesson in project identification is to avoid self-censorship too early in the process. It is imperative that the basket of potential opportunities be as large as possible. In fact, a good process will generate a healthy mix of opportunities; the challenge is to convert as many of them into worthy projects as possible.

The best way to get a large basket of ideas is to keep project identification inclusive, systemically seeking out ideas from every corner of the organization. One way to do this is to use both top-down and bottom-up techniques to compile the initial list of ideas:

- **Top-down:** Idea generation and development start from corporate priorities and a high-level assessment of the business and its value streams.
- **Bottom-up:** Idea generation from existing projects and the employees.

	Pros	Cons
Top-Down	Intrinsically linked to strategy/goals: yields a high NPV Involves a "fresh eyes" approach, gets you "outside the departmental box" by design New insight gained from a fresh look at markets and customers	Requires a new diagnostic process that champions must learn, execute, and educate others on Requires a cross-functional team
Bottom-Up	Good mix of quick hits and projects Allows a wide audience to contribute Self-generating	Bias towards what you already know Tends to surface "pet projects" Typically not driven or supported by data Many ideas are the "persistent pain"—irritants that may have little connection to important value streams

Table 8-1. Comparing top-down and bottom-up approaches for identifying projects

Each approach has pros and cons, as shown in Table 8-1.

Because each approach has its strengths and weaknesses, it's best to incorporate both into your project selection strategy. The top-down approach is more intricate, represents principles and methods that will be new to most people, and therefore is discussed first below.

TOP-DOWN PROJECT IDENTIFICATION

The structure of top-down project identification combines traditional decision-making elements (such as creative thinking and rating ideas against criteria) with elements unique to Lean Six Sigma (such as assessing potential contributions to process cycle efficiency). The goal is to identify performance gaps and then to develop projects that will close those gaps.

The approach described in the next few pages has its heritage in

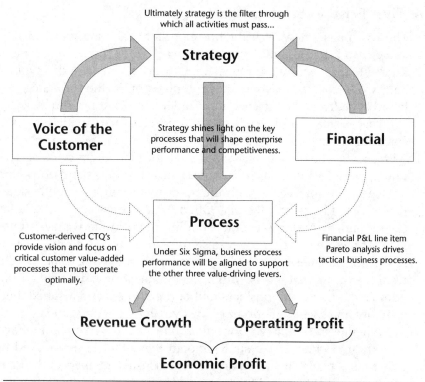

Figure 8-2. Balanced scorecard for project identification

the concepts embodied in the *balanced scorecard*,[1] which promotes organizational governance based on a set of diverse, representative metrics. Similarly, the *project identification balanced scorecard* (Figure 8-2) guides you in examining your business through multiple lenses:

A. Strategy
B. Financial
C. Customer
D. Process

Each lens will reveal a different set of potential projects, allowing us to compile an exhaustive list of project ideas. In nearly every case, the items listed will have many common themes that will help us converge upon the problems that are consistently impacting performance. While it is possible to utilize only a subset of these different aspects, the synergistic effects of convergence will be lost as will some of the unique ideas that spring only from one technique.

A. The "Existing Strategy" Lens

The first phase of project identification is to examine your existing strategy to bring to light *high-potential-NPV value streams* or business segments that require improvement. Our usual source of this type of data would be the existing strategic plans or, in their absence, the broad agendas of the business unit leader and his or her staff.

The existence and detail of strategic plans vary widely among companies. We have successfully launched Lean Six Sigma programs with clients who had no formalized strategic planning process or documentation. In these cases, it is necessary to understand corporate strategy from interviews with the management group, public statements, SEC filings, and the like. Often these discussions lead to a far clearer and more current understanding than do the written strategies. At the other extreme are those companies with a strategic planning process intertwined with the annual budgeting process, the result being that all levels within the organization have applied the grand strategy to their business unit or department and justified their activities and focus in support of the overall corporate agenda.

Whether the strategy is formal or informal, most companies have a pretty good idea of the strategic path they want to travel. And in either case, it helps if your champions are trusted advisors of the P&L manager so that they will fully understand and execute the manager's strategy.

There are multiple ways of analyzing strategy. The best advice is to keep it simple. Strategy, at its core, is simply about charting a path from a current state to a desired state.

One approach for helping champions understand the magnitude of the opportunity for value creation is having them work with the controller to determine the current ROIC of the business and the amount of capital employed. The data can be graphed, much like the value mountain described in Chapter 4.

What comes after a good understanding of the overall health of the business is the level of analysis depicted in Figure 8-3, which portrays market attractiveness vs. the ability to compete in those markets. This analysis is most effective when done for a single business unit or product line with multiple components. It is a good method of identifying key value streams that ought to be considered for improvement before launching a detailed NPV analysis.

The vertical axis of Figure 8-3 portrays *market attractiveness*, defined by the size of the market and the aggregate profitability of the

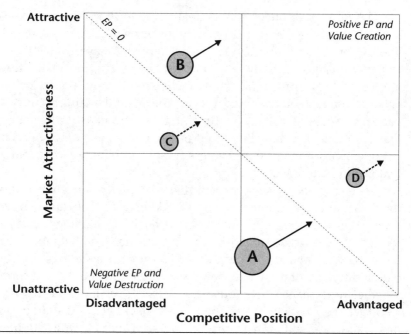

Figure 8-3. 2x2 matrix for competitive position vs. market attractiveness

market (the sum of all participants' profits minus the cost of capital employed). This is often an estimate, since many competitors are not reported separately.

To illustrate this concept, consider some extremes. The airline industry is a very unattractive market (large, but ROIC is much smaller than WACC) that destroys value, while pharmaceuticals are highly attractive (large and ROIC is much greater than WACC) and create value. However, even within an unattractive market, executing a low-cost strategy can create shareholder value (e.g., Southwest Airlines). The terms "value creating" and "value destroying" can be summed up by asking whether sufficient returns are generated by an investment (ROIC) to compensate for the risk undertaken (WACC). Given the two examples above, over the last decade or two, investors would have fared far better investing in a basket of pharmaceutical stocks than in airline stocks.

The horizontal axis portrays *competitive position* relative to your competition. This would encompass your relative cost position, market share, brand equity, and the like. The size of the symbol plotted on the chart represents the relative size of each component of that business unit, on a revenue basis.

The final component of this analysis is to ascertain the desired future state of the graph, as shown by the arrows. In this case, it looks like A is an unattractive segment. The company may desire either to exit that business entirely or to harvest its returns and invest them elsewhere. Segment B is a fairly attractive market and perhaps could benefit from more investment. It should be noted that, unless the company is a monopolist, it is very difficult to make a market more attractive, so the focus is usually placed on how to improve the cost competitiveness of the current business or shift into an adjacent market that is more attractive.

We recommend that this exercise be completed quickly based on the data and understanding that is already at hand. The data will typically be good enough to provide direction. This simple exercise can identify the key value streams within the business and help the champions, the P&L managers, and the CEO drive the direction of Lean Six Sigma implementation. Its greatest value may be in indicating whether a segment of the business is worth retaining or devoting resources (i.e., black belts and their projects). Often times, market segments like segment A in Figure 8-3 are such that executing defined projects will still not cause the segment to create value. For example, if a division is already earning 10% on revenue in one segment and not earning cost of capital, that segment is a better candidate for divestiture and capital redeployment than for process improvement.

B. The "Financial Analysis" Lens

Another lens within the project identification process is the use of financial analysis. It has the virtue of being universally applicable, since all businesses are required to maintain financial and accounting information. Your goal in this stage of the project identification process is merely to ascertain which areas are most likely to spawn suitable high-value projects. At this point, you want to focus on the big picture. A more detailed financial analysis occurs once you have screened numerous project ideas to identify a smaller, more manageable pool of candidates.

Assessing the financials is a two-stage approach for identifying opportunity areas related to financial drivers:

1. Find the big buckets of money from the financial statements.
2. Decide which of those you can reasonably hope to influence.

This is tantamount to identifying the largest "value levers" and then assessing how much we can move each lever. (See Figure 8-4.)

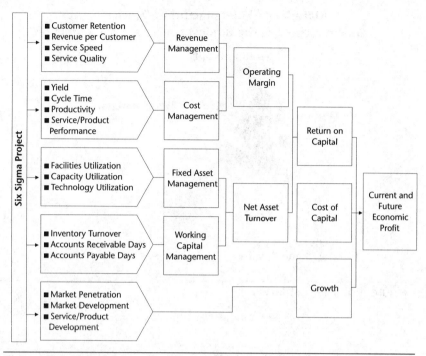

Figure 8-4. Value driver tree (financial)

Identifying the "Big Buckets of Money." By examining the income statement, balance sheet, and cash flow statements, you can quickly isolate the highest-impact line items. Typically, for a manufacturing company, the largest cost value levers will be found in raw materials and manufacturing overhead—and less likely in direct labor. We suggest the champion build his or her "pie chart" of opportunity, much like that presented way back in Chapter 1, reprinted in Figure 8-5.

An element often overlooked when performing this analysis is the impact of sales price on profitability. As can be seen in Figure 8-6, for an average manufacturing company, selling price has the largest impact of all the value levers. The graph depicts the impact of a 1% improvement in various value levers for a generic manufacturing company. Can we gain a price premium by cutting delivery times by 80% or increasing the quality that we deliver?

Evaluating the Likelihood of Influence. The next task is to consider your ability to change these high-impact line items. By doing this, you can determine the overall size of the opportunity pools, as shown in the simple formula and example below:

**Material and Manufacturing Overhead and
Quality Costs Are the Biggest Levers of Cost Reduction**

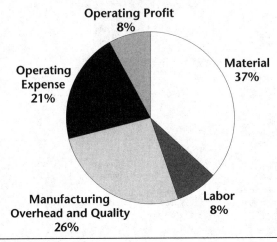

Figure 8-5. The cost levers

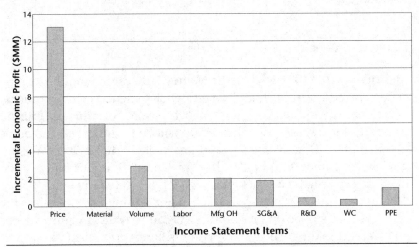

Figure 8-6. 1% change applied to income statement items

size of lever X percent improvement = size of pool

$50,000,000 in raw materials X 6% reduction = $3,000,000 potential

The estimates of improvement potential in each value lever are based on a combination of statistical data (e.g., from the value stream map analysis) and structured team discussions and judgment. Some companies possess excellent sources of benchmarking information that allow us to compare our performance with that of others. In many cases, we need not even look outside the company for this, as we can leverage the performance characteristics of similar plants or assembly lines to establish an internal "best in class" performance that will form the basis of our performance improvement efforts.

Focusing on Projects with High Financial Potential. The result of this simplified financial analysis is to establish a list of opportunities, each with its own pool of potential savings. Each of these pools will ultimately form an area where you should look for additional ideas that will generate the savings possible. Keep your Pareto hat on here: focus your idea generation on the larger, most promising pools. The main benefit here is to ensure that you do not tire yourselves out trying to move an immovable lever or waste time pulling on lots of lower-value levers.

C. The "Voice of the Customer" Lens: What Works, What Doesn't

Listening to the Voice of the Customer is an integral part of the Six Sigma methodology, so it is not surprising that it plays a central role in project identification and selection. This phase of the diagnostic process typically yields the greatest new insights into the business and may surface project ideas that radically impact the business.

In an ideal world, reams of data would be available on our customers' requirements and the relative importance of each. Using this data you could evaluate yourself against the competition and thereby identify performance gaps that would spawn projects—an approach known as *key buying factor* analysis. Unfortunately, performing this type of analysis *well* can consume several months.

Another tool often used to identify projects that will directly affect customers is Quality Function Deployment (QFD), a methodology most closely identified with product development and competitive assessments. However, QFD can be formidable and, based on our observations, an impractical undertaking for initial project selection.

Frankly, we have found both key buying factor and QFD analyses to be too slow to achieve the type of first-year impact required of Lean Six Sigma, especially since markets move very fast. However, both of these tools may be required in maturing Lean Six Sigma efforts to get to the next level of performance.

There is a simpler, less formal approach that can accelerate the process of making the Voice of the Customer heard in the project identification and selection process. Within the company there are numerous sources of marketplace and customer preference data: warranty logs, satisfaction surveys, call center logs, etc. In addition, everyone who interfaces with the customer directly can contribute pieces to the puzzle. All of these data sources can be used to create a list of customer requirements and establish a relative importance among them.

Start by scouring your existing sources to collect as much "tribal" knowledge of customers as you can. You can then validate this information through discussions with the P&L manager and marketing people. This quick analysis can be systematized by plotting the data on a Kano chart, which can help create an initial representation of customer desires. Figure 8-7 shows a sample Kano analysis from the auto industry to illustrate the key concepts and their application to project identification.

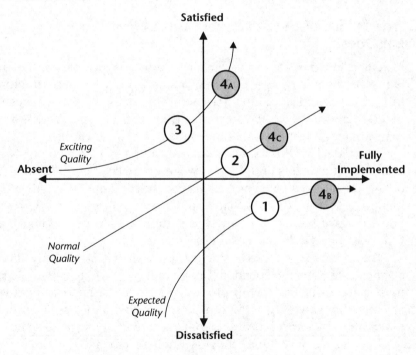

Figure 8-7. Kano chart

In our example, three customer requirements are identified for the automobile:

1. Braking
2. Acceleration
3. Night vision

Braking is considered "*expected* quality," because it is unlikely to make the customer happy at any level of performance, while its absence would be immediately noticed and cause grave dissatisfaction. Acceleration is considered "*normal* quality," because the customer can be either pleased or displeased by it and the more of it in the automobile the happier the customer. Night vision is considered "*exciting* quality," because its absence will not displease the customer, but if it is available it delights the customer.

The first lesson to learn from a Kano analysis is to take care of your customers' expectations in sequence from *expected* to *normal* to *exciting*. In the automobile example, for instance, any car company that ignored a performance gap in its brakes or anything else in the "expected quality" area will not last long enough to work on "exciting quality." Similarly, companies must understand the need to address "normal quality" sufficiently before embarking on the search for new "exciting quality" differentiators. Differentiation is a key component of establishing or maintaining brand equity, but it is secondary to ensuring a consistency of message and performance, as depicted by "normal quality" and "expected quality."

Kano is a powerful model because it provides a framework to think about both "spoken" and "unspoken" customer requirements. If you think about what customers ask for, they typically focus on the "*normal* quality" items; it's rare that customers will tell you about something that is "*expected* quality" (because they just assume you will provide it) or "*exciting* quality" (because they have not thought of it).

A Kano analysis is not something you can do just once. One lesson learned from doing repeated analyses in a given area is that customer expectations change: quality that is at first "exciting" becomes "normal" and then "expected" as the technology matures and features become more common. This can be seen on the graph by 4A-4C, detailing the evolution of expectations around audio systems: where once a stereo was "exciting," it's now "expected." The same is true of brakes in the earliest period of the automobile: at first they were exciting quality, but they soon became expected!

Applying Kano analysis to project identification allows you to understand in a structured manner what influences your customers' behavior and buying decisions. Once you understand the dynamics of each requirement, you can assess the performance of your unit or the company, *from the customers' perspective*, in meeting those needs. Identifying where you fall short leads you to gaps. You can focus your project identification around the most critical influencers of customer satisfaction and retention.

D. The "Process Analysis" Lens

The final lens for top-down generation of project ideas is to look at core processes. The sequence of lenses here is deliberate. People tend to gravitate toward what they know, so idea generation would naturally be confined to existing projects. The reason for leaving the process analysis lens until the end is that insight gleaned from the financial, customer, and existing strategy lenses will enhance the output from this step.

Before you can delve deeply into process analysis, you need to define your core business processes. The first consideration is what a process is and is not; the tendency is to define processes in functional terms, such as "engineering" or "sales." But lessons from Lean Six Sigma tell us that the customer is indifferent to the methods or structures we use to meet their demands. We must first abandon these functional definitions in favor of descriptors that more closely portray what the customer perceives. This is the value stream concept (sets of activities, such as different product lines, that turn a customer opportunity into a delivered outcome), as discussed numerous times throughout this book.

Through a process lens, something that used to be labeled "engineering" could become "design new products" and "sales" may actually be "tailor products to my needs." One helpful hint during process definition is to cast your activities as verb/noun constructs, which will help overcome the legacy of functional structures. At the highest level for a generic manufacturing company, for example, the overall value stream may consist of the following processes: "take orders," "acquire materials," "make products," "deliver products," "collect payment." Viewing the business this way may help break down traditional functional silos and speed the realignment of processes to customer demands. Each of these processes would need to be further decomposed once or twice before they are small enough to contain meaningful LSS projects.

Identifying processes instead of functions is just the first step in applying a process lens. The real goal is to identify the business processes that

- are most critical to your success.
- can be most readily improved by Lean Six Sigma tool sets.

The overlap between these two criteria is where you should dig deeper to generate projects that will close the performance gaps.

One approach to finding this overlap is adapted from the book *The Process Edge: Creating Value Where It Counts*, by Peter G.W. Keen, and depicted in Figure 8-8.

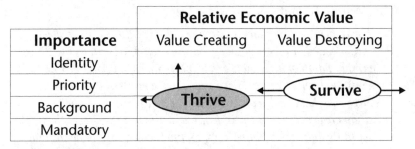

Importance	Relative Economic Value	
	Value Creating	Value Destroying
Identity		
Priority	Thrive	Survive
Background		
Mandatory		

Survive by eliminating processes that destroy value, then thrive by building processes that create value.

- **Survive** – Minimize the number of Value Destroying processes either by improving (moving them to the Value Creating Side) or by eliminating/ outsourcing them.

- **Thrive** – Improve, change, or move appropriate processes upwards (toward identity) or increase their returns (create even more value).

Figure 8-8. Process classification via Process Edge approach

Processes that enhance or protect a franchise or a differentiated product are the greatest value creators in a business. If a process improvement has the potential for protecting or creating differentiation, it will tend to have a high value and should be executed. In a sense, these processes define the company from the customers' perspective and hence have a high priority; they are your key value streams.

You can determine whether a process is creating or destroying value via value stream mapping. You may also want to use process cycle efficiency (introduced in Chapter 3) as a good indicator of whether a process is efficient or not. It is also possible, in theory, to perform a detailed financial analysis on processes, which would dis-till them to a common denominator, like NPV or EVA. In practice, these latter approaches may require a good deal of time, so they are usually not undertaken lightly. For our purposes, we will assess processes based on indications of variability and waste and by benchmarking them against internal and external competitors.

Priority processes like "scheduling machines and assembly" or "acquiring raw materials" are important and may be indirectly visible to the customer, but do not define the company. They are important because their shortcomings can cripple the business, spoil the relationship, and provide an opening for a competitor. To create the highest shareholder value, a firm will strive to create a franchise, a preferred brand, or a recognized reputation for excellence. Remember what Warren Buffett said on this subject:

> It was not the fair market value of the inventories, receivables, or fixed assets that produced the premium rates of return. Rather it was a combination of intangible assets, particularly a pervasive favorable reputation with consumers based upon countless pleasant experiences they have had with both product and personnel. Such a reputation creates a consumer franchise that allows the value of the product to the purchaser, rather than its production cost, to be the major determinant of selling price.
>
> —Warren Buffet, Berkshire Hathaway
> Letter to Shareholders, 1983

To recap, in selecting processes, we need to ensure that we are addressing first those processes that are destroying value, especially those that are identity or priority processes from the customer perspective. Once we have addressed those necessities, we can consider ways to enhance shareholder value by increasing the inherent value of a process via differentiation or by harvesting hidden value.

Compiling the Input

As you work through the top-down analysis, document the key value streams identified and the project ideas that arose from applying each of the four lenses—strategy, finance, customers, and process. These will be fed into an evaluation and screening process. (See p. 146.)

BOTTOM-UP PROJECT IDENTIFICATION

The top-down project identification methods just described involve concepts and methods that are new to most organizations. But the analysis is always worth it, because the project ideas are clearly linked to strategic priorities.

Still, you can't ignore the other approach to project identification: bottom-up approaches (including the commonly used suggestion box) are usually simpler to understand and more accessible to people throughout the organization. Many of the projects that arise from a bottom-up method will reflect projects that existed before Lean Six Sigma.

For our purposes in launching a performance improvement initiative like Lean Six Sigma, we will differentiate between two resource groups: senior management and the broader organization. Each will be able to contribute unique insights to the project identification process.

Soliciting Ideas from Senior Management

The role of senior management—whether at the corporate, business unit, or local level—is to supply information on both the projects currently under way or planned and any problems they are aware of from their spheres of influence or control.

You need to capture information on current or planned projects so they can later be assessed from a number of perspectives:

- Some projects will lend themselves better to the DMAIC methodology than the prevailing approaches and can therefore be pulled into the Lean Six Sigma realm.
- Projects that do not fit the DMAIC methodology will likely consume resources that could conflict with the soon-to-be-launched Lean Six Sigma projects. Management will need to make hard decisions about the relative priorities of these competing demands for common resources, be they capital, human, or management attention. (An impact/effort chart will be prepared to help filter out the best projects.)

Regardless of the disposition of an existing or planned project, projects identified through bottom-up approaches are typically aimed at solving a specific problem, not contributing to an important value stream. Their utility stems from the fact that they may shed light on related problems or offer the possibility of extending the solution to an adjacent area or problem that lends itself to the Lean Six Sigma methodology.

Management is also in a unique position to have a bird's-eye view of the business and can often contribute ideas on where to look to solve the persistent ills of the company. Canvassing the management groups within the organization will not only generate numerous ideas for improvement projects but also ensure that organizational commitment and buy-in are widespread.

Soliciting Ideas from the Broader Organization

The detailed process knowledge of any company is embedded at a much lower level than the management ranks, and many good ideas can surface from the grass-roots level. However, this source is somewhat problematic during the initial stages of a program launch, primarily because, unfortunately, the broader organization will not be very aware of the goals, methods, and constraints of the not-yet-launched Lean Six Sigma program and therefore may not propose projects well-suited to Lean Six Sigma.

If you include the broader organization even at the early stage, take care to ensure that the status of ideas submitted is conveyed openly throughout the organization. Failure to do so will create antipathy or hostility to the nascent program and can cause serious resistance down the road.

For these reasons, we recommend that the broader organization initially be involved on an ad hoc basis during the project definition and scoping phases. Once the program is established, the broader organization can be effectively tapped to augment the structured project identification process.

GROUPING AND SCREENING IDEAS

As a result of both the top-down and bottom-up analyses described above, most business units find themselves at this point with more ideas than they can easily pursue, typically several hundred. These ideas will take the form of high-potential-NPV value streams, opportunities, and projects and will be largely undefined or scoped. Our task is now to isolate the projects suitable for Lean Six Sigma implementation and to select the most promising ones for further definition and scoping.

To illustrate, let's assume that we have uncovered 300 opportunities and project ideas within one division and plan to train and assign 10 black belts to that division. Our ultimate goal is to come out with two to three projects per black belt, for a total of 20 to 30 projects. Since we will likely eliminate some ideas after more detail becomes available, the first screening should probably include five ideas per black belt. This means we'd need somewhere on the order of 50 project ideas to carry forward into the project definition phase.

Step 1: Convert Opportunities into Specific Projects

It is likely that some of the original ideas from the four-lens diagnostic or bottom-up approaches describe "opportunity areas" (see p. 136). rather than specific projects. But black belts don't get assigned *opportunities*; they get assigned *projects*. Throwing out the opportunity suggestions could eliminate a valuable project; it's far better to develop each opportunity into one or more projects.

Focused brainstorming exercises, in which you challenge people to identify manageable pieces of the broader opportunity, often yield good results. Doing these in a small group or team often works better than having people work individually, because the creative process is more dynamic and greater clarity is gained when the projects are discussed.

Step 2: Sort the Ideas

Once you have milked the opportunity suggestions for all they are worth, assemble a complete list of project ideas. Our original list of 300 ideas may have grown to 350 or 400 by now!

To work more efficiently, you need to assemble the list in a format that you can easily manipulate. For some, that means writing the basics of each idea on a separate card or self-stick note; for others, it means entering them into a computer spreadsheet. In either case, you want to then sort through the project ideas to eliminate redundancies and perhaps group similar projects.

One tip: keep the project descriptions short at this stage. Remember that you're winnowing a long list of potential projects down to just a few, so trying to come up with detailed project descriptions here would be a big waste of time. You'll get a chance to flesh out the most likely project ideas just a bit later in the process.

Step 3: Apply Screening Criteria

There are a number of valid screening criteria that can be used to winnow our list of 300-plus project ideas down to our goal of 50. Depending on the initial priorities of the business, some combination of the following benefit/effort criteria will likely be used:

Benefit
- Financial (NPV or annual cash flow impact)
- Customer satisfaction
- Potential to leverage across the business
- Strategic fit (applies more to the bottom-up ideas)

Effort
- Resource requirements
- Duration of project
- Risks
- Capital required
- Special skills/tools required

Regardless of the exact criteria employed, it is often useful to classify each project into one of three broad categories (high, medium, low) for both benefit and effort. You can then graph the results on a *benefit/effort matrix* like the one in Figure 8-1 (p. 128).

The results are far from scientific, but the goal at this stage of the project selection process is to be *directionally correct*—that is, to help concentrate your efforts on the highest-potential projects.

(By way of analogy, this process resembles the Bowl Championship Series, which seeks to determine the top college football teams in the nation each year. Its goal is not to make a definitive judgment or final ranking, but rather to converge upon the top teams in the country and then to allow those teams to compete for the title. While one can always argue about the specific rank of any given team, it is almost certain that the top two or three teams are included in the BCS final four. Being directionally correct is preferable to being precisely wrong.)

Step 4: Identifying the Top Candidates

Ideally, at this point a number of "high-benefit" project ideas will leap out at you. Usually, you would give preference to those that rate low on the effort scale (these promise quick-hit gains), but don't abandon ideas yet simply because they may require a lot of effort. In our illustration, we would look for approximately 50 project ideas to carry forward for further research.

PROJECT DEFINITION AND SCOPING

Project ideas need to be better defined before they will be ready to undergo a final prioritization. The task will be to turn a "postcard" of information into a more robust description of a Lean Six Sigma project, for two reasons. You need to be able to convey the essence of the project to new audiences, like a project selection committee, the management of the Lean Six Sigma program, and the company's senior management. You also need sufficient detail to be able to make informed decisions about which projects to launch first.

The use of a *project definition form* (PDF) is a key component of the overall project selection process. This form will be a living document that evolves as the project teams are formed and begin work on their project. Although PDFs capture more information than was represented on the postcard or in a spreadsheet, it is not necessary to go into excruciating detail yet, because the project teams will augment and refine the information as they proceed.

Another reason to keep it simple is the burden that will be placed on the selection committee to become familiar with each project it must prioritize. An ideal PDF therefore is just a single page, with an absolute maximum of two pages.

In technologically sophisticated organizations, the PDF forms are linked directly to project-tracking software, a sample screen of which appears below (Figure 8-9). This form is input to the software by the master black belt or champion to become accessible to the unit and corporate champions. Usually a team will provide additional detail in attachments (perhaps in PowerPoint) that describe the project. Thus anyone with access to the software can drill down and understand any project in the company.

The contents of the PDF will form the core of the traditional Six Sigma project charter and include information such as the following:

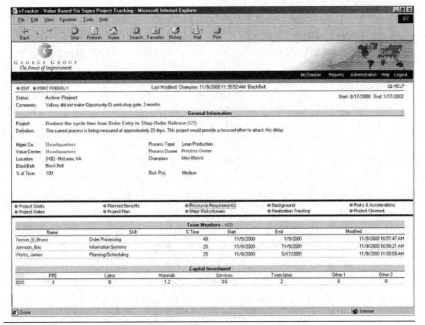

Figure 8-9. Sample PDF graphic from software

- Problem statement*
- Project scope*
- Background information
- Key measures*
- Benefits*
- Effort*
- Assumptions*
- Risks/accelerators
- Resource requirements
- Project duration/timeline

(Items marked with an asterisk are considered essential to a complete and useful PDF, but each company is different.)

The champions have been orchestrating the project identification and selection process up to this point. In many cases it will now be necessary to augment the resource pool with others who can help fill out the PDF, for the following reasons:

1. To ensure that sufficient capacity exists to pursue the projects.
2. To establish cycle time to completion, which will determine the number of projects in process.
3. To tap into detailed process knowledge others may have that the champion lacks.
4. To start gaining involvement and buy-in from the wider organization. Those tapped to assist with PDF creation will often become project sponsors or team members when the projects get launched.

The time required to complete a PDF in adequate detail will generally range from two hours to two days, depending on what decisions have been made regarding its content, the knowledge of those completing the form, and what information is readily available. The amount of effort will vary from project to project and will often be related closely to how clear-cut the project idea is. Ambiguity will considerably increase the time required and will often necessitate several iterations of rescoping—or perhaps the abandonment of the idea if it proves to be intractable or unattractive.

For those of you familiar with Six Sigma programs, this activity will sound like what the project team traditionally does in the Define phase. The initial PDF does address some of the same goals but stops far short of what a project team would accomplish during Define. However, by moving some of this Define activity forward into the project selection process, we achieve several benefits. The primary benefit is creating a better sense of the projects' boundaries, costs, and potential. This knowledge results in a higher yield of projects coming out of the Define phase—90% or more, compared with yields as low as 40% in some programs where the black belt charters a team to investigate project ideas. Another key benefit is to ensure healthy debate about the merits of the projects being launched and gain commitment to the program and support for the project teams.

Refining the Financial Analysis

The most problematic aspect of the project definition process is typically the valuation of benefits. It is also the most crucial, as the majority of the selection criteria will focus on the net benefit to be realized from each project. Financial guidelines will vary from program to program, but they generally mirror the criteria the company uses in its budgeting or capital allocation request processes. Regardless of the criteria used, it is imperative that the calculation be made consistently and in compliance with the goals of the Lean Six Sigma initiative.

The importance of establishing a consistent set of financial guidelines early in the life of a Lean Six Sigma initiative cannot be emphasized enough. Unfortunately, it is rarely done this way, primarily because it involves the resolution of many difficult issues. Good financial guidelines will address the following questions and many others:

- What types of cost reduction savings "count"?
- How are "soft" savings or benefits (cost avoidance, revenue increases, effective capacity increases, lead-time reductions, etc.) treated?
- How long are results to be tracked and credited? Who tracks and reports them?
- Will we use different criteria to select projects than to report savings?
- Will we "charge" projects for team members' time?
- What level of detail is required to substantiate financial estimates?
- Who will approve them?

The purpose is to fashion a set of financial principles that capture the many aspects of value creation, so that you can make good project selection decisions and have a useful yardstick for measuring the success of the Lean Six Sigma initiative.

Revisiting the Link to Corporate Goals

Chapter 4 emphasized the need to link projects with increasing share-holder value. One of the graphics that made this point was the "value mountain" (reproduced in Figure 8-10), which used empirical stock market data to demonstrate how companies that earn an ROIC that is 5% greater than their cost of capital command much higher market values—three to five times higher—than companies in comparable industries that merely earn their cost of capital. The resulting value mountain graph shows that value creation is a function of economic profits and growth.

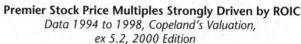

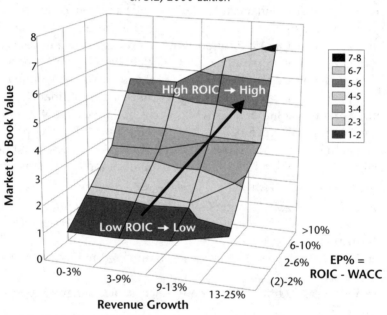

Figure 8-10. Value mountain chart

We refer to the spread between ROIC and WACC as the *economic profit %*, which is the primary determinant of corporate valuation. The value mountain graph also shows that companies that grow at more than 10% per year have an even higher multiple. Our overarching purpose in project selection is to find and execute projects that help us climb the mountain by increasing ROIC and revenue growth.

The practical consequence of the value mountain is that the preferred method of distilling project benefits down to a single number for comparison and tracking purposes (and which is highly correlated to value creation) is the use of net present value (NPV). NPV has the further advantage of providing an analytical method for comparing and selecting the projects to pursue (see the examples in Figure 8-11). It comprehends ROIC, WACC, and growth as well as the timing of cash flows.

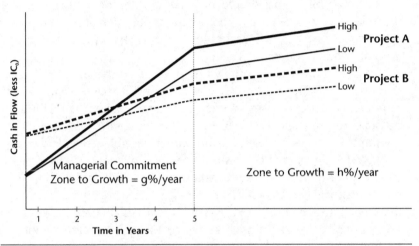

**Power of Prioritizing Projects on NPV and EVA:
Project A Should Get Funded**

Figure 8-11. NPV chart with two projects

FINAL PROJECT SELECTIONS

Before getting into final prioritization, here's a recap of the process that brings us to a sufficient level of detail to be able to proceed confident that the best projects will be selected:

1. We identified high-potential-NPV value streams and generated project ideas that would close any performance gaps detected.
2. We eliminated redundancies from our list of projects and did a cursory valuation of each idea by bucketing it into high/medium/low categories for benefit and for effort.
3. Having selected several projects per black belt to investigate further, we completed a simple project definition form on each one, which included a more detailed appraisal of all costs and financial benefits associated with the project, as well as specifying known risks and all assumptions made.

The entire process was facilitated by the Lean Six Sigma business unit champion with appropriate involvement of others as required.

The approach used for final prioritization is not substantially different than what was employed for the initial screening. You will still employ a comparison of benefit and effort to determine which projects will yield the greatest returns for a given unit of effort. However, there are some key differences from the screening exercise, on both the benefit and the effort sides.

For one thing, you should now have a decent financial analysis that allows you to better gauge the benefit potential of a given project. As discussed earlier, it is desirable to condense all projects to a common denominator, like NPV.

Also, in many cases, you'll want to capture as benefits those issues that do not readily lend themselves to financial analysis, such as customer satisfaction or competitive advantage. While it is theoretically possible to translate these types of benefits into NPV terms, the assumptions necessary to do so are numerous, subjective, and open to endless debate. Part of the Lean Six Sigma philosophy is to make the debate among managers more data-driven; so, to avoid endless arguments, capture "soft" benefits separately and give them less weight than the "hard" benefits. To arrive at an overall "benefit index" score, you can use a weighted average of scores for hard savings and soft savings categories, each of which has its own unique operational definitions as to what dollar amounts constitute a specific ranking.

The same analysis is applied to the effort associated with a given project, with the effort categories remaining largely unchanged from those discussed in the screening phase of the process. Management discussion usually hinges on the risk factors associated with each project. Risks come in two basic guises: risks to schedule and risks to benefit realization. Resource availability is another component of risk, which usually is handled by assigning a higher risk score to those projects that require scarce resources. All these components are then distilled into an overall "effort index" score.

All projects will be plotted on a common benefit-to-effort graph and their relative merits explored. Because these projects are plotted using a composite index for both benefit and effort, the display will only be directionally correct because it tries to display a multi-dimensional data set in only two dimensions. It should be noted that the project's position on the chart is not really a point but a "neighborhood" centered on the point represented by the coordinates. The size of this neighborhood reflects the confidence one has in the estimates of benefits and effort. It is not unusual (or discouraged) for the management team to slide projects around on the graph to reflect their collective assessment of the PDF analysis. This entire process will rapidly separate the wheat from the chaff and allow management to debate the final prioritization on just a subset of the projects under consideration.

Prioritization will actually occur in "flights" of projects, making the decisions less onerous and contentious. This is true because most organizations will have multiple black belts available to deploy to projects and the goal is to generate two or three projects per black belt per year. Using our previous example with 10 black belts and 50 PDFs, our goal would be to exit the session with 20 to 30 projects ranked in relative order of attractiveness. The main concern is to ensure that the top five to seven projects are placed in the top 10 slots so that they are launched immediately by one of our black belts. The prioritization process will deliver to us a queue of Lean Six Sigma projects. However we will launch only those numbers of projects consistent with the cycle time to attain results. If you err, err on the side of too much resource applied to too few projects.

By ensuring an adequate inventory of projects in the hopper, whenever a black belt finishes one project he or she can immediately be given another project to launch. The projects thus launched will be selected easily, based on their relative priority from the ranking described above and the "fit" to the individual black belt who has become available.

Monitoring Implementation

Once the projects have been selected, the business unit champions can begin acting as portfolio managers, examining their basket of projects under way and in queue, to ensure diversification and optimization of the short- and long-term value of that portfolio. One way to do this is to prepare a Gantt chart of the projects in process (to help you manage your "work in process"!). This would be useful in forecasting benefits to the division and highlighting any capacity constraints that may arise due to resource scarcity. We would recommend that the champion and business unit manager adopt a formal project launch/review process.

PROJECTS SUITABLE FOR LEAN SIX SIGMA

As a final check in your project selection process, consider asking these simple questions:

- Does this project address customer critical-to-quality (CTQ) issues?
  Yes —> Lean Six Sigma project
  No —> not Lean Six Sigma strategically focused
- Does this project address revenue growth?
  Yes —> Lean Six Sigma project
  No —> not Lean Six Sigma strategically focused
- Does this project address cost reduction?
  Yes —> Lean Six Sigma project
  No —> not Six Sigma strategically focused
- Can it be completed within three to five months?
  Yes —> Lean Six Sigma project
  No —> stop or rescope
- Is there sufficient "value creation" at stake ($150-$250K annual operating profit)?
  Yes —> Lean Six Sigma project
  No —> stop or rescope

SELECTING THE RIGHT RESOURCES AND PROJECTS

Do you remember the "indicators of commitment" discussed back in the introduction to Part Two? Two of three are covered in this chapter. Besides closely observing whether your company leaders are living and breathing Lean Six Sigma, your employees are going to pay particular attention to the following two considerations:

- Whether it's the best people who are chosen as Lean Six Sigma resources.
- Whether the projects selected are important to the company.

In other words, do not rush these decisions. Pay careful attention to the criteria you use to select black belt and champion resources and take the time to work through the project selection procedures carefully. The implications are far broader than gaining employee support and commitment for your effort; they will determine your ability to deliver on the Lean Six Sigma value proposition of delivering bottom-line improvements in under a year!

Note

1. Robert S. Kaplan and David P. Norton, *The Balanced Scorecard: Translating Strategy into Action* (Cambridge, MA: Harvard Business School Press, 1996).

Chapter 9

Predicting and Improving Team Performance

With Max Isaac[1]

The soft stuff is the hard stuff.
>—Chris Cool, Vice President
>Quality and Lean, Northrop Grumman

DMAIC is the heart of Six Sigma, leadership effectiveness is the soul.
>—Nori Morimoto, ITT Champion

T alk to people who have *been* there, who have successfully implemented Lean Six Sigma or one its predecessors, and they'll all tell you the same thing: having the best data, tools, and improvement methods in the world won't help you much if you don't have black belts who are effective team leaders. Lean Six Sigma is about leveraging the knowledge, energy, and passion of the *whole* team: the green belts, process owners, and other team members. Time and again, at company after company, experience shows that being able to deal effectively with the human element of improvement is a more critical determinant of team success than the rational, analytical processes and tools.

Steve Hochhauser, currently a senior vice president at Johns Manville, learned this lesson when he worked on one of the earliest implementations of Six Sigma. "AlliedSignal has become one of the premier examples of effective Six Sigma implementation in the world," says Hochhauser. "We started seeing much faster, better results once we had black belts who had been through leadership training. The skills and tools they learned helped them make the transition from having a narrower engineering perspective to having a true *business* perspective across the organization. They really blossomed and were able to lead their teams to issue resolution." Hochhauser also points out that in companies like GE and AlliedSignal today, experienced black belts who have extensive leadership training are looked upon as the pool for future corporate leaders.

The simple fact is that while good technique is critical in achieving Lean Six Sigma levels of performance, change and improvement happen through people, not data. In fact, leadership skills and effective team performance are key elements in the Six Sigma infrastructure and culture (discussed in Chapter 2) that are necessary for successful implementation of Lean Six Sigma.

Leadership and team effectiveness are too critical to the achievement of your Lean Six Sigma goals to be left to chance. The subject has been the focus of attention of managerial thinking since the 1960s. The advent of the quality revolution in the 1980s increased the interest in the issue. There are many dimensions to team effectiveness—basic facilitation skills, conflict resolution, goal setting, problem solving, etc.—most of which you can learn about from myriad resources. This chapter focuses on just two areas that aren't given as much attention:

A. Understanding how team members' strengths and weaknesses can either complement each other to make for an effective team or conflict and lead to failure despite the talent of individuals.
B. Building leadership skills so that black belts can fully utilize team members on projects. These skills include self-management skills, inquiry (rather than advocacy) skills, and communication skills.

UNDERSTANDING INDIVIDUAL PERFORMANCE

There are many approaches to understanding individual performance such as Myers-Briggs, Grid, Teleometrics, and Belbin among others. That so many different researchers would have such a wide area of agreement argues for the validity of their conclusions. As a practitioner of team effectiveness, I have actually seen it work in practice. Although my personal experience is limited to the use of Belbin's analysis, other models are no doubt equally valid.

Though the use of teams has become standard in most business-es, there are two competing models that represent polar opposite views about how to structure teams to obtain optimum performance.

PREFERRED TEAM ROLES AS PREDICTORS OF TEAM SUCCESS OR FAILURE

The first, intuitive model would suggest that assembling brilliant individuals creates a great team. However, that approach can fail.

The failure of the "collection of brilliance" approach to team effectiveness was first analyzed in an industrial setting at Imperial Chemical Industries (ICI) in the UK. ICI recruited only the absolute top chemical talent, but the result was very poor team performance. This phenomenon attracted the attention of Dr. R. Meredith Belbin of Cambridge University, with far-reaching consequences.

Belbin and his team of researchers spent nine years in an intensive study of management teams undergoing executive development and working in simulations that mimicked real world challenges. Every individual involved in the team exercises also underwent detailed psychometric and mental ability testing prior to participating in the simulations. During team activities, an observer tabulated data on the subjects' behavior at 30-second intervals. Belbin was able to amass a huge amount of information on the relationship among team success, personality factors, mental capabilities, and creativity.

He describes this work in his book, *Team Roles at Work*. When Belbin concluded his research, he had achieved his goal of being able to accurately predict which teams would succeed and which would fail in his simulations. *The fundamental discovery was that individuals have one or more preferred roles and that, to be highly effective, a team must achieve a balance of these roles.*

Belbin, in fact, identified nine roles, mentioned briefly back in Chapter 2 and repeated in Table 9-1.

You'll note that Belbin discovered that the personal attributes that enable a person to make a particular type of contribution also create weaknesses that must be accommodated. In other words, our strengths are often accompanied by associated weaknesses. The footnote to the table points out another important lesson: seldom is an executive (or anyone else, for that matter) strong in all nine roles. Finally, every person's preferred role is a good role, *if* they are aware of it and play it on the team.

Role	Team-Role Contribution	Allowable Weaknesses
Plant	Creative, imaginative, unorthodox. Solves difficult problems.	Ignores details. Too preoccupied to communicate effectively.
Resource Investigator	Extrovert, enthusiastic, communicative. Explores opportunities. Develops contacts.	Overoptimistic. Loses interest once initial enthusiasm has passed.
Coordinator	Mature, confident, a good chairperson. Clarifies goals, promotes decision-making, delegates well.	Can be seen as manipulative. Delegates personal work.
Shaper	Challenging, dynamic, thrives on pressure. Has the drive and courage to overcome obstacles.	Can provoke others. Hurts people's feelings.
Monitor Evaluator	Sober, strategic, and discerning. Sees all options. Judges accurately.	Lacks drive and ability to inspire others. Overly critical.
Team Worker	Cooperative, mild, perceptive, and diplomatic. Listens, builds, averts friction, calms the waters.	Indecisive in crunch situations. Can be easily influenced.
Implementer	Disciplined, reliable, conservative, and efficient. Turns ideas into practical actions.	Somewhat inflexible. Slow to respond to new possibilities.
Completer Finisher	Painstaking, conscientious, anxious. Searches out errors and omissions. Delivers on time.	Inclined to worry unduly. Reluctant to delegate. Can be a nitpicker.
Specialist	Single-minded, self-starting, dedicated. Provides knowledge and skills in rare supply.	Contributes only on a narrow front. Dwells on technicalities. Overlooks the "big picture."
Strength of contribution in any one of the roles is commonly associated with particular weaknesses, called "allowable" weaknesses. Executives are seldom strong in all nine team roles.		

Table 9-1. Nine team roles

The obvious conclusions are that teams will do best with a combination of roles and that imbalances need to be recognized and dealt with. In fact, Belbin's research identified specific team dynamics that were predictive of team effectiveness (or lack thereof):

Factors contributing to ineffective teams

1. No *Monitor Evaluators*: the team is unlikely to carefully weigh options when making decisions.
2. Too many *Monitor Evaluators*: "paralysis by analysis" outweighs creative ability.
3. No *Completer Finishers* and *Implementers*: teams that create good strategies can't execute.

Factors contributing to effective teams

4. Teams with *Plant* role: more ideas lead to better strategies. (Note: Team with *Plants* require *Monitor Evaluators* and *Coordinators*.)
5. Teams with *Resource Investigator* role: external orientation.
6. Teams with *Shaper* role: recognize need for urgency, which leads to significant impact on results, approaching high-performance teams.
7. Too many *Shapers* leads to excessive conflict, so a *Team Worker* is needed to facilitate relationships and allow team to succeed.
8. Teams with *Specialist* role: crucial in many situations where specialized knowledge is required, to become effective technical team.
9. Each role has "allowable weaknesses" that require compensation to result in highly effective teams, but weaknesses are OK because they result from strengths.

If the team does not have a balance of roles, this can be detected by software testing and a compensation strategy can be devised.

Belbin's findings show the following:

- It is necessary to understand a person's preferred team roles. (There are usually more than one.) These are the roles for which that person has natural and learned skills as well as an aptitude.
- The structure and composition of a team need to be carefully considered.
- The team must consciously use the different strengths of its members and manage their weaknesses.
- A team that does not have a balance of these roles or a plan to address the team deficiencies can be *predicted to fail.*

APPLYING BELBIN'S RESEARCH

The process of evaluating team strengths and weaknesses has been made practical and inexpensive by software that automates the process. Using that software, you can …

- Determine an individual's preferred role, as perceived by both the individual and his or her teammates.
- Evaluate team dynamics, suggesting who should fill which role.

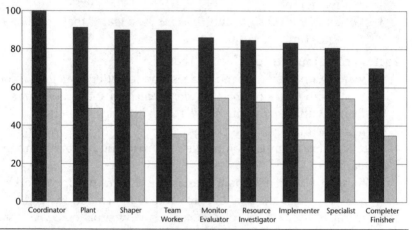

Figure 9-1. Team role combinations report

Figure 9-1 shows a sample preferred roles report from one team. Each of the roles is represented by a bar. The bar on the left represents the individual with the highest score; the bar on the right represents the average score of the whole team.

This team shows pretty good balance. However, it shows a much higher average on Monitor Evaluator than in Team Worker and is just average as Shaper. The report will warn that this team will be prone to "paralysis by analysis" and make specific recommendations by person on who should be empowered as a Shaper, etc.

A preferred roles chart helps a team to understand where it is strong or weak and where specific individuals can contribute. For example, where an individual score is much greater than the team on a particular role, the team will have a better opportunity for success by leaving that activity to the individual with the strength. For the team depicted in Figure 9-1, for example, it can be predicted that they will need to empower their stronger Shaper to force the group to a decision.

After a team is evaluated, you'll be able to decide what types of corrective actions, if any, would help improve the team's chances of success. In some cases, you'll find that the team composition is off; in other cases, you'll find that a person's self-perception differs markedly from the perception by teammates. For example, a team dominated by Shapers will need to take appropriate steps to rebalance the team, such as by adding Coordinators, Team Workers, and Resource Investigators as team members or mentors.

Another strategy would be for certain team members to "flex" into roles that may not be their preferred roles. Belbin identifies three levels of aptitude for a role: *preferred*, *manageable*, and *least preferred*. It is possible for an individual to assume a role that falls into the manageable category, although this will result in a certain amount of stress on that team member. It is not advisable to have an individual fill a role that falls into the least preferred category—it is highly likely that the team member will under-perform in this role.

Understanding preferred roles is an eye-opener for most people! At last they are able to understand why their teams have succeeded or failed. They are also fascinated to learn their own preferred roles and the strengths and weaknesses and all that these imply. There is a sense of liberation in realizing that they have weaknesses *because* they have strengths … and that these weaknesses are OK as long as they are managed. In fact, the strategies described suggest there are no bad traits, just roles that need to be comprehended to make the Six Sigma teams effective.

Most importantly, each team needs to be aware of each individual's preferred role(s) and use that knowledge to improve its effectiveness.

THE IMPORTANCE OF TEAM LEADERSHIP

Next to understanding how to structure a team based on preferred roles, the biggest determinant of team success is linked to the team leadership skills (especially productive problem solving and team facilitation) exhibited by the team's black belt. Organizations experienced in the implementation of Six Sigma programs, ITT Industries and Starwood Hotels & Resorts, have found that the team leadership component of Six Sigma training is capable of driving higher levels of performance by

- Increasing trust.
- Facilitating the sharing of knowledge.

- Generating synergistic solutions and innovation through productive problem solving and high-performance teamwork.

As depicted in Figure 9-2, team leadership can improve the quality of thinking that forms strategy and has a direct impact on the ability of the team to carry through on its commitments (execution). In short, Lean Six Sigma programs are integrated into the company's culture and strategy through team leadership.

Figure 9-2. Team leadership and team dynamics

Beware of Dictatorial Black Belts

Most leadership training includes exercises that challenge black belts to reconsider their own ideas of the problem and its solution in the light of input from the team. The development of inquiry skills (in which black belts learn to first understand others' positions) rather than solely advocacy of their own positions is a key success factor in team performance. No one person, not the black belt or the process owner, can know all the issues that may affect cost, quality, or delivery time. Leadership training creates the awareness of the power of collaborative, inclusive thinking—which is a powerful latent source of energy within the team—and tests the black belt's ability to subordinate his or her original thesis to a new thesis based on team input. Taking the contrary point of view, a black belt who cannot achieve this goal will be at best an individual performer with extra "hands" carrying out his or her orders and will not achieve the performance made possible by using the team members heads. You can expect that about 20% of your black belts will need remediation and about 5% will, despite their intellect, be unqualified to lead teams. There is a vast body of research that supports this conclusion.

IMPLICATIONS FOR BLACK BELT TRAINING

This chapter focused on the lessons of Belbin's preferred team roles because we have found it to be an effective tool in helping organizations improve performance. You may have other instruments for testing team leader or team group effectiveness that you prefer. No matter which approaches you use, the bottom line is that you have to pay attention to team effectiveness in your Lean Six Sigma efforts. Team and leadership skills should be provided to all your black belts and champions. For example:

- Use the Belbin technique or other instruments to identify team members' skills and aptitudes. Incorporate the lessons into how you structure teams, making sure that the roles necessary to your team's success are filled.
- Include a one-week *Increasing Leadership Effectiveness* (ILE) workshop in black belt training and encourage participative decision making. These courses explain the impact of employing various management and social styles in managing teams and allow participants to develop their skills in a workshop environment.
- Make your workshops interactive so the potential team leaders can develop inquiry skills (where they seek to understand someone else) over advocacy (where they seek to be understood). Good inquiry skills can draw out the best ideas of the team rather than constrict solutions to those already formed in the team leader's mind. Such skills prepare black belts to address complex situations such as identifying opportunities, involving process owners in projects, and successfully managing their sphere of influence to ensure project completion.
- Train participants to handle various forms of defensiveness. For example, people need to express their frustrations before they can deal more objectively with issues that are influenced by defensive routines—yet many leaders have a very low tolerance for what they perceive as whining. Experienced facilitators intuitively understand this fact and suppress any intolerance they have in favor of allowing team members to vent.

■ Monitor the effectiveness of black belts as team leaders. In our experience, about 20% of the trainees require additional training or coaching beyond the one week ILE course, and about 5% never succeed in the role.

Remember: Your champions and black belts will become the catalysts of your culture change, bringing new ideas to their teams and creating a positive chain reaction of improvement in your organization. These skills will enable them to maintain the momentum for improvement as they assume leadership roles in the future.

If you do a good job, you'll likely get feedback from your new black belts similar to these from real participants who received ILE training as their first week of the standard black belt curriculum:

As we approach Black Belt certification, we have reflected on the training we have received. It is our belief that the week of ILE Training was the strongest package we attended. In our opinion Value Based Six Sigma relies on a structured methodology, detailed statistics, but most of all the ability to lead, facilitate, and create synergy within a cross-functional team.

ILE has helped with the following:

■ *Creation of self-awareness and the value of personal feedback.*
■ *Understanding of social and behavioral styles.*
■ *Facilitation skills.*
■ *Development of effective meeting tools/techniques.*
■ *Decision making.*

—Peter Bounsall and Mark Bracey
ITT Jabsco (UK)

Note

1. Max Isaac has developed the Team Leadership Practice within the George Group. His clients include Estée Lauder Cosmetics Ltd., Shawmut Bank, Honeywell, Liebel-Flarsheim, Praxair, Valmont Industries, Ingersoll-Rand, Starwood Resorts, Nitronex Corporation and ITT Industries. Before entering the field of consulting, he had 14 years experience in senior financial management positions with Imasco, Warner Lambert Canada Inc., and the Molson Companies. Within the Molson Companies, he held the position of Senior Vice President and CFO in its Retail Division He is a member of the Institute of Chartered Accountants of Ontario, Canada.

Chapter 10

Implementation: The DMAIC Improvement Process

Recently, a manufacturer was facing the kind of problem that most companies *want* to face: an increase in orders was overloading the production scheduling process. Customers could not find out promised dates of delivery, order status, etc. The whole order entry process encompassed many functions (an engineering review, purchasing status, etc.) that affected production capacity and lead time. This company was concerned about customer retention: customer satisfaction was well below a six sigma level. Immediate action was needed, but their key question was whether process improvements could speed up the flow or if they needed to start hiring more staff.

Another company had a much different situation, but faced similarly dire consequences. Their manufacturing process relied on the precise alignment of high-frequency communication diodes, which are about the diameter of a pin. Because these diodes are so tiny, it's easy for them to land on an edge, creating a defective connection and thus becoming scrap. The yield at the key workstation was about 87% (about 2.7 sigma). This company wanted to be at six sigma levels, because that would mean tremendous savings in terms of scrap, rework, cost, and capex investment.

At first glimpse, these process improvement challenges sound quite different. One company is dealing with a transactional process where the goal is to quickly and accurately transfer information among groups; the other is concerned with highly specialized technology at a single workstation. Yet both of these situations can be (and were) improved using the same basic model of Define-Measure-Analyze-Improve-Control, known more familiarly as DMAIC.

But it was more than just having a model that made improvement possible. What these companies had in common was the knowledge of when to use the Lean Six Sigma tools and when to call for additional firepower. The results?

- The order fulfillment challenge was solved by use of some simple process tools, which led to an improvement in cycle efficiency from 7% to 22%. Since the company could handle more work much more quickly, they did not need to hire any additional staff. More details are included at the end of this chapter (see pp. 178-181).
- The diode challenge was met through the application tool known as mistake proofing (described in Chapter 11). The loss of yield at this step fell to about 3 per million, compared with the initial 130,000 per million failure rate.

You might recall the tier-one auto supplier case study in Part I, where it was critical to achieve breakthrough performance improvement in quality problems, excessive lead time, and high overhead costs. The whole value stream was improved by first containing the customer critical-to-quality problems and using diverse DMAIC tools to attack the top 10 time traps in the process.

These disparate applications demonstrate that the Lean Six Sigma DMAIC process provides the framework for solving *any* process problem.

THE CONTEXT OF IMPROVEMENT

Before getting into the specifics of DMAIC, it will help if you try to imagine the context within which the process and its tools will be used.

At the broadest level, the corporate champion, business unit managers, business unit champions, and others will identify numerous opportunities that are clearly linked to customer needs and core value streams and that have high potential for contributing to shareholder value. Once approved, these opportunities are assigned to specific black belts and their teams by the business unit champion (working closely with the business unit manager). In turn, these teams are expected to apply the Lean Six Sigma improvement process to deliver on the projected benefits.

The highest-priority projects are most often critical-to-quality issues, such as the leaking brake hose fittings example discussed earlier in the book: in that case study, the leaking hoses affected the relationships with and retention of customers and the good reputation of the company. In other cases, the opportunity may be in the form of internal failures or high-cost problems that affect the bottom line rather than the customer. These Hidden Factory costs are completely valid for projects even though they are not related to customer critical-to-quality issues. In fact, this is a very common type of Lean Six Sigma project. Attacking these opportunities usually results in a simultaneous and dramatic reduction in variation, cost of quality, and cycle time.

Transitioning to the Black Belt Team

Part of becoming a Lean Six Sigma organization means incorporating a Lean Six Sigma mentality into every aspect of your work, not just what happens in a designated project. And part of Lean Six Sigma is managing the boundaries between process steps, not just what happens within each step. Therefore, as you look at transferring projects from the initial scoping work done by champions and/or managers to an assigned project being handled by a black or green belt team, there are several process boundary issues you will need to address. For example, you will need to document what information has already been used to bring the project idea this far already and what issues and/or assumptions you expect the black belt or team to investigate further.

Between the selection of projects and team implementation there are several key steps:

- Each business unit champion must decide which opportunities will create the greatest value in the least time and then assign a black belt or green belt to each selected project.
- Once those assignments are made, the black belts become involved in confirming the goals and generating data. Although the responsibility for project selection should initially lie with the champion, the black belt can use this information to validate the business opportunities to the champion and provide direction to the green belts and teams.

The confirmation work requires close analysis of the data, discussion with the process owner, and ultimately good judgment when the data is not clear-cut. It can be relatively simple if you have data that confirms the problem is critical-to-quality and existing records that document customers' complaints and/or existing data that can be plotted to expose undesirable trends. In other situations, confirmation might require extensive investigative work, which might be conducted by a black belt team rather than the unit champion or a master black belt.

THE DMAIC PROCESS AND ITS TOOLS

No matter how you handle the transition from a selected project *idea* to an active *project*, at some point the black belt and his or her team will take over. Their job is to deliver on the opportunity. And the best way to do that is almost always to follow a structured improvement method that leads them logically from a definition of the problem to implementing solutions that address the underlying causes. One of the most widely used improvement models is DMAIC:

Define: Confirm the opportunity and define the boundaries and goals of the project.

Measure: Gather data to establish the "current state," what is actually going on in the workplace with the process as it works today.

Analyze: Interpret the data to establish cause-and-effect relationships.

Improve: Develop solutions targeted at the confirmed causes.

Control: Implement procedures to make sure the improvements/gains can be sustained.

Teaching the full DMAIC process and all the tools usually takes four or five weeks of training. So, rather than attempt to provide a full exposition, for the remainder of this chapter, we'll review the overall DMAIC improvement process. Chapter 11 describes common tools used in the Define, Measure, and Analyze phases, and Chapter 12 covers the Improve and Control phases. As a manager or executive, it will help if you are familiar with the names and purposes of some of the DMAIC tools, though you need not understand in detail how they are constructed.

Figure 10-1 gives you a high-level view of DMAIC, which consists of 17 steps divided into five phases; Table 10-1 lists some of the tools associated with each of these phases.

Tollgate Reviews

One other feature of the DMAIC overview in Figure 10-1 you may

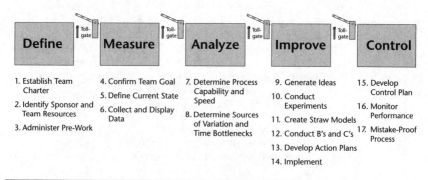

Define	Measure	Analyze	Improve	Control
1. Establish Team Charter 2. Identify Sponsor and Team Resources 3. Administer Pre-Work	4. Confirm Team Goal 5. Define Current State 6. Collect and Display Data	7. Determine Process Capability and Speed 8. Determine Sources of Variation and Time Bottlenecks	9. Generate Ideas 10. Conduct Experiments 11. Create Straw Models 12. Conduct B's and C's 13. Develop Action Plans 14. Implement	15. Develop Control Plan 16. Monitor Performance 17. Mistake-Proof Process

Figure 10-1. The DMAIC process

have noticed is the "tollgate" that occurs *between* each major phase and the next. These tollgates represent critical stages in each process, where the ongoing project is linked back to the corporate goals. During these reviews, the appropriate managers, master black belts, and champions have a chance to …

- Listen to a team present its work.
- Ask questions to ensure that team is staying focused on the CEO's priorities.

The purpose of these reviews is manyfold. The managers and Lean Six Sigma resources need to …

- Ensure that the project is on track toward the original goals.
- Evaluate whether the team seems capable of performing the work necessary to deliver on the potential benefits of this project. (If not, the answer is *not* to abandon the team, but to determine what additional training and coaching/mentoring will help them fill any gaps.)
- Help guide the team as appropriate by suggesting particular tools, sources of information, techniques, etc., that they may find helpful.
- Identify organizational barriers to the team's success and develop strategies for intervening on the team's behalf.
- Perform critical time checks to keep projects moving along on schedule. (The reviews serve as a tool for champions/sponsors to keep things flowing.)

It is vitally important that these gate reviews are done in a timely manner. The burden is on the gatekeeper (champion, MBB, sponsor, etc.) to do this, not the black belt. However the black belt should be

Process	Activity	Tools	
Define	1. Establish Team Charter 2. Identify Sponsor and Team Resources 3. Administer Pre-Work	Project ID Tools Project Definition Form NPV/IRR/DCF Analysis	PIP Management Process SSPI Toolkit
Measure	4. Confirm Team Goal 5. Define Current State 6. Collect and Display Data	SSPI Toolkit Process Mapping Value Analysis Brainstorming Voting Techniques Pareto Charts Affinity/ID	C&E/Fishbones FMEA Check Sheets Run Charts Control Charts Gage R&R
Analyze	7. Determine Process Capability and Speed 8. Determine Sources of Variation and Time Bottlenecks	C_p and C_{pk} Supply Chain Accelerator Time Trap Analysis Multi-Vari Box Plots Marginal Plots Interaction Plots	Regression ANOVA C&E Matrices FMEA Problem Definition Forms Opportunity Maps
Improve	9. Generate Ideas 10. Conduct Experiments 11. Create Straw Models 12. Conduct B's and C's 13. Develop Action Plans 14. Implement	Brainstorming Pull Systems Setup Reduction TPM Process Flow Benchmarking Affinity/ID DOE	Hypothesis Testing Process Mapping B's and C's/Force Field Tree Diagrams Pert/CPM PDPC/FMEA Gantt Charts
Control	15. Develop Control Plan 16. Monitor Performance 17. Mistake-Proof Process	Check Sheets Run Charts Histograms Scatter Diagrams	Control Charts Pareto Charts Interactive Reviews Poka-Yoke

Table 10-1. Lean Six Sigma toolset

communicating progress well enough for the gatekeepers to anticipate when gate reviews should be scheduled. It is the role of everyone involved to ensure effective and timely communications.

Most importantly, each tollgate review serves as an official stamp of approval, an acknowledgment that people in charge of the company's resources understand what it will take to complete the next phase of work and have approved the use of resources for that purpose.

Boundaries and Iterations

Note that the outcome of each tollgate is confirmation that the team has met the requirements of the phase and that it is OK to continue work in *the next DMAIC phase*. It is not a blanket approval for the team to plow through to Control unchecked.

But while tollgate reviews acknowledge the transition of a team from one phase to another, don't expect the boundaries between phases to be clean-cut. Often the team must delve into subsequent phases to complete the current phases. The reverse is also true. It is not uncommon to revisit and revise work done in an earlier phase because of what is learned in later phases. By dividing the reviews/approvals into stages, Lean Six Sigma recognizes that (a) teams will be gathering information that may influence the feasibility or projected impact of a project and (b) other business circumstances arise that may cause you to shift priorities. Your responsibility as someone guiding the teams is to make a call about whether this use of resources is still appropriate for your organization at this time.

A WALK THROUGH DMAIC

In Chapters 11 and 12 you'll find more detail about the tools associated with each of the DMAIC steps; here we'll look at the overall process from the view of a champion or a master black belt.

Define

The purpose of Define is for the team to clarify the goals and refine their understanding of the potential value of a project. As noted above, you need to determine for your organization who will do what portion of this Define work. In any event, someone needs to confirm the magnitude of the value opportunity in a given value stream, check the assessment of resources required, and develop a plan for how this project will be implemented using DMAIC.

Define Tools. The tools associated with the Define stage primarily serve the function of "information documentation." The team needs a clear *written* charter that documents the business case for working on this project, the expected returns, team membership, the project sponsor, and so on.

Define Tollgate Review. The final step in the Define phase should be a tollgate meeting between a team (led by a black or green belt) and a guiding team, usually composed of the unit manager, unit champion, master black belt, and process owner (if appropriate). At this stage, the review should focus on the following points:

■ How the project definition has been altered or refined (if at all)
■ What evidence exists to confirm the value opportunity and resource requirements
■ The team's plans for conducting the Measure stage

Measure

The purpose of the Measure phase is gather data that describes the nature and extent of the problem. As such, many of the data-collection tools will be used first in this phase, with subsequent data collection used to confirm improvements in later steps.

Measure Tools. There is a broad range of data and process tools used in Measure, including …

■ Brainstorming techniques, to encourage creativity.
■ Process mapping tools, to document how the process works today.
■ Numerous data tools, to collect and display different types of data.

Measure Tollgate Review. Perhaps no portion of the DMAIC process is as variable as the Measure phase and its tollgate review. The reason is simple: there is no predefined sequence or set of tools that each team *must* use. Rather, teams must apply their logic and knowledge to create their own path and select tools appropriate to their particular challenges.

In the Measure tollgate, the reviewers have their own challenge: to trace the logic the team pursued in deciding what data to collect and where that data led them. They should be using such investigative statements and questions as the following:

■ "Explain to me where you got that data."
■ "How is your measurement system?"
■ "What lessons did you take away from that data chart?"
■ "Show me your cause-and-effect diagram. How did you decide which of these causes to pursue with data collection? What data did you collect and what did you find out?"
■ "Why did you decide to collect that particular kind of data?"

Analyze

As you can tell, by the time a team reaches the Analyze phase, it should have a lot of data and information gathered in the Measure phase. The goal here is to make sense of all that information and to track down the cause-and-effect relationships that produce the targeted defects, process delays, and so on.

By the end of the Measure phase of DMAIC, the team should have a much clearer picture of exactly what is going on in the process and which steps are contributing the most to delays, quality problems, etc. In Analyze, the goal is to develop knowledge that will help a team use its time in Improve most effectively—where they will want to develop countermeasures that address the underlying causes of problems linked to customer needs and cycle efficiency. Therefore, much of the Analyze phase is devoted to exploring the relationships between input and output variables.

Analyze Tools. It should be noted that the Analyze tools are often used to analyze *historical* data—that is, data that already exists. Using existing data is still appropriate because you are looking for "clues" that will help you determine potential causes of problems. Historical data is an obvious source of potential "clues."

Sometimes these "clues" can give us breakthroughs; but you have to be careful because historical data can be laced with many problems and inherently has some weaknesses. (When I was in Japan, one of my hosts exclaimed: "Don't use dead data!") When we simply can't get the information we need from historical data or there is too much risk of misinterpretation, we use some "power tools" that appear in Chapter 11 (such as Design of Experiments, for statistically determining true cause-and-effect relationships).

Analyze Tollgate Review. The Analyze tollgate continues the theme of emphasizing linkages:

- What causes is the team going to target in the Improve phase?
- Why did they focus on those causes? What are the links to the data/conclusions reached during the Measure phase?
- What other potential causes did the team investigate? How do they know those were not actual causes?
- What data do they have that links the targeted cause to the problem under investigation?
- What data indicates that improving the identified cause(s) will have the desired impact on the targeted improvement measure (e.g., how do they know that addressing the cause will reduce lead time)?

Improve

Throughout most of Measure and Analyze, a team is challenged to think creatively and inclusively in deciding what potential causes to investigate, what data to collect, how to display that data, and how to interpret its messages. In the Improve phase, the team has to switch from thinking broadly to a focused, practical mindset: now that they know what the causes are, what specific changes can they make in the process to counteract those causes and what methods will achieve the desired effect?

Improve Tools. Of all the tool sets associated with DMAIC, those most commonly used in Improve represent perhaps the broadest mix of both Lean and Six Sigma tools. Pull systems, setup reduction, and Total Productive Maintenance, for example, are traditional Lean tools used in Improve to eliminate work-in-process and time delays; tools such as Design of Experiments and process mapping represent approaches inherited from the Six Sigma/quality improvement tradition.

Improve Tollgate Review. Predictably, the Improve tollgate picks up where the Measure tollgate left off in pursing the logical links between causes and actions, *plus* there is a new focus on implementation:

- What countermeasures did the team develop?
- How did they decide which ones to implement (e.g., the criteria used to select among options, pilot tests used to see whether the changes had the desired effect)?
- How do they *know* that those measures would affect the causes confirmed in Measure?
- What happened when the countermeasures were first put into practice? What changes did the team make to refine the improvements?

Control

The purpose of Control is to make sure that the gains made will be preserved, until and unless new knowledge and data show that there is an even better way to operate the process. The team must address how to hand off what they learned to the process owner and ensure that everyone working on the process is trained in using any new procedures.

Control Tools. The tools used in Control are focused on implementation: how to document the new procedures, what data to collect regularly on the process to monitor performance, and so on. In many cases, the team will be using tools used earlier in DMAIC (such as control charts), but switching the emphasis to "ongoing monitoring" instead of "cause investigation."

Control Tollgate Review. The Control tollgate is both a formal closure to the project and a forum where the process owners and other key managers can see what it will take to make sure the process doesn't backslide to its former, unacceptable performance. Four key elements of the review are:

- **Measures:** What indicators will be tracked to evaluate process performance?
- **Monitoring:** Who will collect data on the indicators? Do they know what to do depending on what the data shows them?
- **Sustainability:** What measures have been taken to ensure that all process staff/operators are trained in the new procedures and that any new staff will be similarly trained?
- **Leveraging the Learning:** What best practices were established in the project? How are they being documented? What other lessons did the team learn? How is this information going to be shared?

DEVELOPING FOCUS: THE DMAIC FILTER

The simple flowchart of Figure 10-1 and the tools of Table 10-1 are sometimes combined into a graphic that provides a better pictorial representation of what DMAIC allows a team to accomplish (see Figure 10-2).

In the diagram, *KPIV* stands for key process input variables or, in common Six Sigma terminology, the process factors (X's) that affect the process output (Y). When a project begins, the KPIVs are really not "key" variables yet; they are raw ideas for improvement, the *potential* factors that might have a big influence on quality and/or time. As depicted in the figure, what happens in a DMAIC project is that a team starts with a defined opportunity. At that point, there are lots of ideas for potential improvement—everyone on the team will have their own ideas about what's causing the problem with the output. By using the tools and logically linking causes and effects, the team gradually narrows its focus to those ideas or KPIVs that are *most* critical or have the largest effect on output. The rest of the KPIVs are essentially "filtered" out as the team collects data showing they are unimportant in terms of CTQ quality or improving cycle efficiency.

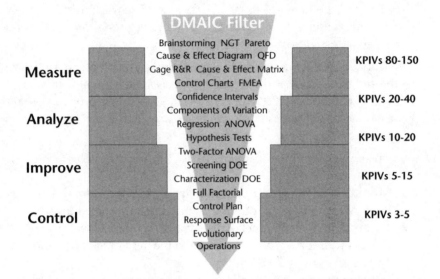

Figure 10-2. The DMAIC filter

BIG GAINS WITH SIMPLE TOOLS: TWO EXAMPLES

Here is one example of how some of the simple tools described above can nevertheless produce impressive results. At the beginning of this chapter, you read of a company that was facing the imminent need to add personnel to keep up with the purchasing load. One of the first steps they took was to map the flow; as expected, it showed a lot of non-value-added steps. Figure 10-3 shows the original process flow and what steps were taken to improve each type of problems:

- *Light gray* symbols are non-value-added steps that were subsequently eliminated.
- *Black* symbols are steps that were reduced in terms of time.
- *Dark gray* symbols are steps that were moved to a more logical flow elsewhere.

The resulting flow diagram is shown in Figure 10-4.

The results were amazing. The number of steps in the process was reduced from 21 to 7. With a simpler, more streamlined process, the company did not have to hire additional people, achieving savings of $240,000 per year. Process lead time was reduced by 72% and the cycle efficiency increased from 7% to 22%.

How were such gains possible? One of the most important improvement opportunities in most organizations is the fact that few

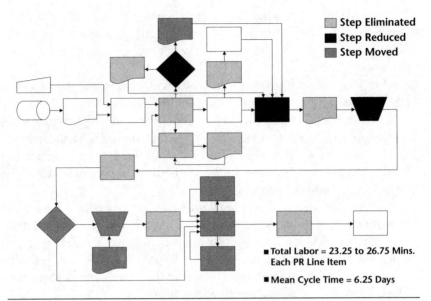

Figure 10-3. Pre-improvement flowchart

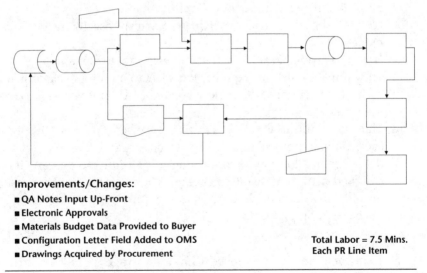

Figure 10-4. New process flowchart

non-manufacturing processes have been mapped! That is, there is no single document that shows all the steps in how the work flows. Simply mapping that flow opens people's eyes to low-hanging fruit that can be picked to improve process speed.

In addition to lacking any form of process map, organizations generally have very little data. When a modicum of data is collected to build a Pareto chart of delay time, for example, immediate solutions become apparent.

Let's look at another example. One of our clients was doing a poor job of responding to customer inquiries. Should they hire more people to do a better job? This would be equivalent to putting more machines and people in a plant in hopes of speeding up deliveries—it won't work. Remember the Third Law of Supply Chain Acceleration (Chapter 3): overall process lead time is directly proportional to the number of "things in process."

Given this knowledge, the client knew exactly *what* to measure: how much work there was in process! They discovered they received more than 12,000 requests per year, which consumed 6,000 hours of employee time. It was estimated that $350,000 was lost each year due to customer irritation, not even counting the lost follow-on business. The company then took the following steps:

- They divided the process into three major chunks:
  Phase 1—Inside Sales receives customer inquiry and requests information from Production Control.
  Phase 2—Production Control provides response to Inside Sales request.
  Phase 3—Inside Sales provides final response to Customer.
- They implemented an expedite log sheet to monitor cycle time for each phase with SAP Workflow created (SAP in this case) to control process.
- They determined Phase 1, which comprised 60.5% of the total cycle time, to be a "Pareto delay" (accounting for the majority of delay time). Along with continuing to monitor the process, they assigned dedicated inside sales reps to handle expedited requests, developed strict guidelines for handoffs, and provided training in the expediting process.

Results:
- Total cycle time was reduced from an average of 5.8 days to 1.5 days.
- They expect $267,500 incremental sales and $83,300 labor cost reduction in the first year.
- Incremental sales and labor savings will result in $147,000 operating income.

This improvement required only one black belt for four months, with the assistance of 10 people from within the process who devoted about 10% of their time.

IMPLICATIONS FOR BLACK BELT TRAINING

As you read through the next two chapters and learn more about DMAIC and its tools, keep in mind the following advice:

- First, it is important to establish a standard improvement process in your black belt training. DMAIC, the process described here, is currently the most common of these processes, but there are other, equally valid models you may already be using. The key point is to make it a *standard* process that *everyone* uses or you'll soon be caught in a quagmire of conflicting methods and approaches.
- Second, give priority in black belt training to the simpler tools that teams are most likely to need and use; reserve training in the advanced or more specialized tools (such as those described in the next chapter) to teams that have a demonstrable need for them or for black belts and master black belts who want to cultivate their knowledge in those tools. (One recent Six Sigma book spent 640 pages on tools likely to be used by 10% of black belts at most, leaving just 160 pages for tools useful to the other 90%.)
- Last, it isn't necessary for line managers, executives, or perhaps even champions to understand the ins and outs of all the Lean Six Sigma tools. However, they will be unable to guide a team through offline coaching and the formal tollgate reviews if they are completely ignorant. You will therefore probably want to adapt some elements of the black belt curriculum to provide awareness training for those who need some knowledge of these new methods and tools, but don't have to apply them themselves.

Chapter 11

Implementation: The DMAIC Tools

"But how the devil did you deduce that, Holmes?"

"I see that you are a medical doctor, Watson, by the stethoscope bulging in your pocket and a cane engraved with CCH for Charing Cross Hospital. I see that you are returned wounded from India because you are brown as a berry and walk with an exaggerated limp...."

"Ah Holmes, I thought you'd done something clever there for a moment."

—Arthur Conan Doyle

When you pose a quality or lead-time problem to people who have not been trained in Lean Six Sigma tools, they are initially incredulous and believe the goal of achieving three failures per million or an 80% reduction in lead time is impossible. After all, the problem they are confronting has probably been around for a long time and has never been solved!

But as they complete their black belt training and have seen and used Lean Six Sigma methods under the guidance of an expert coach, they become more like Watson: "For a moment, I thought this required something clever." They develop a sense of power and they feel exhilarated. This change in attitude is a moment of success, when Lean Six Sigma starts to become part of the way they

182

think, part of how they do their everyday work. And *if* the proper project was selected (based on potential for shareholder value), powerful financial results will soon ensue.

The same reaction occurs when people first learn about many of the Lean Six Sigma tools described in this chapter. While some of these tools are simple and straightforward, others can be intimidating. But with training and guided practice, black belts and team members soon come to think, "What's the big deal?"

These tools are worth the effort. They have been proven in practice, time and again, that they can bring nearly miraculous progress to what you thought were "intractable" problems. They are the tools that can achieve breakthrough performance improvement in quality, cost, and lead time. In keeping with the basic premise of this book—that a combination of Six Sigma and Lean is needed to achieve the best results—you'll find here a mixture of tools from both of these disciplines.

DEFINE TOOLS

The tools used most often in Define serve two purposes:

- Documenting key information about the project (project definition form).
- Providing a high-level view of the value stream being targeted in the improvement effort (SIPOC diagram).

Project Definition Form

This form was introduced back in Chapter 8 because it's likely that the people responsible for selecting projects will have begun documenting information relevant to the project. As shown in Figure 11-1, the project definition form (PDF) captures key information relevant to the project, such as the problem statement, scope, assumption, resources, and schedules.

If a PDF and/or a team charter has not been completed, the team itself can take on the responsibility to prepare a draft to submit to its champion and unit manager for review and approval. This is generally accomplished using a Web-based tool.

SIPOC Diagram

A core principle of Lean Six Sigma is that defects can relate to anything that makes a customer unhappy—long lead time, variation in lead time, poor quality, or high cost, for instance. To address any of the problems, the first step is to take a process view of how your company

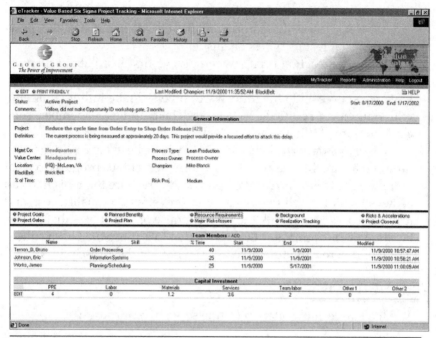

Figure 11-1. Project definition form

goes about satisfying a particular customer requirement. Because many organizations still operate as functional silos and because no one person owns the entire process, just steps in the process, it's likely that few if any people will have looked at the process from start to finish.

The tool that black belts use to create a high-level map of process is called SIPOC, which stands for:

Supplier: The person/process/company that provides whatever is worked on in the process (raw material, a subassembly, information, etc.). The supplier may be an outside vendor or another division.

Input: The material or information provided.

Process: The internal steps (both those that add value and those that do not add value).

Output: The product, service, or information being sent to the customer (preferably emphasizing critical-to-quality features).

Customer: The next step in the process or the final customer.

Figure 11-2 shows a SIPOC diagram for an organization that leases equipment. As you can see, it not only shows all the S-I-P-O-C ele-

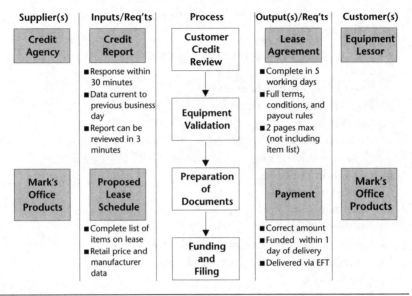

Figure 11-2. SIPOC process diagram

ments, but also critical-to-quality (CTQ) indicators (such as "complete in 5 working days").

A SIPOC diagram usually takes shape during the Define stage of DMAIC, but its impact is felt throughout the rest of the improvement project as well. In the Measure phase, the team will be measuring the lead times and quality levels wherever the process fails to meet (CTQ) requirements of the customer. In the Analyze phase, the team will be relating each CTQ and each time trap (the output, or Y, in Six Sigma parlance) to a few process parameters (the X's) whose change will improve the CTQ or time trap. In Improve, the team makes changes to the inputs and process steps that affect the critical output. These improvements are then, in Control, the target of measures to make sure the gains are retained.

MEASURE TOOLS

The Measure phase of DMAIC is symbolic of a critical shift in thought patterns that has to occur in order for any project to deliver on its desired goals. No longer can team members go from thought to action; they have to go from thought to *data* to action. Data comes in all shapes and sizes, with a corresponding array of tools used to collect, display, and analyze it. We'll look at examples of five types of tools, both simple and sophisticated, that your teams will likely use in their Measure work:

A. Describing a process and its characteristics
   Process mapping
   Lead time/cycle efficiency
B. Focusing and prioritizing
   Pareto charts
   Cause-and-effect matrix
   Failure modes and effects analysis (FMEA)
C. Generating and organizing ideas
   Brainstorming
   Nominal group technique
   Multivoting
   Cause-and-effect diagrams (fishbones)
D. Collecting data and ensuring accuracy
   Checksheets
   Measurement accuracy (gage R&R)
E. Understanding and eliminating variation
   Run charts/control charts
   Process capability

A. Process Characteristics Tools

Process Mapping. The foundation of the Lean Six Sigma—and virtu-ally all modern improvement methods—is the process map (often called *flowchart*). Process maps are similar to SIPOC in that they show process steps, inputs, and outputs, but are different in being both more detailed and more localized. The importance of a process map to any improvement effort cannot be overemphasized: it is simply too difficult to work on a process without having a picture of it. It is often amazing to witness the constructive discussions and revelations aris-ing from the simple exercise of getting people together to build a process map. In non-manufacturing applications, a process map gen-erally does not exist; hence the opportunities for improving speed, reducing cost, and increasing value are all the greater.

The process map (Figure 11-3) clearly illustrates the steps making up the process, the inputs necessary to carry out each step, and the outputs resulting from each step. In addition, it is usually very bene-ficial to indicate critical measures, interaction points, options, times, and other key aspects of the process on the map. This level of detail is usually sufficient for the first version of a process map. As the project

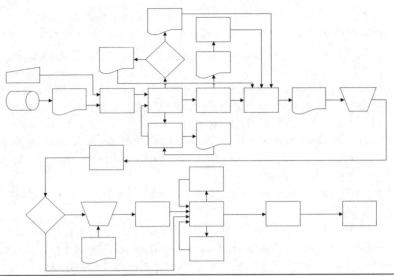

Figure 11-3. Process map

progresses, more detail will likely be needed for steps and inputs singled out by the other Lean Six Sigma tools as being critical. At that juncture, the detail and data will be added to convert the process map into a value stream map.

Process Lead Time and Cycle Efficiency. Some projects may be defined to directly attack process cycle time, lead time, or other speed issues. As you might recall from Chapter 3, the key Lean metric is *process cycle efficiency*, which is determined by comparing the value-added time with the total lead time (see pp. 36-38).

Measuring total lead time will sound daunting if you think it involves time-coding every piece of paper or material that enters a process and tracking how long it takes to come out the other end. But, in truth, it is not as difficult as it might sound at first, because you don't have to wait for a product (or report, order, etc.) to go through a full manufacturing process cycle (which could take many weeks). Instead, you can get a fairly accurate estimate of lead time by comparing work in process (WIP) with the number of completions per day (this was the Third Law of Lean Six Sigma, p. 49):

lead time = WIP/completions

At this time in a project, a team reaches a point where they want to calculate cycle efficiency. Some of these calculations may have already been performed as part of the value stream mapping (conducted during project selection). If the calculations were never done or if only preliminary data was collected, the team should do the following:

- Confirm that the value stream map includes all the non-value-added steps, such as rework, moving to stockrooms, retrieving, etc. These non-value-added steps will provide the foundation for estimating what cost can be driven out of a process by *Leaning* it. While the MRP (Material Requirements Planning) routers are useful for information on the value-added steps, it is best to include people who actually work in the process to confirm all the non-value-added steps.
- Estimate the value-added time and WIP at each step in the process.

After the data is recorded, the team should meet to discuss the results. A one-line diagram of the process should be written on a large white board, with Post-it® notes placed along the diagram to depict value-added and non-value-added steps. A lot of discussion will ensue: steps have been missed, the diagram is wrong, the times are wrong, etc. However, the heat of this discussion will also generate some light and a clear picture of the process will emerge.

Once the team has agreed on how the process is depicted and how time is allocated between value-added and non-value-added steps, they are ready to calculate the cycle efficiency:

process cycle efficiency = value-added time/total lead time

Measuring process cycle efficiency is a way to benchmark your process performance against world-class standards. As you may recall from Chapter 3, a Lean process is one in which the value-added time in the process is more than 25% of the total lead time of that process. Knowing the cycle efficiency, therefore, lets you judge how much improvement is possible and perhaps needed.

B. Focus/Prioritization Tools

The "funnel" diagram in Chapter 10 showed how one purpose of the DMAIC process is to narrow down from the dozens of *possible* causes (X's) to just the few that contribute the most to the key customer issues (outputs, or Y's). The tools below will help your teams where to focus their efforts to get the biggest impact.

Pareto Charts. The Pareto chart is simply a bar chart in which each bar represents the *relative* contribution of each cause or component to the total problem, with the bars arranged in descending order of importance.

Pareto charts are named for the Italian statistician who asserted the *Pareto 80/20 principle*: that 80% of the problem can be explained by just 20% of the causes. They are, therefore, a tool of focus and leverage, allowing us to devote our energies to the areas that will have the biggest impact—in essence giving us five times more leverage than would be possible if we spread our energies equally among all the causes contributing to a result.

You can see this Pareto effect in Figure 11-4: nearly 80% of the billing errors are due to just the first two causes (using a carrier that isn't often used and missing codes).

Pareto charts are extremely simple to construct and interpret and

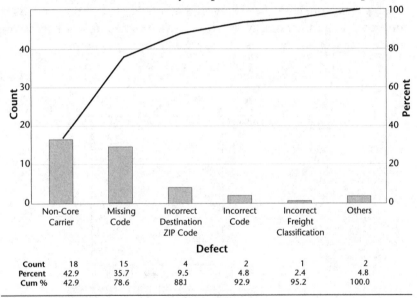

Defect	Non-Core Carrier	Missing Code	Incorrect Destination ZIP Code	Incorrect Code	Incorrect Freight Classification	Others
Count	18	15	4	2	1	2
Percent	42.9	35.7	9.5	4.8	2.4	4.8
Cum %	42.9	78.6	88.1	92.9	95.2	100.0

Figure 11-4. Pareto chart of freight billing errors

therefore are one of the tools you should expect nearly every team to use early in its project.

Cause-and-Effect Matrix. A very effective method of capturing the Voice of the Customer and relating it to process input variables is the *cause-and-effect matrix* (see Figure 11-5). This type of matrix helps you filter out less important steps and inputs so you can focus on the parts of your process containing the relatively few critical input variables that truly have an effect on your key process output variable.

To create a cause-and-effect matrix, list customer-related outputs across the top of a grid, along with their rating (1-10) in terms of importance to the customer. These outputs will include the key process output(s) for your project. Then list process inputs or steps along the left side of the matrix. These process steps or inputs will typically come from the process map as well as additional brainstorming. Rate each step or input based on its relationship to the customer output, using a scale of 0, 1, 3, or 9, where 0 means no correlation and 9 is strong or heavy correlation. Finally, multiply the process correlation times the customer weighting and add the scores across the row to get a total score for each process input.

In this way, a cause-and-effect matrix acts much like a Pareto chart by providing focus. Here, as with other tools, the inputs or steps with the highest score have the strongest relationship to customer needs, so improvements in those areas will go the furthest toward achieving gains that will be noticed and appreciated by customers.

Example: Truck Stop

Process Step	Process Input	Temp of Coffee 8	Taste 10	Strength 6	Process Outputs Importance
		Correlation of Input to Output			Total
Clean Carafe		0	3	1	36
Fill Carafe with Water		0	9	9	144
Pour Water in Maker		0	1	1	16
Place Filter in Maker		0	3	1	36
Put Coffee in Filter		0	9	9	144
Turn Maker On		3	1	0	34
Select Temperature Setting		9	3	3	120
Receive Coffee Order		0	0	1	6
Pour Coffee into Cup		3	1	3	52

Process Step Correlation Scores
A higher number indicates stronger correlation

Figure 11-5. Cause-and-effect matrix

In this context, the term "customer" does not mean only those external to the organization. Here, the customer for an internal process may well be the next downstream workstation as well as the external customer.

Many readers may recognize the C&E matrix as a simplified version of the Quality Function Deployment (QFD) method of capturing and relating the Voice of the Customer. This version is far simpler and, unlike QFD, most teams can use it without a consultant/coach.

Failure Modes and Effects Analysis (FMEA). Like several other tools described previously in this chapter, failure modes and effects analysis (FMEA) is a primarily a tool of focus (see Figure 11-6). FMEA is used to prioritize risks to the project and document recommended actions. Each potential type of failure of a product or process is assessed relative to three criteria on a scale of 1 to 10:

- The likelihood that something will go wrong (1 = not likely; 10 = almost certain).
- The detectability of failure (1 = likely to detect; 10 = very unlikely to detect).
- The severity of a failure (1 = little impact; 10 = extreme impact, such as personal injury or high financial loss).

The three scores for each potential failure are multiplied together to produce a combined rating known as the Risk Priority Number (RPN): those with the highest RPNs provide the focus for further process/redesign efforts.

Process/Product
Failure Modes and Effects Analysis (FMEA) Form

| Process or Product Name | | | Prepared by: | | | | | Page ___ of ___ | | | | | |
| Responsible | | | FMEA Date (Orig): _____ (Rev):_____ | | | | | | | | | | |

Process Step/ Input	Potential Failure Mode	Potential Failure Effects		Potential Causes		Current Controls			Action Recom-mended	Respon-sible	Actions Taken				
			Severity		Occurrence		Detection	RPN				Severity	Occurrence	Detection	RPN
What is the process step and input under investi-gation?	In what ways does the key input go wrong?	What is the impact on the key output variables (customer require-ments)?		What causes the key input to go wrong?		What are the existing controls and procedures (inspection and test) that prevent either the cause or the failure mode?			What are the actions for reducing the occurrence of the cause or improving detection?		What are the completed actions taken with the recalculated RPN?				

Identify Failure Modes and Their Effects   Identify Causes and Failure Modes and Controls   Prioritize   Determine and Assess Actions

Figure 11-6. FMEA form

C. Idea-Generating and Organizing Tools

During the Define stage of DMAIC, the team is mostly confirming or fleshing out information that has already been collected. The amount of creativity required by the team is minimal at that point, a situation that reverses once the team reaches the Measure stage. Here and throughout the rest of DMAIC, a team needs to be sure that it is getting high-level involvement from all team members. There are a variety of so-called idea-generating and -organizing tools that a black belt can use to foster productive interaction with the team and help ensure the ideas that will actually result in improvement are captured.

Brainstorming. *Brainstorming techniques* are used to solicit *unconstrained* input and ideas from each team member, even ideas with which other team members (including the black belt!) might disagree. The trick to effective brainstorming is record all ideas, *without discussion or comment*, until a complete list is constructed. A brainstorming session may be the first time a newly minted black belt is called on to be an impartial facilitator and to actively manage team member participation—skills that take some practice to fully develop. You may want to have an experienced black belt or a master black belt act as a coach/observer during this first team facilitation to help guide the new black belt.

Idea-Selecting Tools. There are some common and very simple prioritization tools often used in conjunction with brainstorming:

- *Nominal group technique* (NGT) is a way to add a quantitative element to the decision making that often follows brainstorming. It is used when teams have a number of contentious members or controversial issues. During an NGT session, discussion is limited; people may ask questions of clarification and state their own personal reasons for supporting a given option, but there is no back-and-forth discussion about the pros and cons. Once everyone is clear about what each element on a brainstormed list means, they are given a limited number of votes to cast. Then, the choices that receive the most votes are singled out for further attention. The advantage of NGT is that it uncouples ideas from the team member personalities, so an idea gets evaluated on its merits, not according to the person who suggested it.
- *Multivoting* is a means for closing in on a conclusion when confronted with either an initial brainstormed list or one that has been semi-prioritized through NGT. Once the team has boiled the list of possible sources of a problem down to a manageable number (anywhere from about five to 10), each team member gets a third as many votes to cast in the final vote as there are items. If there were nine items, for example, each member would have 9/3 = three votes to cast. The results are then put on a Pareto chart.

Idea-Organizing Tool. *Cause-and-effect (C&E) or fishbone diagrams* are a specialized idea-organizing tool that helps a team identify *potential* causes they need to investigate. The ideas from brainstorming are typically grouped into categories known as the Six M's—Methods, Manpower (personnel), Machines, Materials, Measurement, and Mother Nature (environment)—and then organized in related categories into a diagram that looks like a fish skeleton (see Figure 11-7). One of the major outcomes is a consensus by the team members to collect some more data to resolve the issues.

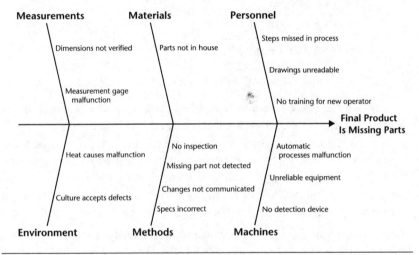

Figure 11-7. Cause-and-effect diagram

It's important to note that C&E diagrams are structured brainstorming tools, *not* data! Just because something is listed on the C&E, that doesn't mean it is an actual cause of the problem. The team still needs to collect data to verify which potential causes are actual contributors.

D. Data Collection/Accuracy Tools

Obviously if a team is going to be collecting data, it should have standard procedures for measuring and logging the data. There are many tools for establishing common data-collection procedures and for ensuring that the data collected is a reliable indicator of what's really going on in the process. We'll highlight just two of these tools here.

Checksheets. A major activity in Measure is gathering lots of data. A simple data recording method is the *checksheet* (Figure 11-8), which can detect trends and allow good questions to be posed to the team in a manner understandable by all. A checksheet can take many forms. It suggests additional collection points and data that should be taken.

Employee Benefit Issue Tracking – June

Defect	Week				
	1	2	3	4	Total
Incorrect SSN	I		I	I	3
Incorrect Address		I			1
Incorrect Work History	I			I	2
Incorrect Salary History	II	I	III	II	8

Figure 11-8. Data collection checksheet

Checksheets are commonly needed early in a project when certain key data is not available. For example, a manufacturer was interested in reducing waste in a particular key operation. The pounds of waste being produced were known, but no information was being recorded to indicate the amount of waste resulting from the various sources within the operation. A simple checksheet was implemented at the different workstations to capture the contribution of each to overall waste.

Gage Repeatability and Reproducibility (R&R). In some ways, it might be argued that gage repeatability and reproducibility (gage R&R) should appear first on everyone's tool list, because it's of fundamental importance. Implicit in our discussion is the assumption that the measurements being taken are accurate and consistent. But this assumption is not always true. Gage R&R is the method by which physical measurement processes are studied and adjusted to improve their reliability. "Repeatability" means that someone taking the same measurement on the same item with the same instrument will get the same answer. "Reproducibility" means that different people measuring the same item with the same instrument will get the same answer.

A gage R&R assessment is relatively simple to perform. For example, you could have two or three operators measure 10 parts three times each and enter the results into a statistical package (such as Minitab). The analysis determines the total amount of variation present in the measurement system and the relative contribution of the two components of measurement variation, repeatability and reproducibility. This variation is then compared with total process variation and the tolerance range. If measurement system variation is less than 10% of the specification range and process variation—the measurement system is considered good: it can reliably measure whether the data you collect will accurately reflect the actual process performance. If the measurement variation is above 30%, the measurement system definitely needs improvement. Any measure process that has a gage R&R between 10% and 30% *may* be OK, but you'd be better off to take action.

If you are a champion, sponsor, or other manager who will be reviewing a team's work, it's not essential that you understand how to perform a gage R&R analysis, but you *should* make it a habit to ask a team how much confidence they have in their measurement system and how they can tell whether their measurements are accurate.

E. Understanding and Eliminating Variation

As you probably know by now, there are many ways in which "variation is evil":

- Variation in product quality leads to scrap and rework, which are significant contributors to manufacturing overhead costs, delays in lead time, and product that does not meet customer requirements.
- Variation in time—arrival time, processing time, etc.—contributes to congestion and other delays that prevent a process from operating at optimal speed.

In order to reduce variation, you first have to identify it, then understand what causes it. There are several classes of tools used to understand variation. The most common are of two types:

- Graphic tools used to plot data over time (and expose patterns of greatest variation) and even relate process capability to customer specifications.
- Statistical analysis tools that can help pinpoint important differences in variation.

These two types of tools overlap. There are, for example, statistical tests used to analyze data on a graphic chart and results from some statistical analyses are sometimes displayed graphically. Here are some examples of these tools.

Run Charts. By definition, a process is something that is repeated periodically over time. It stands to reason, therefore, that much of the data a team collects will be produced over time as well—such as key process measures taken each shift, number of defects produced per hour or per day, total lead time each day, and so on.

There is a special subset of tools useful for displaying and analyzing data that is time-ordered, the simplest of which is called a *run chart* (Figure 11-9). A run chart simply displays observed data points in the order in which they are collected.

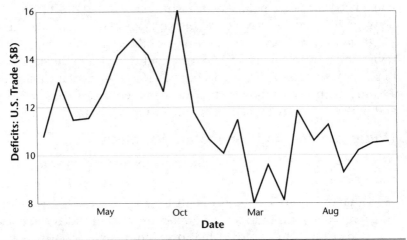

Figure 11-9. Run chart of the U.S. trade deficit

You can learn a lot simply by plotting data in time order, such as …

- The general range of scatter (variation) in the points.
- Whether the data points are generally stable around some mean or if there are clear trends upward or downward.

Besides these simple visual impressions, there is a set of statistical rules used to interpret the patterns (or lack thereof) on a run chart. However, detailed statistical analysis and interpretation are normally done with *control charts*.

Control Charts. Control charts are the high-power version of run charts. The purpose of a control chart is to help a team determine whether the variation seen in the data points is a normal part of the process (known as "chance" or "common cause" variation) or if something different or noticeable is happening ("special cause" or "assignable" variation). There are different improvement strategies depending on which type of variation is present (common or special cause), so it is important for a team to know the difference. There are several simple statistical rules used to analyze the patterns and trends on the control chart to determine whether special cause variation is present.

The basic structure of a control chart (see Figure 11-10) is always the same. The charts show the following:

- *Data points* plotted in time order.
- A *centerline* that indicates the average.
- *Control limits* (lines drawn approximately 3 standard deviations from the average) that indicate the expected amount of variation in the process.

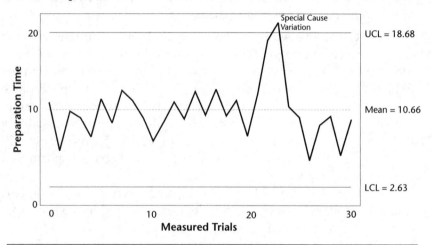

Figure 11-10. Control chart of pizza preparation time

What differs from chart to chart is the type of data plotted on the chart and the specific formulas used to calculate the control limits. Being able to know what kind of data to collect and the best way to calculate control limits is a skill that a black belt will develop only through special training or under the guidance of a master black belt or other statistical expert.

It takes time and effort to create a control chart, so the first and most important decision to make is when to create one. When control charts are used as part of a DMAIC project, that decision should be fairly clear: you want to monitor variation in characteristics of the process and/or its output that are critical to quality in terms of your project goals. In other words, don't have black belts create control charts just because they can! Pick and choose where to use these tools.

In and of itself, creating a control chart does you no good. You have to understand what the chart is telling you and take appropriate action. We create control charts for one purpose: to help us distinguish between two types of variation: common cause variation and special cause variation (also known as assignable variation).

■ Common cause variation is inherent in the process; it is present all the time to a greater or lesser extent.
■ Special cause variation is a change that occurs because of something different or unusual in the process.

As mentioned above, the reason we need to tell the difference between special and common cause variation is because there are different strategies for reacting to them.

Process Capability Analysis. *Process capability* tells you how well the natural process variation fits within the range of customer specifications. A capable process is one where all of the natural variation fits within the customer-defined target range; in a six sigma capable process, the natural process variation is only half as wide as the target range. An important point to remember is that we must have stability (no special causes) before we can assess capability. Therefore, capability analysis will be conducted only after control charts confirm that the process is stable.

There are four possible relationships between the actual process capability (determined by the process variation) and its desired capability (determined by customer specifications):

■ **Ideal state:** The process is in control and meets customer specs. Even though you are meeting customer specs, there will still be opportunities for reducing cost and improving process speed if you are not yet operating at six sigma capability. But you'll have to dig hard!
■ **Threshold:** The process is in control, but the process output data is wider than the spec limits. Use DOE or other problem-solving tools to tighten up the distribution (reduce variation).
■ **Brink of chaos:** The process is out of control but meets customer specs. Continue using control charts to identify and eliminate special causes of variation. This will make the process more predictable.
■ **Chaos:** The process is not in control and doesn't meet specs. Remove special causes first to bring the process in control, then work on additional improvements to meet specs.

The tier-one auto supplier described in Chapter 1 had a *threshold* process: the output was centered at the right point and there weren't any special causes, but it was not meeting customer specifications. As you can see in Figure 11-11, through the use of DOE, they were able to

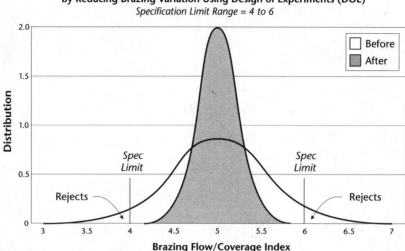

Figure 11-11. Variation and capability

achieve the *ideal* state: the process is in control and it meets customer specifications. (In fact, it is operating at a six sigma level of quality.)

ANALYZE TOOLS

The data and process tools used in Measure help a team focus on process factors that are most likely contributing to the problem at hand. But that belief is just a *theory* until it is tested with additional data. Two types of tools used in Analyze are *causal analysis tools,* used to confirm which potential causes actually contribute to a problem, and *time trap analysis tools,* used to locate the biggest sources of delays in the process.

Causal Analysis Tools

Scatter Plots. The *scatter plot* is a simple tool that can help determine if a relationship exists between two sets of data. For example, does the backlog of work correlate with the error rate of computer data entry?

The data displayed in Figure 11-12, for example, was gathered to investigate whether pizza preparation time was dependent on equipment, methods, personnel, or some other factors. In this case, the scatter of points appears almost randomly arranged, indicating that there is no relationship between this input (how busy store is) and output (pizza prep time).

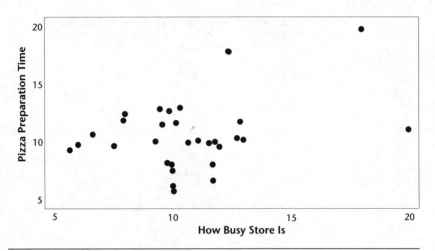

Figure 11-12. Scatter plot

Scatter plots provide a powerful visual image of how potential inputs variables are or are not related to the targeted process outcomes. Often, the visual impression is enough to confirm or rule out a specific course of action—such as whether a potential cause should be specifically addressed by countermeasures. If necessary, more advanced statistical tools, such as *regression analysis*, can be used to quantify the degree of relationship between the two factors. Keep in mind that you can see a trend between variables without a cause/effect relationship. For example, share bites and ice cream sales would show a correlation in a scatter plot. This is because both increase in warmer temperatures.

ANOVA (Analysis of Variance). Let's say that we have a machine that is used on all three shifts and that the average value of its output differs from one shift to the other. Like all processes, there will always be *some* variation present. The important improvement question is: Are the differences in averages *among the shifts* significant—that is, should you investigate further and try to standardize procedures *among* those shifts?

What if, in addition to shifts, we have several operators, three other machines, and different ways to set up these machines? The important question becomes: Which input, or *factor*, has the greatest effect on my key output? Is it shift, operator, machine, or setup? Which of these areas should I explore further?

Such questions are much easier to answer with simple statistical packages like Minitab. Where once you would have had to perform complex calculations, now it is simply a matter of inputting the data, asking for an Analysis of Variance (ANOVA) evaluation, and interpreting the answer.

Regression Analysis. ANOVA methods help us to identify which factors, or input variables, affect our output. Regression analysis carries this a step further by providing us with a mathematical model that quantifies the relationship. For example, in a polymer manufacturing process, ANOVA could tell us that temperature and line speed both have a significant effect on the tensile strength of a polymer. ANOVA alone will not tell us how much the tensile strength changes for every unit change in temperature or line speed, but regression analysis will. Regression will provide us with an equation that mathematically relates the inputs to the output. This allows us to predict process performance resulting from any changes we make in our input variables.

Time Trap Analysis: Supply Chain Accelerator Software. One of the major themes of Lean Six Sigma is that slow processes are expensive processes. In most processes, the material spends 5% of its time in "value-added." By increasing value-added to 20%, you can reduce manufacturing overhead by 20%. How to achieve such a substantial increase in value-added time in a process? The Second Law of Lean Six Sigma taught us that 80% of the delay is caused by a few time traps. By identifying these time traps (using the First Law of Lean Six Sigma for Supply Chain Acceleration equation), you can define those improvement projects that will drive the cycle efficiency over 20% and hence make a major impact—typically improving operating profit by 5% of revenue and reducing WIP and finished goods inventory by 50%.

The trick to identifying time traps was described back in Chapter 3. We looked at a simple press-to-assembly operation that produced a single part from four components. As part of that illustration, we focused on a single workstation where the four components were produced; the process had a constant demand. We used examples of spreadsheet calculations to show how to calculate the delay time of any activity, which is how we identified the few time traps that contributed 80% of the delay time. In reality, the company then applied improvement methods and applied a rapid setup method (described later in this chapter) to reduce the delay time of that time trap by 90%.

You may have thought at the time that that example was a bit simplistic. After all, a real workstation may build dozens of different parts, each requiring its own setup, each with its own percentage of scrap, rework, downtime, etc. Moreover, a real factory typically has hundreds of workstations producing thousands of parts. Doesn't it seem like it would be too complicated to perform similar calculations on a real process, even using a spreadsheet?

The answer is "not any more."

Over the last decade, virtually every supplier of ERP systems has supplemented the old infinite-capacity MRP systems with Advanced Planning programs that use real capacity. These systems typically store all the data necessary to perform the minimum batch size calculations described above.

In addition, specialty *supply chain accelerator* (SCA) software is available as a supplement to Advance Planning (AP) programs. SCA software not only calculates the minimum batch size, but also helps you identify the hidden time traps, the steps that insert the most delay time (the "20%" we want to identify according to the Second Law of Lean Six Sigma). As you'll see in Chapter 13, SCA software also helps establish a true pull system, where materials are released into the process on demand.

In short, SCA software can provide a value link between traditional materials planning capability that your company likely uses already and the new information needs associated with Lean Six Sigma projects. A schematic of the data flow within the whole Lean Six Sigma process is shown in Figure 11-13.

One key insight of the press example was that supply chain accelerator software helps us break out of the mindset that batch sizes are fixed and instead look at them as a dynamic variable we can alter as we improve process efficiency. To achieve smaller batch sizes, howev-

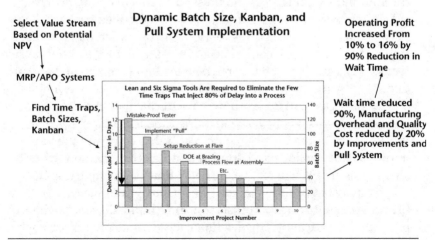

Figure 11-13. Using SCA as the linchpin of Lean Six Sigma

er, you first have to reduce the delays at the time traps:

1. Make the improvement (e.g., setup reduction).
2. Calculate the new, smaller batch size that will allow the workstation to produce at the same rate.

If you don't reduce the batch size, you will not reduce the delay time appreciably. One of the reasons why companies make such slow progress in reducing lead time is that they are wedded to fixed batch sizes, or economic order quantity batch sizes. These take no cognizance of the number of different parts flowing through the workstation (see Figure 3-5). A workstation that produces five different parts will have the same batch sizes as one that produces 20 different parts, thus resulting in four times the delay! Conclusion: *dynamic batches are required to reduce lead time and inventory.*[1]

IMPROVE TOOLS

The tools associated with Improve are incredibly diverse. They fall into two broad categories:

- Simple data collection/analysis tools used to confirm improvements.
- Specialized tools targeted at specific types of process problems.

Examples of simple data collection tools were covered under Measure and Analyze, so are not repeated here. Just be aware that many teams will reuse tools in this stage that they used earlier in the project, as a way to establish how much improvement has been seen. For example, a team that started a control chart in Measure will likely continue plotting data on that chart and look for changes in the amount or pattern of variation as a result of changes they have made in the process.

Knowing which of the specialized tools is appropriate in any given situation will only come with experience. Here is an overview of five common Improve tools used to make both process and product improvements.

Mistake Proofing

The assertions of mistake proofing are both bold and startling: *"To engineer and instrument an activity or workstation so it is incapable of supplying a defective product or service."*

Mistake proofing really applies to any process, but it grew up in manufacturing, so people have mistakenly thought it was correspondingly limited. Actually, the concept of mistake proofing applies to any human endeavor. The modern version of mistake proofing evolved in Japan, where it is known as *poka-yoke*. But it should be pointed out that the key concept was widely used by Ford in Model T production as early as 1908, and later in the Rouge plant.

So how does mistake proofing work? Here's a quick example involving a grinding operation. At the most basic level, mistake proofing would involve installation of an independent optical gauging system that automatically measures each part after machining and kicks rejects into a "bad" bin. This at least would prevent assembly problems downstream. This would enable downstream workstations to achieve six sigma quality, but it wouldn't eliminate the cost of scrap and rework. The next step toward Lean Six Sigma quality and cost would be to optically or mechanically measure the part *during* grinding and provide a dynamic feedback loop to compensate for abrasive wear. By this means, no bad parts are produced, which is the basic premise of mistake proofing. Signals can be provided to alert the Total Productive Maintenance process (see below) of the degrading status of the consumable abrasive material.

Because optical and electronic gadgets are so cheap and inventor types are in such good supply, we are far better equipped for mistake proofing than was Henry Ford. Scrap and rework have a devastating impact on process speed, so the better we are at preventing them, the better our process capability and efficiency will be!

Mistake Proofing Case #1: Semiconductor Diode Chip Misorientation. The start of Chapter 10 introduced a real-life case where mistake proofing had significant impact. (It's so wonderful that the client insisted on patent rights!) Here are the details on that example.

High-frequency communication diodes are about the diameter of a pin. They are supposed to be oriented in the bonding machine such that they lie flat. But because they are so tiny, they can land on an edge or on end and the bonder will not make a proper connection. Yes, you will catch these problems through testing, but it is still scrap, with all the implications for cost, machine capacity, delivery time, and inventory.

In fact, the yield at this workstation was acceptable by pre-Six Sigma standards, at about 88% (2.7 sigma), because most of the time the chips landed on the correct side due to a mechanical vibrator. Fixing a minor problem with cleaning rollers improved this yield somewhat, but nowhere near six sigma capability.

This problem was presented to a black belt class at this company; participants were asked to break into teams to come up with solutions and then come back together to present their ideas. In these situations, new ideas and fresh approaches always come to the fore, and sometimes offer improvements to the actual solution. If you want, take the time to write down your own idea before reading what this group developed.

Solution: One of the most powerful tools of mistake proofing is to exploit or introduce asymmetry. In this case, the chips had three unequal dimensions (length of the flat face, width, and depth). The participants with an understanding of basic physics knew that because of this asymmetry, the chip would react differently depending on the frequency of vibration. So rather than using the crude vibrating machine in place, our coach suggested using transducers at much higher frequencies to create micro-vibrations. The chips were first vibrated at one particular frequency that resonated with the edge dimension and caused the chips to flip onto their flat face or, less frequently, on end. To correct those chips that landed on end, they also introduced vibrations at a second frequency that resonated with the end dimension and caused the end-aligned chips to also flip onto their flat face.

Through these clever but simple steps, the failure rate at this step due to misorientation fell below three per million (above six sigma capability!), compared with the initial 80,000 per million (see Figure 11-14).

Mistake Proofing Case #2: Asymmetry in Design. The first case showed how a company exploited existing asymmetry to achieve six

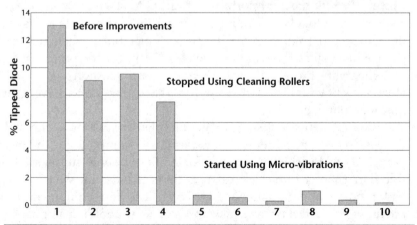

Figure 11-14. Tipped diode yield improvements

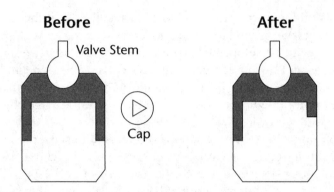

Before

Valve Stem

Cap

After

In the assembly of the single-handle faucet control valve, the cap was often installed backwards, thus creating a leak.

10% Defects

To prevent the defect, the cap was made asymmetrical, so it could only go on one way—the right way.

0% Defects

Figure 11-15. Defect prevention through mistake proofing

sigma levels of quality. You can take this principle one step further by introducing asymmetry to product design. Figure 11-15 shows an example in which a cap was often installed backwards onto a faucet control valve, resulting in leaks. The process had about a 2% rework rate. The question asked of the team was "How can we prevent caps from being installed backwards?" The answer was to modify the cap design so that it would fit onto the valve *only* in the correct orientation. After making this change, defects dropped to 0%.

Mistake Proofing: An Important First Step. Mistake proofing reflects a key mindset that has to imbue a Lean Six Sigma orientation: it's one thing to stop defects from reaching a customer, but a whole different game when you can *prevent* those defects. The impact on process speed and capability are significant. Therefore, one question you should always ask of your black belt teams is "What can we do to prevent this mistake from happening?"

The first step in a Lean Six Sigma implementation is to eliminate the customers' critical-to-quality issues. Mistake proofing is the most powerful tool to achieve this goal. For the tier-one auto supplier introduced in Chapter 1, the leak testers at the end of the line were passing bad product and failing good product. The test equipment was attempting to detect if washers were installed by applying air pressure and detecting a leak, but the test was far too crude (not enough precision, accuracy, or consistency). The pressure sensors were replaced by an optical system using light-emitting diodes and detectors that could directly sense the absence of a washer.

How important is scrap as a source of delay and the creation of a time trap? We have mentioned that a 10% scrap rate can cause a 38% time delay and a 50% increase in inventory in a factory. Using the First Law, you can derive an equation for the average time delay due to scrap. The relationship is depicted in Figure 11-16. You will notice that, as scrap is eliminated, the delay time falls dramatically.

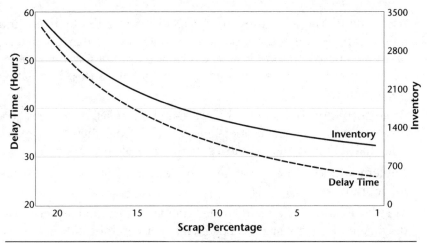

Figure 11-16. The impact of scrap on delay time

Rework is even worse, because the time to process each unit is usually greater than to build the part and an additional setup is often required.

Kaizen

"Kaizen" means "continuous improvement" in Japanese. The kaizen process is modeled after quality circles, the team-based continuous improvement vehicle utilized in the Toyota Production System. The secret to Kaizen is that it *emphasizes creativity before capital.*

Kaizen is an intensive, rapid improvement model. Here's how it works. A cross-functional team is assembled to improve a process or problem identified within a specific, limited area. The team meets full time for three to five days and works rapidly through the following phases/gates:

Training: The team receives specialized training that is specifically intended to be directly applied during the kaizen event (setup reduction methodology, defect prevention, etc.).

Discovery: The team "discovers" the kaizen project area by going on a guided tour in which the guide explains the current state. This establishes a common team understanding around basic process flow, products produced, machines used, etc.

Analysis: The team gathers data required to assess the current situation (demand, defect history, downtime history, machine processing times, etc.).

Assessment: The team uses the data and information to assess and identify opportunities for improvement in the project area (calculating takt time and comparing it with workstation processing time, determining present state scrap rate and potential causes, calculating downtime, etc.).

Brainstorming: The team uses cause-and-effect fishbones and five why's analysis to uncover root causes of problems, then brainstorms potential solutions and prioritizes them for implementation.

Implementation: The kaizen team divides into sub-teams to implement prioritized ideas.

Standardization: The team creates standard operational procedural documentation or visual management and control systems to help sustain implemented improvements.

Results: The team documents results (e.g., 25% productivity improvement, 40% scrap reduction).

Follow-up: The team creates follow-up plans to complete implementation of solutions not completed during the kaizen event.

Parking Lot: The team parks items out of solution scope for other teams or management consideration (e.g., ideas that may require capital expenditures).

Presentation: The team prepares and delivers a presentation to local top management to communicate project area findings, improvements, and results. The presentation is also a forum for management to question changes and, more importantly, publicly recognize and thank team members for their contribution.

Kaizen is a process that generates a considerable amount of momentum and organizational energy. Kaizen is a great vehicle for driving quick-hit value and, to be truly effective, should be used unendingly to make improvements and truly involve employees in

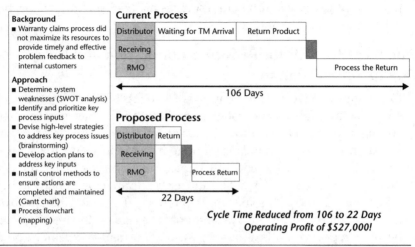

Figure 11-17. Benefits from a kaizen effort

improving the enterprise (part of the culture).

Figure 11-17 shows the results from one kaizen effort. You will notice that the team's progress was validated by the business unit controller to have reduced cost by $527,000 per year and yielded other quantitative benefits.

Using Kaizen. Kaizen efforts are often treated as an adjunct or supplement to an ongoing larger project, a time when a black belt or a champion will select resources to attack a high-priority time trap and devote an intensive week or weekend to addressing that bottleneck. The work may be done by a team that is already working on the main project, but more often is done by a larger ad hoc team composed of non-dedicated green belt resources as well as operators who have a lot of process knowledge, the line manager, and perhaps a supplier and a customer.

Generally the black belt will define and organize a few kaizen events in support of a larger black belt project. In preparation for the kaizens, the black belt will present key data to the ad hoc team members and provide training on specific tools they will need during the event. The "standardization" phase of a kaizen event is synonymous with the Control phase of a black belt project. The black belt's core Lean Six Sigma team translates the kaizen team improvement into standard procedures that will lead to sustained reduction in lead time and cost and improvement of quality.

Kaizen can create a lot of tangible benefits as well as energy in the organization. But you have used it judiciously, on time traps that have the highest priority and where resources are available for a short but concentrated period of time.

Queuing Methods for Reducing Congestion and Delay Due to Time Variation

Congestion at a workstation happens when lots of different part numbers flow through the workstation, each with its own separate batch. As an activity or workstation approaches its maximum capacity, any variation in demand can cause a huge increase in wait time, as was briefly discussed at the end of Chapter 3. Congestion is usually the greatest single source of delay and is the framework on which all other sources hang. It's like the Hollywood Freeway: the speed of travel is determined more by the number of cars on the freeway than by their type—you'll be traveling slowly no matter whether you're surrounded by Pintos or Corvettes.

Often congestion occurs because of variation in timing, much like the effect that variation in arrival time and check-in times had on the hotel check-in process described much earlier in the book (p. 42). In that case study, though the average check-in time was five minutes, guests often had to stand in line 10 minutes or more, due to congestion at the check-in counter.

Part of the supply chain accelerator analysis described earlier is identifying exactly where in your process congestion occurs. Once identified, there are three principle techniques for reducing congestion that arises from time variation:[2]

- Pooling
- Triaging
- Backup capacity

Pooling. In the hotel check-in example described earlier in the book, the hotel prepared for irregular but certain "overloads" of customers by pooling (or cross-training) its staff. Having staff who could step in as needed provided an alternate path through the process and eased congestion.

The same principle works in manufacturing. When any workstation receives a statistical variation peak (an excess amount of work), the peak load can be routed to another workstation. This simple step cuts delay time approximately in half with no additional investment in staff or equipment! This "something for nothing" sounds too good to be true, but it works easily in practice.

Triaging. Another way to attack time variation is to triage the work by sorting jobs into three categories: "easy and small problems," "real problems," and "catastrophic problems." Then develop different routings, strategies, or resources to deal with each. Triaging reroutes the terrible jobs so they do not bottle up the easy jobs and create huge variation in overall lead time and inventory and wreak havoc downstream. For example, you could pool two workstations to take on the easy and small problem jobs and then reroute the harder jobs.

Triaging typically results in another 15% to 20% reduction in overall wait time, and at times it can be much more.

Backup Capacity. Pooling and triaging are very effective in knocking the peaks off the delay due to demand variations. But what happens if the excess demand for a given product is sustained? You've already used up all the possible alternate sources of capacity through pooling and intelligently quarantined the troublesome products by triaging. You could use overtime for short periods of time to cover a peak, but this is an expensive and non-sustainable approach.

To deal with a sustained peak, the best approach is to cross-train operators who work on all of your stations that have high demand fluctuations. By juggling scheduled downtimes (such as lunch, coffee breaks, etc.) among your various lines, you can then staff these lines, which can add 20% more capacity. Finally, if the demand is truly sustained, you will have to add equipment.

Pre-Testing the Solutions. If you have access to supply chain accelerator software (p. 55), you can play "what if" games with ideas for reducing congestion. In effect, you can measure the effectiveness of each method before spending any resources or capital expenditures or disrupting work.

The Four-Step Rapid Setup Method

The four-step rapid setup method was initially developed to reduce the setup time of large presses used to stamp out parts like fenders in auto plants. The method is of general application and has been used in everything from time manufacturing to medical devices. The generality and power of the method is amazing, given the simplicity of the process.

Step 1: Separate Internal and External Setup. Observe the setup process and categorize each step as either *internal* setup or *external* setup work by asking the question, "Can this step be accomplished only with the machine shut down, or can we do this while the machine is working on the previous batch?"

- *Internal setup* is work that can be accomplished only while the machine is shut down.
- *External setup* is work that can be done while a machine is operating. For example, if the operator has to find material, a work order, the correct tool, or fasteners, etc., to begin the setup, each of these steps could be done while the machine is operating—e.g., material could be brought up by another worker whose machine is in the middle of a run, tools can be brought by the tool crib, etc.

By finding alternative ways to accomplish external setup, you can often reduce setup time by 30% to 50%. We were recently involved in such a cleanup process, where the overall setup time of the punch press was reduced by 60% just by cataloguing, classifying, racking, and precleaning of the die.

Step 2. Convert Internal Setup to External Setup. Some steps will currently require the machine to be shut down before a step can be accomplished. For example, in an automatic molding machine, a new die may have to be heated before it can be operated. This heating step can be converted to external setup by preheating the die and using a system of rails to safely load it into the machine.

As with Step 1, the work of converting internal to external setup starts with a simple question: "Why do we have to shut the machine down to take this step?"

Just asking this question of the team inevitably raises many ideas that are supported by a lot of *tacit knowledge* team members have encountered. Typically, the ideas require only a modest amount of capital. The amount of setup reduction accomplished by this step can vary from 10% to 60%, depending on the machine.

Step 3. Streamline Internal Setup. By now, you will have organized the flow of material and information *to* the machine, but the machine is still shut down for what appears to be an irreducible period for internal setup steps.

For example, if you are changing the dies of a press, you clearly have to stop the machine. However, you can still reduce the time needed by streamlining the process. Dies are often fastened with bolts through holes that are internal to the die. Attaching these bolts requires the operator to stand in the press window and make the connections, which takes 20 turns to remove the bolts on the current die, time to switch dies, then another 20 turns to fasten the new die.

You can streamline the process by welding "ears" on the die and cutting a pear-shaped hole in the ears. The large part of the hole is large enough to clear the head of the bolt. The die is then slid forward until the bolt is against the small end of the pear-shaped hole and the motor is energized, which tightens the die.

This is a fairly complex example, but other changes can be as easy as using cam-operated clamps in simple assembly processes.

Step 4. Eliminate Adjustments. The final step in this method is another example of using intelligence instead of money to solve problems. The setup is not complete until the output of the process is "in spec" and under statistical control (meaning the amount of variation is within predictable limits). After a machine or process is set up, the first few parts or feet of output is not "in spec" and the operator needs to make adjustments to the machine. Whether or not you count such adjustments as part of setup time or not, it is still time when the process is not producing "in spec, in control" parts that can be sent to the downstream process or customer.

Part of a Lean Six Sigma mindset is looking at non-value-added work and asking why it is necessary. In this case it means questioning whether adjustments really are necessary to produce high-quality output.

The reason that people need to make adjustments is that they don't know enough about the process to "set" the machine correctly so the first part is good. That may sound like an impossible goal, but method, example, intellect, energy, and teamwork conquer all!

Let's return to the example of a press operation, although the idea really applies to any process. These ubiquitous machines stamp flat metal into a shaped part using upper and lower dies that squish the parts together. After the roll steel is loaded, the operator sets the "shut height" that sets how close the upper and lower dies will meet. If it is set too close, the part may be damaged; if too far apart, that part may not form correctly. To complicate matters, the rolled steel may vary from lot to lot in terms of key physical properties like ductility and springback (e.g., if you want a 45° bend, you may have to bend it by 47° because it "springs back" 2°).

The operator takes a stab at the right settings, runs a test part, measures it, adjusts the press, and tries again. If there are competing parameters, this wandering in the dark can take a long time, sometimes longer than the whole mechanical part of the changeover.

The way you eliminate (or at least minimize) adjustments is by adding intelligence—using data to investigate the reasons why adjustments seem necessary. In our press example, it means looking at the relationship between the variation in input and the machine settings. We could collect data by measuring and recording the springback, ductility, and other physical properties of each roll of material versus the final shut height and other adjustments that are required to finally get that part "in spec and in control." With not too much effort, we can build up a reference table, as shown in Table 11-1.

Springback Rating	Ductility			
	1	2	3	4
1	735	740	751	765
2	755	762	765	790
3	790	790	800	840
4	828	838	855	870

Table 11-1. Press shut height versus variation of supplier input

Using a table like this, we can measure the physical properties of each roll as it comes in, then set the "shut height" fairly close to the final value. The operator can use an interpolation table to make the second or possibly third shot nearly dead on. If it takes more than two or three tries, it's likely that something different or unique is happening and the operator may need help from a black belt. Using the batch-size/inventory workstation turnover equation of the First Law, we can graph the impact of setup time reduction on delay time and inventory (see Figure 11-18). Note that a 90% reduction of setup time *and* a subsequent reduction of batch size will reduce the delay time at the workstation by 90%.

Total Productive Maintenance

Did you know that roughly 35% of machine capacity is lost to downtime? As you might expect, reducing downtime speeds up process speed. Once again, the First Law can be applied and it shows that reducing machine downtime from 20% to 2% will reduce delay time from 70 hours to 29 hours!

An even more insidious result of machine downtime is that it effectively makes the machines run at a higher percentage of available

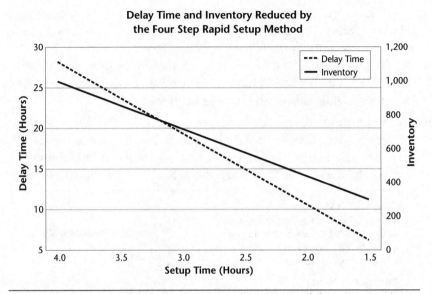

Figure 11-18. Impact of setup time reduction on delay time and inventory

capacity. A machine that is running at 65% of capacity is really running near 100% of *available* capacity—because the other 35% of the time is downtime! All of the effects that variation in arrivals and service times has on total lead time are enormously amplified if a workstation is operating near capacity.

Machine downtime not only impacts the output of the station itself, but if it is severe enough it may cause a significant variation in the arrival of parts at the downstream workstations, leading to congestion and delay (problems discussed above). This problem can cascade throughout the whole factory. As interim measures, we may be able to reduce variation of output as much as possible, understand the maximum capacity, and provide downstream buffers of material to cover times when capacity is exceeded. Ultimately, however, the goal is to remove the need for such buffer inventories by making the machine more reliable.

Machine downtime can have a bad impact on quality, as a degrading machine is more likely to produce out-of-control parts. Moreover, machine downtime robs a plant of productive capacity and leads to the procurement of "newer, better, more reliable" machines. Our estimates show that as much as 50% of the capital expenditures budget is wasted in unnecessary expenditures that freeze capital.

What can be accomplished with Total Productive Maintenance (TPM)? Some factories have reduced the number of unscheduled downtime events from 300 per month to fewer than 10.

Together, steps taken to reduce machine downtime act on all of Lean Six Sigma's shareholder value drivers, increasing productivity and profit while decreasing invested capital.

Implementing TPM. TPM implementation occurs through a wide variety of specialized tools, listed in Figure 11-19, including some standard Lean Six Sigma tools and some that are unique to TPM. Describing each of these tools and their purposes is beyond the scope of this book.

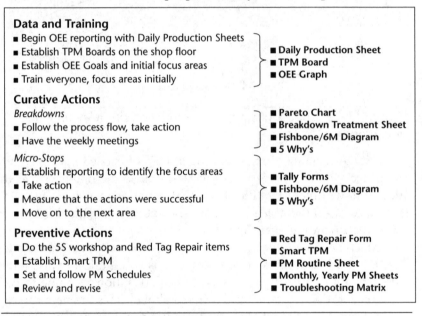

Data and Training
- Begin OEE reporting with Daily Production Sheets
- Establish TPM Boards on the shop floor
- Establish OEE Goals and initial focus areas
- Train everyone, focus areas initially

  - ■ Daily Production Sheet
  - ■ TPM Board
  - ■ OEE Graph

Curative Actions
Breakdowns
- Follow the process flow, take action
- Have the weekly meetings

  - ■ Pareto Chart
  - ■ Breakdown Treatment Sheet
  - ■ Fishbone/6M Diagram
  - ■ 5 Why's

Micro-Stops
- Establish reporting to identify the focus areas
- Take action
- Measure that the actions were successful
- Move on to the next area

  - ■ Tally Forms
  - ■ Fishbone/6M Diagram
  - ■ 5 Why's

Preventive Actions
- Do the 5S workshop and Red Tag Repair items
- Establish Smart TPM
- Set and follow PM Schedules
- Review and revise

  - ■ Red Tag Repair Form
  - ■ Smart TPM
  - ■ PM Routine Sheet
  - ■ Monthly, Yearly PM Sheets
  - ■ Troubleshooting Matrix

Figure 11-19. Information and diagnostic tools

After training on the tools and TPM principles, the next step is to take curative actions to stop the breakdowns that currently occur. As with all Lean Six Sigma actions, this starts with data on just when and which breakdowns occur and investigations into why. Breakdowns come in two flavors:

- Breakdowns of extended duration (> five minutes)
- Micro-stops (< five minutes)

The long breakdowns get significant attention, but generally account for less total downtime than do micro-stops, which go virtually unnoticed. TPM reverses that emphasis.

The last component of TMP is prevention, methods that make it unlikely that breakdowns will occur in the first place. These methods include techniques like the 5S method: sort, set in order, shine, standardize, and sustain.

Design of Experiments

In many improvement projects, the true causes of the problem jump out when a team uses simple methods like creating process maps and charting data. But in other situations, it's not totally clear what caused the problem or there are so many process parameters to consider that it appears nearly impossible to find the right combination to provide optimum performance.

The tool of choice in these situations is Design of Experiments (DOE).

To understand what DOE is and how it can help, let's consider a simple simulation used in training courses: trying to improve gas mileage. In this simulation, students are told that initial data suggests that five factors (or inputs)—speed, octane rating, tire pressure, driver habits, and whether the radio is on—are mostly like to have the biggest impact on gas mileage (the output, or response).

The class is charged with improving the current process and finding an optimal combination of the five factors under consideration and is given a reasonable budget for performing experiments to find this optimal combination. (The budget emphasizes that, in the real world, resources are always limited—and ultimately drives home the point that there's only so much time a team can spent attempting to solve this problem without a methodology.)

Most classes will use one of two approaches to finding the best combination:

- **Trial-and-Error:** People randomly manipulate all five inputs, often all at once, and hope they stumble on a combination that seems to work. This approach is time-consuming and requires quite a bit of luck to achieve an improvement.
- **One-Factor-at-a-Time:** People who remember their school science classes commonly use this method of experimentation. It involves holding all of the input variables constant except one—so they change one input, then observe the results, reset everything, change a different input, observe the results, and so on.

What do think the odds are that either of these methods leads to the best combination? If you guessed "close to 0," you're right!

- Neither of these approaches can tell you which of the factors are significant and which aren't. In this case, most people would guess that whether the radio is on or off would have little impact on mileage, but it's seldom that obvious in real situations.
- Trial-and-error is least likely to be successful, but used amazingly often, even in serious improvement efforts conducted by smart people. Think about this way: without an analysis plan, it is impossible to track the source of a change in output.
- The one-factor-at-a-time approach is more organized and helpful than trial-and-error, but is much less successful than you might think. It misses the mark completely when two of the inputs work together, or interact, to affect the output. A textbook example is baking a cake, popularized by the success that Duncan Hines had with experimentation on cake mixes in the 1950s. To bake a good cake, you need to consider both oven temperature and bake time. If you tried testing oven temperature and bake time *separately*, you wouldn't get an accurate result.

A Designed Experiment. DOE is the best alternative to both trial-and-error and one-factor-at-a-time approaches. With DOE, all factors are tested *simultaneously* in very specific patterns.

Table 11-2 shows the design for basic experiments on the five factors associated with the gas mileage example. There are eight *runs*, or trials, in this experiment, each representing a different combination of the factors. Note that each factor is tested at only two settings, or *levels*: speed is set at either 55 mph or 65 mph, octane at 85 or 91, and so on. This restriction is a critical element of DOE. The point is that you don't set levels for each factor randomly, but rather select specific settings you want to test.

To conduct the experiment, the factors are set at one of the combinations shown in the table and the car is operated to determine the gas mileage. Then the factors are reset to a different combination and again the output (gas mileage) is measured.

After the factors have been tested at each of the combinations, the gas mileage for each run is entered into a statistical software package. (Actually, it's fairly easy to do the calculations by hand, because you just need to calculate averages, but most people use software these days.) The most common output from such software is graphical images that depict the relationships between the factors and the output.

Run	Speed	Octane	Tire Pressure	Driver	Radio
1	55	85	30	2	N
2	65	85	30	1	Y
3	55	91	30	1	N
4	65	91	30	2	Y
5	55	85	35	2	Y
6	65	85	35	1	N
7	55	91	35	1	Y
8	65	91	35	2	N

Table 11-2. Experimental matrix for an eight-run DOE

The first such image is called the *main effects plot*. This output for the gas mileage is shown in Figure 11-20.

Interpreting these plots is straightforward: the *steeper* the slope of the line, the *more significant* the input factor. The *direction* of the slope indicates whether the relationship is positive or negative. From Figure 11-20, for example, you can tell at a glance that average mileage improves with higher octane and tire pressure, but decreases at higher speeds. More specifically:

- Speed has a *strong, negative* effect on average gas mileage. The slope is very steep and it angles downward from left to right, meaning that the higher the speed, the lower the mileage.

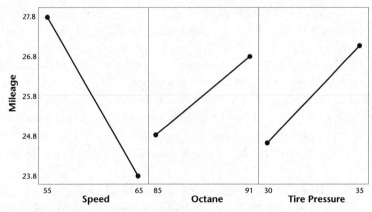

Figure 11-20. Main effects plot for gas mileage

- Both octane and tire pressure have *less strong* (but still significant), *positive* effects on mileage. The higher the octane and the higher the tire pressure, the better the average gas mileage.

Often it is equally important to learn which of the inputs have no effect on the output variable. In this case, both driver and radio are insignificant. You can easily see this in Figure 11-21, because both of the lines are flat. Finding insignificant factors like these in a designed experiment is a good thing, because it means you can set them at whatever level is most convenient and/or least expensive without affecting the output.

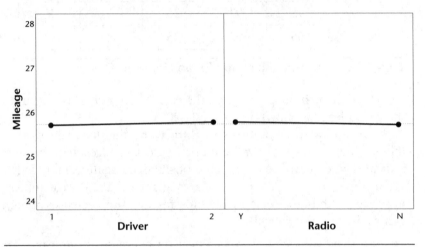

Figure 11-21. Main effects plot for the effects of "driver" and "radio" on mileage

Based on the main effects plot, the best gas mileage will still be obtained driving at 55 mph, with 91 octane and 35 psi tire pressure (as shown in Figure 11-20). Driver and radio have no effect.

The analysis of the designed experiment will provide important information needed to optimize a process. The black belt can understand which inputs affect the average and the standard deviation. These can be the focus of the improvement process and additional experimentation, if necessary. It is often valuable to understand the factors that have little effect as well, as these can be significant opportunities for cost savings.

Applications of DOE: Robust Design. Modern experimental design methods are broadly used in manufacturing, product development, marketing, and transactional applications. They are used to determine input values in an existing process to optimize results and minimize costs. DOE can also be used to define the optimum set of tests that will verify whether a new design meets spec much faster and more reliably. Common applications have grown, from scrap/rework reduction and scientific method for setting tolerances to the improvement of the capability of any process.

The machining process is often a target of black belt improvement projects, and Design of Experiments is used both to reduce defects and to increase throughput. Machine parameters significantly impact both, but often parameter settings have not been evaluated in many years or are frequently changed based on operator preferences.

Machine settings can be optimized with a small experiment, improving tool life and reducing machine downtime by 25%. This performance is possible because the cutting parameters (e.g., cutting angles) are chosen such that tool life is not only maximized but also not materially affected by the normal variation in cutting angles that will occur due to vibration, temperature etc. Figure 11-22 shows that there is a portion of the tool life curve that is fairly flat, with little variation. We would select the cutting parameters in the center of this flat zone. We have picked a portion of the *response surface* where the design is *robust*—which means normal variation in the environment (*external noise*) will have little impact on tool life. These principles can be applied to product development, so that the system can meet customer specifications across a broader range of external noise parameters. Software tools such as Minitab can generate the response surface based on data from the designed experiment.

Knowing that you have good data and statistically significant results is a powerful tool for making objective management decisions and obtaining buy-in. Data transcends politics and personal likes and dislikes and encourages a focus on the process, not the people.

For example, warranty reduction projects are frequently selected for black belt initiatives. These situations can easily degenerate into heated discussions with vendors, with each side going back and forth claiming that the other's products are defective. For a hydraulics supplier, data-driven decision making based on Design of Experiments completely changed this process, removing ambiguity and focusing on the root cause. The statistical results were leveraged to get a corrective action with the vendor in question and warranty claims dropped by over 200 per year.

Using designed experiments in stress analysis resulted in a 15%-30% improvement in capacity in a crane specially designed for the

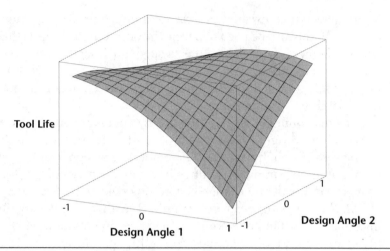

Tool Life

-1

0

Design Angle 1

1

-1

0

1

Design Angle 2

Figure 11-22. Example of response surface methodology

European market. Design for the European market required consideration of many additional requirements with which the American design and analysis team was unfamiliar. Analysis of these additional criteria was time-consuming and, since the requirements were unfamiliar, the solutions tended to be extremely conservative. This conservative approach added cost to the European machines that made it difficult to compete in that market. DOE focused the team on the few requirements that were really significant and allowed the others to be optimized for reduced cost. The result was a significant capacity increase at a lower cost. (You find more details of this example and applying DOE to product development in Chapter 15.)

CONTROL TOOLS

The purpose of Control tools is very simple: to make sure that any gains made in process performance are maintained (until and unless new knowledge reveals an even better way to carry out the procedures). One issue the team has to think about is all the ways that knowledge of operating the process is learned by the process staff/operators: through formal documentation, training, procedures/diagrams posted at work stations, instructions encoded into software, and so on. The other key element is providing ways for the staff to monitor the process performance so they'll know when something happens that must be resolved. One of the most common tools for that purpose is Statistical Process Control (SPC).

Statistical Process Control

The important lesson to remember is that the power of SPC lies in applying it to the *key process input variables* (KPIVs) identified with the DMAIC process. A common mistake is to try to use SPC on the process *output* variables only. Process control will be achieved only through the key inputs. After all, uncovering these key inputs was the path to dramatic process improvement in the first place!

There are three main components of SPC:

1. Creating a control chart.
2. Isolating and removing special (assignable) causes of variation.
3. Instituting procedures for immediate detection and correction of future problems.

1. Creating a Control Chart. The basics of control charts were covered earlier in this chapter. Very briefly, someone working on the process has to know what data to gather and how to plot that data (e.g., by hand or through graphing software).

2. Isolating and Removing Special Causes of Variation. The key to using control charts is understanding the meaning of the control limits. These lines are determined by moving out from the average approximately three standard deviations (3σ) on both sides. Finding one or more points outside the control limits is just one *signal* that a special cause has appeared. (There is a whole series of tests that look for more subtle patterns or signals. These tests are taught in the black belt curriculum.)

The obvious question is "So what?" Once you have a signal of a special cause, what do you do?

To eliminate a special cause of variation, you need to investigate what is different or changed in the process—something that isn't always evident. There are specific statistical techniques (also taught to black belts) that help them identify patterns of cause-and-effect related to when the special cause appears and when it doesn't. Once the source is isolated, they can use standard DMAIC techniques to come up with creative ways to minimize or prevent that source of variation.

After all of the special cause variation has been removed, a process is left with only common cause variation and is said to be *stable* and *in control*. Common cause variation is predictable: it is always present in the process to some degree because of the way the process is structured—the steps followed, the equipment used, the training given to staff, etc. The only way to reduce common cause variation is to make a fundamental change in the structure of the process.

Control charts tell us if our process is stable and predictable, not if the process is acceptable to our customers. If you want to know how well the process is performing relative to customer requirements, you would need to conduct a process capability analysis (discussed in the Measure phase).

3. Instituting Procedures for Immediate Detection and Correction of Future Problems. By now, your process should be in control and producing output that meets customer specifications. But just because the process is operating well today, that doesn't mean something new won't happen tomorrow. So the last ingredient in SPC is making sure that immediate action is taken should the process drift in any way or a new special cause appear. The elements of this step include the following:

- Train operators to use control charts (including who will be responsible for collecting and charting the data).
- Provide clear instructions on how to respond if a special cause appears, including both ...
  - *Damage control:* How can any poor output be prevented from affecting the next process and the ultimate customer?
  - *Remedial actions:* Who should be notified? Can the process be stopped? Who will be responsible for tracking down and eliminating the special cause?
- Provide clear instructions on when and how to update process documentation to make sure new corrective actions are preserved.

USING THE LEAN SIX SIGMA TOOLS

There is one way in which these advanced Lean Six Sigma tools are identical to the basic tools described in the previous chapter: their effectiveness is limited only by the intellect, imagination, and effectiveness of the team that is attacking the problem. No matter how daunting the task, a solution is possible.

Some of these tools may appear too difficult or time-consuming to apply. But remember: you are going to apply them judiciously on the *leading quality problems and time traps*—representing the biggest opportunities for improving shareholder value. You also don't need to use them on every process, every step, or every workstation in the factory; rather, as you know from the Second Law of Lean Six Sigma, you'll need to use them only on less than 20% of the workstations that are contributing to 80% of your problems. In addition, the black belts and their teams will be trained in these tools; they will receive expert coaching on their first few projects. The Lean Six Sigma culture leaves nothing to chance.

Notes

1. You can find out how to do these calculations at www.profi-sight.com
2. Much of these practical results of queuing theory are due to Professors James Patell and Mike Harrison of Stanford University Graduate School of Business.

Those who want more details on the tools introduced in this chapter should see *The Six Sigma Handbook* by Tom Pyzdek (McGraw-Hill).

Chapter 12

Institutionalizing Lean Six Sigma

L ean Six Sigma can deliver increased operating margins and growth that will drive the intrinsic value of the company. But the key to having the stock market *recognize* that value is to sustain the growth in ROIC and revenue. And that means *institutionalizing* Lean Six Sigma so that the company can continue to improve performance year in and year out.

One of the biggest concerns we hear from our clients is "How do we make sure that our people don't think this new initiative is just the latest flavor of the month?" This telling comment reminds us that nearly every company will have tried to implement a change program or two at some point in the past. In many cases, these programs faded away and the initiatives became "flavors of the month." The experience tends to create an immunity in the company to making change.

This immunity to change is not because people are opposed to doing the right thing. In fact, many of the skeptics of the program probably have tried to do the right thing many times in the past. The immunity is created by the conviction that this initiative is merely wasting time and committing effort to an initiative that is destined to fade away.

Institutionalizing the new methods encompassed within Lean

Six Sigma will prevent it from becoming another flash in the pan. Lean Six Sigma is institutionalized through the CEO's visible commitment, management's resolve to use the Lean Six Sigma infrastructure as a means to improve their business, and the design team's efforts in up-front planning. Lean Six Sigma is institutionalized through the black belts' success in generating quick results from projects and an organizational commitment to extending Lean Six Sigma into everything the company does, from its customers and suppliers into every facet of the company (including Design for Lean Six Sigma).

The approach that Caterpillar has taken is an example of an effective approach to institutionalizing Lean Six Sigma. As the graph (Figure 12-1) shows, Caterpillar focuses relentlessly on keeping the arrow pointed up and ensuring that its Six Sigma program leads to transformational change in the company. Caterpillar sees institutionalizing the process in four major phases: Comply, Commit, Embed, and Encode.

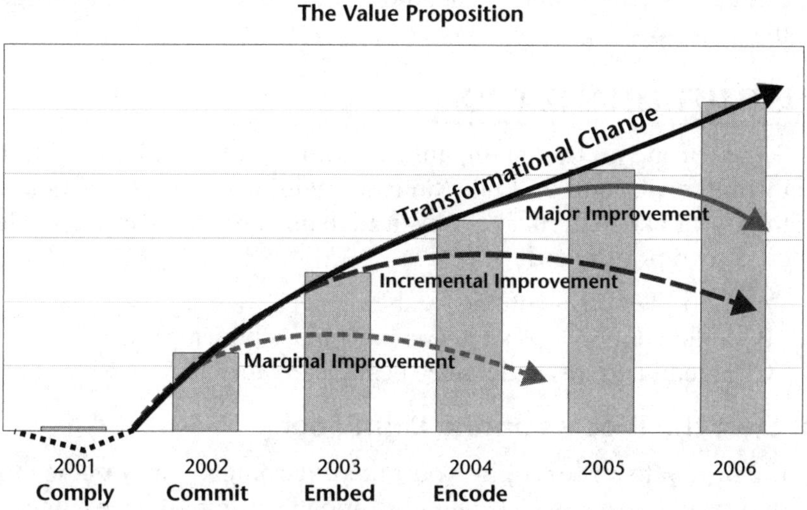

The Value Proposition

Figure 12-1. Caterpillar's institutionalization process

Comply. This is the up-front process in which the executive team must be willing to make the necessary investments and, to some degree, enforce their will on the company to give Lean Six Sigma a try.

Commit. Commitment comes from a true belief that all of this work is paying off, personally and organizationally. This second stage in the process can come only as a response to seeing valuable results from Lean Six Sigma. That is why it is so critical to establish and publicize project successes as early as possible and to reward those who established this success.

Embed. Lean Six Sigma must become embedded in everything the company does. The philosophy must be embraced and the actions of the organization must reflect this. This includes ensuring that Lean Six Sigma is the process that drives improvement across the company, in manufacturing, in transactional processes, in customer-facing processes, and in new product development. Embedding Lean Six Sigma also includes driving the process beyond the four walls of the company into customers and suppliers.

Encode. Some companies like to talk about making Lean Six Sigma part of the company DNA. When Lean Six Sigma is in the DNA, you probably won't even have to call it by name. It will just become the way that the company thinks. Encoding takes time. In our observation, very few companies have made Six Sigma part of the DNA in the company. GE and AlliedSignal (now part of Honeywell) are probably the most notable.

INSTITUTIONALIZATION

So, how can you lead an organization through these phases? Clearly, institutionalization will take time and will meet with barriers along the way. I like to think about institutionalization in three "steps," listed here in priority order:

A. Start the process on the right foot.
B. Build confidence that Lean Six Sigma is here to stay.
C. Extend and institutionalize Lean Six Sigma.

A. Start the Process on the Right Foot

If you don't start off right, you put your company at a tremendous disadvantage and all of the effort applied to the other elements of institutionalization will be diluted enormously. Here are three essentials to starting off right:

- **Dedicate black belt and champion leadership positions full time.** Deploying Lean Six Sigma (especially in its infancy, the first one or two years) is not a part-time job—it requires highly respected, highly talented, full-time leadership and management.
- **Select the best people for these roles.** Employees will be watching closely to see if management has the conviction to dedicate their best resources (who are most likely currently in important roles).

- **Select the projects most important to the business.** Utilize Net Present Value justification; do not blindly manage to budget. If one dollar invested today returns two dollars tomorrow, go to the P&L manager, get approval, and spend the dollar!

Each of these actions is an important test of up-front management conviction in the process. If Lean Six Sigma is executed well, the rest of the organization will begin to believe.

B. Build Confidence That Lean Six Sigma Is Here to Stay

Making Lean Six Sigma part of the fabric of your organization involves of a lot of actions, at many levels of the organization, carried out consistently and repeatedly. It's not easy to be consistent, especially when you are just learning a new way of conducting business. Here are few reminders on how to walk the walk:

- **Get and publicize results.** If Lean Six Sigma ends someone's frustration, it's suddenly made a friend for life! So first, use what you can learn from this book to make sure that you *do* get results. Then, as gains start accruing, be sure they are shared throughout the organization. Write up stories in the company newsletter. Post charts in the work areas that show increasing profit, reduced costs, and improved quality.
- **Leaders must articulate what Lean Six Sigma means clearly, simply, and frequently.** Communicate often, frankly, and with many different media to ensure key messages are received by all potential audiences (both internally and externally):
  - Clearly and frequently communicate the need for the change. Why is change necessary and urgent?
  - Clearly explain the need for change and the potential benefits (and risks) to those constituencies that will be affected in the process of transition.
  - Describe what will change, how and when the changes will occur, and what individuals need to do in order to succeed.
- **Involve employees in all aspects of transformational change.**
- **Recognize and reward positive change behaviors and skills.**
- **Integrate leadership training** (including change management best practices) into the Lean Six Sigma curriculum. Lean Six Sigma involves changes to behaviors, as well as technical changes, and all change involves a disruption. Natural discomfort and resistance must be expected and managed.

- **Launch Lean Six Sigma by leveraging existing organizational strengths** (e.g., use existing training modules and existing best practices whenever appropriate). If Six Sigma has already been launched, Lean can be added as an enrichment with no name change.
- **Plan and enforce a focus on transactional processes.** We recommend that at least 50% of all improvement projects should be directed toward transactional processes. This will involve many segments within an organization that might have been left out of improvement processes in the past. This percentage may be high in manufacturing companies during the first year, but manufacturing cycle efficiency can be improved to 25% only if the transactional areas that surround manufacturing are streamlined.
- **Reinforce existing corporate values** (e.g., integrity, customer focus, teamwork) **during implementation.** This reinforces that Lean Six Sigma is part of your existing value set, not some independent short-term program.
- **Integrate Lean Six Sigma into existing business unit strategic planning sessions, operational reviews, and management team meetings.** Use these meetings to hold management and project sponsors accountable for the progress of their projects.
- **Create accountability through visibility.** Often companies deploy project tracking software to collect and publicize the financial wins and losses of the Lean Six Sigma effort. These tools have been indispensable in the deployment of large-scale corporate programs.
- **Proactively plan for Lean Six Sigma communication events.** Do not reactively schedule around existing leadership commitments.
- **Share best practices and lessons learned across the business.** Celebrate the successes openly and frequently.

Here are two examples of how some of these play out in practice.

At a *Fortune* 500 client of ours, the corporate Six Sigma deployment team set new company standards—the most comprehensive set of metrics anyone there had seen. But that wasn't enough. The team *automated* the collection of metrics and linked these metrics hierarchically to the company's financial system (through the sites, divisions and groups to corporate). This gave the CEO the ability to electronically review performance and point-and-click his way down to the root cause of great performance metrics or poor performance metrics. Already, the corporate office is fielding interest from other groups throughout the company, with questions such as "Can we use your metric system?"

The same company uses a comprehensive electronic project tracking system. Project profiles are captured electronically and approval happens through electronic reviews. The same procedure is used to select team members. Milestones, schedules, and results can be viewed and a formal gating process is controlled so that no project can progress without electronic sign-offs from project sponsors or executives. The project tracking system also makes the process "transparent." Everyone from the CEO to coworkers on the front line can follow and compare the results (or lack thereof) in various parts of the company. This kind of tracking system creates significant pressure to move forward quickly. Again, the project tracking system and rigor set a new standard within the corporation.

C. Extend and Institutionalize Lean Six Sigma

As people in your company become more comfortable with Lean Six Sigma, look for ways to extend its use:

- **Enforce a common language.** Make terms such as DMAIC, metrics, dashboards Net Present Value, Lean, variation, and cycle time part of your everyday language when discussing existing operations or future improvements.
- **Integrate Lean Six Sigma plans with business plans.** Ensure that Lean Six Sigma is incorporated into existing strategic plans, operating plans, and budgets. In this way, Lean Six Sigma projects will all directly align with existing business strategy and existing business needs.
- **Extend Lean Six Sigma into your entire supply chain.** Your suppliers and some intermediate customers are part of the larger value stream. If necessary, train black belts for your customers/suppliers or lend them one of your own if they will commit to the process. (This topic is discussed in further detail in Chapter 13 and 14.)
- **Address the need for Lean Six Sigma in the design process.** Lean Six Sigma can both speed up your product design/development pro-cesses and help you improve the designs of products and processes. Since the majority of cost associated with a product is determined in the design stage, applying Lean Six Sigma in those areas can have a dramatic effect on reducing costs. (See Chapter 15.)

PLANNING FOR EACH BUSINESS UNIT LAUNCH

Deployment planning was introduced back in Chapter 6, but in truth the discussion was left incomplete because deployment isn't finished until every business unit is using Lean Six Sigma. However, completion of your deployment plans requires knowledge of the issues raised above and in all the intervening chapters as well, such as ...

- The resource and project selection processes.
- Management team alignment and commitment to projects that get selected.
- What it will take to develop a cadre of trained black belts and champions.
- How to build toward true institutionalization.

In the broadest terms, launch planning happens when the projects are reviewed by the business unit manager and the selected projects, black belt assignments, and resource commitments are pulled together into a coherent package. The business unit manager and his or her team should review the list of selected projects and verify that the range of projects are linked to, support, and will achieve the goals set forth in the strategic plan. They should also review the unit champion's recommendations for project measurements and review mechanisms.

As you complete your deployment plans and contemplate the business unit launches, think about ways to inform everyone in the unit that one or more Lean Six Sigma projects are about to begin within their world and how those projects will be supported. Provide the historical context and explain why these projects have been selected above other projects (including many "pet projects" that weren't chosen). That will help set the stage for successful completion of the first projects.

It is important as well to exhibit management's commitment to the program and to the projects being undertaken, and to answer any questions or concerns that arise from the new course the company is charting. Additional training may be provided to team members and the management staff to broaden the base of Lean Six Sigma knowledge and ensure alignment of individual perceptions with the overall program goals.

THE EXECUTIVE'S ROLE

Everything starts with leadership, and leadership starts with the executive team. The executives in your organization must lead the way. They must continually link their strategy's execution to Lean Six

Sigma and continuous improvement; they must frame Lean Six Sigma as "transformational change"—something that requires hard work over the long haul, not a short-term improvement effort. Lean Six Sigma should be presented as the way the business will be transformed with large-scale integration of fundamental changes throughout the organization—including processes, culture, and customers—to achieve and sustain results.

Here is an example of a clear strong message:

> *Our best bet to create shareholder value was to become a premier multi-industry company. One of the things we had noticed in our analysis was that while some people get a conglomerate discount, there are others like GE who get a conglomerate premium. And guess what? It all depends on performance, and if we could get our performance up significantly from where it was back then, we felt we'd be able to earn those types of premiums as well. So that's become our strategy. We've been making acquisitions. We went out and told the world that this is what we wanted to do. We set what we considered to be significant, aggressive targets for ourselves.*
>
> —Lou Giuliano, CEO of ITT Industries

The importance of communication is highlighted in this message:

> *It's your job to launch this initiative with clarity, consistency, and commitment throughout the extended Caterpillar enterprise, as this impacts everyone—each and every continent, each and every employee, each and every supplier, and each and every dealer throughout the entire value chain. Everyone will be deeply impacted by this new way of working, an undertaking that will transform all that we do to achieve our quality and cost-reduction goals and help us deliver the $30 billion company we have promised by 2006.*
>
> —Glen Barton, CEO of Caterpillar

The CEO and other leaders must also act in ways that support the importance of having the best people fill black belt and champion positions. The experience of being a black belt or champion provides a process view of the corporation that is a very valuable experience in the preparation of the future leaders of the firm. For this reason, it is important that the black belts and champions be selected with this aim in mind; hence they must be among the best and brightest. They will have an experience of increasing operating profit, reducing lead times, etc., that will make Lean Six Sigma a tool they will employ for life. If the next generation of P&L managers have this experience, the institutionalization of the process and the sustainability of results are ensured. Thus the insistence of the CEO on getting the best and brightest assigned as champions and black belts is the most important aspect of institutionalization.

EMPHASIZING THE ULTIMATE GOALS

One characteristic of successful Lean Six Sigma efforts is that the CEO and his or her P&L managers think of Lean Six Sigma as a culture, a way of life, and "the way we operate." Lean Six Sigma is the instrument of transformational change and, ultimately, all improvement efforts should fit under the umbrella of Lean Six Sigma. In the nervous trials of reality, Lean Six Sigma should be looked on as a resource that provides continuity of conception and organic development of strength and that can be applied to solve any business problem. In summary:

- Lean Six Sigma is a key enabler of corporate strategy.
- Lean Six Sigma is driven by both business and customer needs.
- Competitive pressures only increase with time, and Lean Six Sigma enables a competitive advantage.

The ultimate goal is for Lean Six Sigma to become part of the "warp and woof" of the company. (In weaving, as you may know, "warp" is the long threads that provide the structure and "woof" is the crossing threads that provide design and color.) You will know that you have reached this goal when Lean Six Sigma is no longer referred to as a program. In fact, it may not even be referred to by name. It will simply be the way that your organization solves problems and improves processes, all the time.

Part Three

Leveraging Lean Six Sigma

Chapter 13

Total Supply Chain Acceleration

Part Two of this book described basic principles and methods that could be used to bring speed and high quality to prioritized time traps within an activity or a workstation, a process, or a whole factory. Once you've developed internal expertise on accomplishing Lean Six Sigma on an ever larger scale within your company, you can start to gain further leverage across your entire supply and distribution channels, from raw materials until the finished product reaches the customer. This chapter is going to pull it all together.

Just as only 20% of the *workstations* determine the velocity of the factory, the flexibility and velocity of the factory in turn determine distribution and channel inventories. Improving the velocity of your factory will have the same type of impact as improving the velocity of a single workstation. As the factory becomes faster, more flexible and adaptable, it can produce to actual demand (or at least an ever closer approximation) rather than to forecasts. This will greatly reduce the inventory needed in warehouses and distributor channels and improve responsiveness to customer needs.

Traditionally, most supply chain software has *assumed* a given factory velocity, and then optimized the distribution channels around that constraint using mathematical forecasting techniques, etc. In contrast, Lean Six Sigma assumes that factory velocity is *not* given, but rather can be substantially improved by making the factory itself far more *flexible*—which allows even greater customer satisfaction, and inventory and cost reductions in downstream distribution. The ultimate goal is to make the factory and distribution so flexible that the factory operates on pull scheduling, where it *makes to order* with ever diminishing reliance on a forecast. Lean Six Sigma also extends this pull scheduling to suppliers, reducing both shortages and raw material inventory.

This chapter will take you through the principles of expanding your scope of implementation, starting with your entire factory, then reaching out to suppliers and distributors. You'll see how you can produce to satisfy *this* day's demand just as economically as if you built a month's worth of product. In addition, you save all the overhead and quality cost of the Hidden Factory.

PART A: ACCELERATING YOUR INTERNAL SUPPLY CHAIN

Earlier sections of this book have established a list of ills associated with long process lead times:

- Long lead time *automatically creates a high level of variation* in that lead time. For example, if your manufacturing, engineering, or any other process has a 14-day average lead time, it will likely have five days' variation either way—and it's worse for even longer processes.
- Long lead time creates the *obvious* extra costs of overtime, scrap, and rework and high cost of capital in inventory and capital expenditures.
- Long lead time creates the *hidden costs* in manufacturing overhead of excessive plant size, expeditors, stockrooms, and personnel— the *Hidden Factory*.
- Quality improvements can proceed at a slow pace. The large stockpiles of WIP and finished goods are in jeopardy of suffering from quality costs, obsolescence, and low-margin sales.

Because of the revenue and cost implications of long lead time, it is incumbent on management to control and reduce both lead times and variation in lead times.

Where are the levers for improving lead time? We already know the answers:

- The Third Law of Lean Six Sigma—process velocity and lead time are driven by the number of "things in process"—tells us we need to reduce WIP to speed up the process.
- Supply chain acceleration tells us that the process itself (setup times, processing times, etc.) dictates what minimum amount of WIP inventory is required for a given demand.

There are three conclusions from this learning:

1. We need to put a maximum cap on the amount of WIP (or "things in process") to be able to even predict lead time.
2. Maintaining the velocity of the supply chain means maintaining an even flow of WIP: if WIP stops for any period of time, we won't be able to meet demand. WIP must therefore be related to current demand.
3. To prevent excess WIP, we need to release material into the line in amounts consistent with the minimum process batch sizes, etc.

The impact of these lessons is captured conceptually in Figure 13-1. Without a cap on WIP, our lead time will be too slow and have huge variations. With a WIP cap, we can stabilize and reduce cycle time.

No WIP Cap – Cycle time fluctuates with amount of WIP

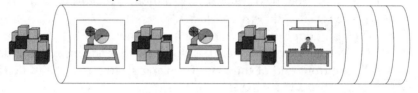

WIP Cap – Cycle time is reduced and stable

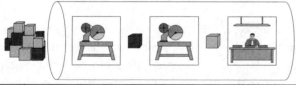

Figure 13-1. WIP caps

Supply chain accelerator software allows us to calculate the minimum batch size needed to (a) compensate for the workstation with the longest time delay (time trap) and (b) release material into the line in the certain knowledge that this will maintain the minimum WIP and the fastest overall lead time.

Meeting WIP Targets: The Pull System of Lean Manufacturing

The linchpin of a produce-to-demand system that minimizes WIP is called the *pull system* (or *kanban*), where each process withdraws from the previous process *only the quantities of parts that have been used*. This principle is illustrated in Figure 13-2.

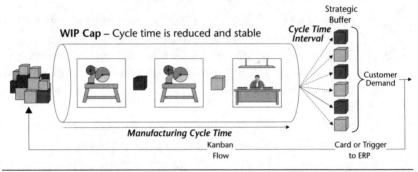

Figure 13-2. The pull (kanban) system

- We have to keep a certain amount of material on hand to serve customers (the next process, operation, purchaser, etc.). This reserve is called the *strategic buffer*.
- When an item is pulled from the buffer, there is a *trigger*, either a physical alert (a card system) or an electronic tracking system, that tells the front end of the manufacturing system that the buffer is low. ("Kanban" is Japanese for "card.")
- The manufacturing system then produces an item to replenish the buffer.

In the discussion below, we first describe the classic pull system as devised by Toyota. This pull system is eminently successful for repetitive manufacturing, where the standard deviation of demand is no more than 30% of average demand. Later in the chapter, we'll look at a pull system more suitable for situations where there is completely non-repetitive demand (each order is unique). In the latter case, the pull system uses inventory levels to drive ERP "order point" releases.

In both cases, however, pull happens at every level of the manufacturing system: one workstation produces only enough to replenish what the next workstation is using; one process replenishes what the next process is using; one factory produces only what the distributor or customer uses.

Determining the Strategic Buffer. The strategic buffer reflects the *maximum kanban quantity* and is an absolute cap on the amount of WIP inventory. How much do you need in the strategic buffer? It has five components:

1. **Manufacturing lead time buffer.** First of all, you need to have enough inventory to service demand during the time it takes a new order to traverse the factory. This is the manufacturing lead time (MLT) in days for that part number times the average demand per day for each part number.

2. **Cycle time interval buffer.** Let's say that the factory just completed a batch of Product 1 and it is now building Products 2, then 3, then 4, etc. It will take some time, the cycle time interval (CTI), for the factory to cycle back to Product 1 and you must have sufficient inventory to service demand. This is the CTI in days times the average demand per day.

3. **Transport time buffer.** If there is some geographical distance between supply and demand, you must have the transport time in days times the average demand per day.

4. **Safety stock.** Each of the above processes has an average time plus a fluctuation around that average. The same is true of customer demand. The safety stock formula must comprehend both. (Most formulas consider only demand fluctuations.) The specific formula will be described below.

5. **Seasonality or promotions.** Additional "look ahead" inventory must be generated based on history and forecasts but modified by actual consumption. The fast factory can put the brakes on faster.

All of these buffers can be obtained empirically and can be confirmed by spreadsheet analysis or modeled in supply chain accelerator software. You can also calculate the quantity of the strategic buffer by using the following equation:

$$\text{Max Strategic Buffer (Kanban)} =$$
$$(\text{Mfg Lead Time} \times \text{Demand}) + (\text{Cycle Time Interval} \times \text{Demand})$$
$$+ \text{Safety Stock} + \text{Seasonality} + (\text{Transport Time} \times \text{Demand})$$

If the amount of inventory in the buffer falls to a level equal to the lead time times usage plus safety stock, we have just enough inventory to keep downstream customers satisfied until a new batch of material arrives. In Japan, where this system evolved, reaching that minimal level triggers a kanban card to be sent to the front end of the process. If the buffer quantity ever falls below the safety stock level, a red card is triggered to the process manager and the plant manager. Employees, material, and suppliers converge on the line to resolve the issue. Many shop floor signaling devices have been used to supplement the card system, but they are all variations on a theme.

Once a pull system is established, you can attack lead time using setup reduction, batch size reduction, etc., on the workstations that contribute the most to workstation turnover.

Using the Pull System. The basic pull system described above is what's most frequently in the minds of advocates of Lean. It was used at the tier-one automotive supplier introduced in Chapter 1 as well. This firm supplied a total of 168 different end items every week and consumed 154 different supplier products. Each product had about 20 steps on its router.

In addition, the variation in demand from week to week was fairly moderate. A standard metric for assessing variation is the *coefficient of variation* (standard deviation of usage divided by average usage). This coefficient was less than 30%.

Our experience, confirmed by simulations, shows that a kanban card system can become unstable when the coefficient of variation is above 30%: when variability is so high, the queue times increase at high-utilization workstations and lengthen workstation cycle time. The upstream workstation becomes less flexible and is eventually unable to react to the high variability in the downstream demand. Trigger quantities are inadequate to sustain the downstream usage, shortages ensue, and the lead time swiftly lengthens.

Nevertheless, in general, a card pull system is quite robust for highly repetitive manufacturing. Within a coefficient of variation of 30%, it signals problems quickly and "pulls" additional resources into the process. For variations beyond 30%, or systems with more than a few hundred part numbers, an electronic trigger pull system is appropriate as described below. The workstations with the longest time delay (time traps) can often be found by trial-and-error rather than with supply chain acceleration calculations (or supply chain acceleration software): Toyota simply started removing kanban cards from circulation and the WIP will decrease until a workstation cannot keep up. In supply chain acceleration terminology, this happens when a workstation's batch size is too small, it is spending too much time in setup, or it is building scrap, etc., to keep up with demand. If this trial-and-error sounds like a painful way to find opportunities, remember that this process is no longer required to find time traps, nor are pull systems limited to highly repetitive processes. The spreadsheet calculations[1] or supply chain acceleration software calculate the time traps, avoiding the trial-and-error process in repetitive manufacturing. In non-repetitive manufacturing, the trial-and-error process is inapplicable and you must calculate time traps.

In short, pull is a wonderful system, one that meets all the Lean Six Sigma criteria of having low-cost, fast-lead-time manufacturing.

Effect of Product Line Complexity. The complexity of most companies' product lines is expanding faster than the unit volume—we're producing smaller numbers of more different things! Inevitably, this means that the variation in demand by stock-keeping unit (SKU) must advance relentlessly.

One approach to handling increased complexity was to build focused factories that produce a limited number of parts (limited SKUs). The problem with focused factories is that you build inflexibility into your system and trap property, plant, and equipment.

Let's say that a company has four car models. It could build four focused factories or one flexible factory that could produce all four cars. For a given fluctuation in each SKU, the fluctuation in the flexible factory will be $1/(N)^{1/2}$, where N equals the number of different parts. For a factory producing four cars, that translates to half the fluctuation in demand as would occur at the focused factory.

One car manufacturer built two focused factories, one in Spain and the other in Germany. Demand fluctuation was such that the Spanish plant was nearly idle and the German plant was over capacity. Had both volumes been combined in one factory, statistics teaches us that the overall volume fluctuation would have been just 70% of that for a single factory ($1/(2)^{1/2} = .71$). Focused factories also require separate, duplicate overhead costs. Rather than pursue a focused factory approach, let us try to deal with the complexity problem using flexibility rather than physical assets—intelligence instead of money.

Synchronicity of Pull Systems and Triggers. You may have noticed a curious aspect of the basic pull system described above: it didn't have any preset timing associated with it. Whenever a customer demanded a part, the pull system supplied that part and replenished the one used. This is known as an *asynchronous* pull system.

In contrast, for applications in which manufacturing is done in stages to meet a final customer lead time demand, we often use a *synchronous* pull system. For example, the assembly of a complex system like a car, an airplane, or construction equipment may progress through four or more stages of assembly. When the unit *actually* moves to the next station, the move will *trigger* the production of an assembly (possibly an asynchronous line) needed at a station downstream. But the lead time of the various subassemblies has to be known in order to be synchronized to match the progression of the total system as it moves down the line. Triggering the production of a subassembly only when a major assembly has passed a certain point lets us know two things:

- There is a real need for the part (i.e., the major assembly made it).
- The amount of WIP in the line, hence the lead time, so the subassembly will meet the major assembly downstream when needed.

The use of a trigger actuated by real process velocity (defined by the physical movement of material) is a first clue as to how to merge pull systems and MRP while still preserving a defined WIP and controlled lead time. The trigger can cause the MRP system to release the subassembly. Since the MRP system is able to handle essentially infinite complexity, pull systems can be applied to any form of manufacturing. The synchronous pull system moves the material forward through the shop at a predetermined velocity or rhythm, which is called the *takt time* (German for "metronome"). The planned moves are usually displayed on a takt board (Figure 13-3).

600 Series Mainline
Weekly Production Sequencing Tracking

INPUTS — UNIT IN PROGRESS

Zone	Unit	Customer	Shop Order	Work Order#	Comments
PAINT	695		15020		3° LOAD
4	695		12029		
3	690				
2	690		16041		SOFT VIEW
END-DEL	692		16089		

OUTPUTS — EXITS

Model Type	5 AVG	12 AVG	19 AVG	26 AVG	2 SUT	9 SUT	Running Exits by Model
695	2	1					695
695	0	0					695

UNITS TO START NEXT

Sequence	Unit	Customer	Shop Order	Work Order#	Comments
2-1	690		16029		
2-2	690		16043		

RUNNING TOTALS

Measurements	5 AVG	12 AVG	19 AVG	26 AVG	2 SUT	9 SUT	Production Averages	
Total Exits	2						Avg Exits	2
Takt Rate	2	1		2	1	1		
Recovery	-2	-2					Carryover	-2
Avg Daily WIP	4	4					Avg WIP	4
Cycle Time (days)	15						Avg CT	4
Notes & Comments							Target WIP	

Figure 13-3. Sample takt board for coordinating production

WIP and Production Control

Obviously, having an effective pull system—one that minimizes WIP so we can improve lead time delivery—depends on having total control over our production streams. *Hence, whatever scheduling and material release system we use must control the WIP*—if not, scheduling is just an idle hope, and deliveries are made real by expeditors and overtime, with significant waste. Modern ERP systems have "order point" and kanban logic that allows the use of shop-controlled release triggers, whereas the older MRP systems did not appreciate that a "time bucket" of excess WIP releases would stall the line. The time bucket was simply too crude. The ability to calculate the time delay at each workstation as a function of total demand allows far more accurate setbacks and can be refined further by shop floor triggers.

Lean advocates have claimed that MRP dumps WIP into the line long before it is needed, decelerating lead time. On time delivery performance above one sigma was only achieved with expeditors, overtime …, i.e., the Hidden Factory. Certainly release of material into a production line without regard to existing WIP is detrimental to lead times. A few Lean and Six Sigma advocates have gone so far as to suggest scrapping MRP. On the other hand, companies are faced with the problems of scheduling thousands of parts per day and are at a loss to know how to operate without their MRP/ERP systems. The conflict of these two factions reminds me of Winston Churchill's insight on the Spanish Civil War (1936-1939): "The worst arguments happen when both sides are equally in the right and in the wrong."

In other words, both Lean and MRP advocates are correct; it is just a matter of applying the proper tool within the context of the variability of demand and process. The elimination of forecasts is a worthwhile goal, but entirely dependent on reducing process lead times, supplier lead times, and order frequencies to levels that may not square with industry dynamics. Supply chain acceleration software calculates the delays and setbacks, creates a methodology for using order point triggers, and hence provides a bridge between Lean Six Sigma and MRP that minimizes cost, inventory, and process lead time. We will review some of the historical antecedents that bear on this important issue.

Origins of MRP. The original idea of MRP was straightforward Material Requirements Planning (you've got to have gray hair to know that!):

- Start with figures on the order backlog and add a forecast of orders by SKU to develop a demand schedule.
- Use the computer to explode the bills of material to develop a demand for raw material and components, usually by month.

If a company is building complex systems, some form of MRP is superior to manual systems based on past usage. We're in a new era, where product designs today have little relation to last year's, so an accurate forward-looking computer system could better cope with both variation and complexity. And besides, raw material is often fungible against several SKU, so if the forecast is off, it is not a fatal flaw. Lean advocates would complain that too much raw material would be at risk too soon, but this might be dismissed as a quibble. We'll refer to *Material Requirements Planning* as *MRP I*.

The next evolution was to expand the planning process to the shop floor: *MRP II* or *Manufacturing Resource Planning*. In this process, the computer controls the release of WIP into the line. The month is divided into time buckets and material is released accordingly … with no concern about capacity at the workstations or about setup time being too long, processing time being too slow, the batch being too big, or any other process variable! As you now know, batch size is one of the most critical Lean Six Sigma calculations because it drives the whole factory lead time. In MRP II, the batch size is determined in one of the following three ways:

- Equal to a week's or a month's usage.
- Calculated using the EOQ formula[2] (batches typically three times too large).
- Picked out of the air.

    In addition, MRP batch sizing …

- Does not consider how many other parts are produced at the workstation.
- Does not consider rework, machine downtime, etc.

The fact that the batch size is always wrong and nearly always too big is what makes it easy to make quick gains with Lean Six Sigma! It is possible to compare the existing batch sizes that have been loaded into MRP with those calculated using supply chain accelerator software and compare the resulting lead times and inventory. Often a 30% immediate reduction of WIP inventory and cycle time is possible.

In fact, there was no evidence that anybody used the knowledge that excess WIP causes long lead times and slow velocity (the Third

Law of Lean Six Sigma). Nobody considered excess WIP during MRP I, so why would it change when we shifted to MPR II? The result was long lead times, large inventories, and slow responsiveness to changing customer demands

The Rise of the Pull System. This all started to change when the pull system appeared to be at the heart of Toyota's superiority. People started to understand the relationship between WIP and lead time. MRP II was pejoratively referred to as a push system that shoved material at workstations that were already overloaded or even down for maintenance.

The fact is that both sides were "equally in the right and in the wrong." The last 10 years have seen the MRP II suppliers evolve to *Enterprise Resource Planning* (ERP) suppliers and adopt the Lean philosophy to varying degrees.

Merging ERP and Lean Six Sigma. The major difference between mechanical pull systems and the older MRP systems is that the demand in a pull system is triggered by the *actual situation on the shop floor,* and MRP (as described thus far) simply pushed the material onto the floor whether it was needed or not. The first step in any successful merger is the recognition that, in fact, Lean Six Sigma and ERP have complementary strengths and weaknesses:

- **Lean Six Sigma:** The great strength of Lean Six Sigma is that it gives us the tools to improve our business performance by successfully reducing lead time and improving quality, which makes material flow through the system much more quickly and smoothly. On the other hand, the kanban card replenishment system is impractical for dealing with highly complex products or product lines where demand fluctuation coefficients exceed 30%. The idea of a replenishment pull system falls apart when you use a part only every three months! To address that limitation, we need to equip ERP with a mechanism to release material in response to a downstream demand signal. This has been accomplished with the order point logic now integrated into most ERP systems. A release is not made until a trigger is received from the shop floor indicating that the generic kanban time buffer is ready to receive more material.
- **ERP:** Enterprise Resource Planning is eminently qualified to deal with near-infinite complexity in the product line and infinite fluctuation of coefficients of demand, since it easily cascades each

order into bills of material and shop releases. On the other hand, it has no inherent brakes for stopping these releases. Incorporating pull system capability will give ERP the order point signals it needs from the floor to control releases. When the two are combined, ERP will release material into the line in response to a vacant kanban card (or presently vacant bin, electronic signal, etc.). That release, in turn, is timed such the next product will be complete before the next request for material is received. The batch sizes will also be calculated with Lean Six Sigma principles in mind (accounting for process variables such as setup time, processing time per unit, scrap, etc.), using spreadsheets or supply chain acceleration software. The SCA-calculated batch sizes can be uploaded into ERP.

A lot of movement has occurred over the last three years, with ERP suppliers developing Advanced Planning and Operations (APO) modules (courtesy of SAP) that include entries for kanban quantities, cycle times, etc.

Data from the shop floor is now collected and transmitted back to the ERP system and can include the "up" status of the workstation and demand for material. Many companies are bar-coding material and scanning batches into and out of the workstations so that a real-time picture of WIP accumulation can be used as a brake on additional releases.

In the past, MRP systems tended to work in splendid isolation, not communicating with any other systems or the actual WIP on the shop floor. Most suppliers now communicate through portals that allow Lean Six Sigma software—such as project tracking software—to upload process data such as setup time, scrap, etc., into the ERP system. (Some companies are even making Lean Six Sigma training materials available through this same portal so both the Lean Six Sigma champions and the ERP suppliers can work to improve the client company's processes.)

The MRP/Trigger Pull System. Given this convergence over the last few years, where do Lean Six Sigma and MRP/ERP now stand? Given knowledge of the amount of WIP in the line and the schedule from MRP, supply chain acceleration software can calculate the lead time of each process in the factory. Because we live in the real world, actual lead times will be influenced by sources of variation that won't affect the MRP software. But we can compensate for this variability in two ways:

1. **Empirical correction:** The actual process flow velocity is sampled

at the time traps, the top 20% of the long-time-delay workstations throughout the plant. This will allow a continual check on actual conditions in case some *special cause* (machine downtime, lack of material, etc.) has occurred that disrupts the schedule.

2. **Safety time stock:** Let us assume that the fluctuation of lead time is normal. No special cause exists and hence no corrective action is possible because the process is in control. In analogy with the safety stock of the kanban system, we release material into the line early enough to compensate for a potential delay equal to one standard deviation in delivery time variation. This is a component of the safety stock formula discussed below.

It should be pointed out that adding safety time stock injects approximately 10% extra WIP and lead time into the system. Thus the hybrid MRP/trigger system is not as effective at lowering inventory as the pure kanban card pull system, but it has the merit of easily handling completely non-repetitive manufacturing. Moreover, as the process is improved and the overall lead time is reduced, the intrinsic variation in the process will also be reduced.

We first applied this trigger system at a GE electric motors plant that had highly non-repetitive production. These were large custom motors with a lot of options that affected core processes as well as options processes. As a core was finished, it triggered the release of subassemblies needed for downstream processes and maintained the correct sequence. If a core was delayed due to a vendor shortage, the subassemblies would not be triggered and hence would not trap supplier parts that were in short supply. In this way the WIP was always known and under control and the lead time was predictable in a virtually non-repetitive process. Lead time and material shortages were reduced by 60%.

Since that time, technology has made the MRP/order point pull system far more practical. The general availability of factory data collection systems (such as bar code tracking) has enabled the process. The increased awareness of ERP suppliers in making pull, kanban, takt, and process data fields available through open portals allows a seamless scheduling system.

Automation of Pull Systems. All the pieces we need to integrate Lean Six Sigma into production control are now available to us: we can apply APO data and supply chain acceleration to dynamically calculate batch size, safety stock, and kanban quantities and use these for release quantities. We can employ order point capability to actually initiate a trigger

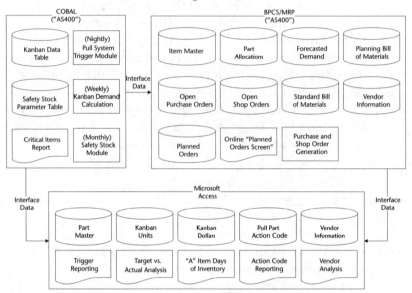

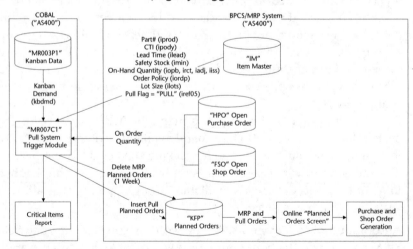

Figure 13-4. Data flows from pull system to MRP

based on factory or downstream distribution consumption.

I first saw a system like this in operation in Japan at Shiseido (see Figure 13-4). Orders from the cosmetics retailers' actual consumption are collected daily by store. Each store's collapsible box is then conveyed down a gantry, which has the top 4000 products loaded into

Figure 13-5. Shiseido gantry

magazines that spit out the replenishment required. This pull actually creates demand for the Shiseido factories (see Figure 13-5).

Safety Stock Calculations

The purpose of the safety stock is to provide a level of buffer inventory such that fluctuation in demand or supply will allow customers to be serviced with better than 99% on-time delivery (three sigma).

Let us say that the cycle time interval (CTI) of a given process was five days and that the supplier lead time (SLT) was 15 days from order to ship. We would then have, on average, three orders' worth of material in our plant, in transit, or about to ship. We would only need about five days' worth of safety stock, since we are pretty well covered and just have to worry about missing one of the supplier's releases of five days' worth of usage.

If the supplier's lead time *really* is 15 days, we need not worry. But what if the timing were reversed?—our CTI is 15 days and the supplier's lead time is reliably five days? Then again we already have three orders in our pipeline, so we have to carry at most a five-day safety stock.

The same logic applies to our distributors' safety stock, where our factory takes the place of the external supplier. If the CTI of a product is five days and the manufacturing lead time (MLT) is 15 days, we already have three orders in the pipeline. At most we just need five days in safety stock because we can always expedite an order in process. If the CTI is 15 days and the MLT is five days, we can always expedite an order forward and again need only five days of safety stock.

Conclusion: For 100% reliable delivery, supply, and consumption, we need two types of safety stocks:

- **Supplier material safety stock:** equal to the average demand times the lesser of *either* cycle time interval (CTI) *or* supplier lead time (SLT).
- **Finished goods safety stock:** equal to the average demand times the lesser of *either* manufacturing lead time (MLT) *or* CTI.

One More Step: The Effect of Variation on Safety Stock Calculations. All the calculations above are logical, but they neglect the problem of variation. Each of the individual components of time in the process of getting materials into, through, and out of your factory are subject to variation, plus there will be variation in customer demand. And all of these sources of variation occur *independently* of what's happening anywhere else in the process. A single order could therefore encounter any combination of delays at the supplier, delays in manufacturing, or a drop or rise in customer demand. In actuality, therefore, the equations given above have to be modified based on determinations of how much variation there is in each of these elements.

Lean Six Sigma measures this coefficient of variation of supply as the standard deviation divided by the mean ($C_S = \sigma_S$ / mean) and the same for demand. These considerations all roll up into safety stock formulas :

$$\text{Supplier Material Safety Stock} = 3 * (\text{Lesser of CTI or SLT}) * (\text{Demand per week}) * [(C_S^2 + C_d^2) / 2]^{1/2}$$
$$\text{Finished Goods Safety Stock} = 3 * (\text{Lesser of CTI or MLT}) * (\text{Demand per week}) * [(C_S^2 + C_d^2) / 2]^{1/2}$$

Sales and Operations Planning

Figure 13-6 shows an 84-day supply chain for a food distributor in which the inventory spends 52 days in various distribution channels.

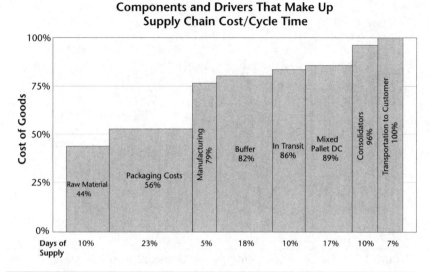

Figure 13-6. Supply chain cycle time in a food distributor

Why is the channel so "stuffed"?

This is an example in which the actual customer consumption does not drive the factory loading schedules. Rather, marketing is using various trade deals: special discounts to distributors to induce them to make large purchases. While these promotions are often a necessary part of doing business (and can be accommodated in Lean Six Sigma), Figure 13-7 shows the results of failing to respect lead time dynamics in a real case.

As you can tell from the graphic, the factory production variation is driven wildly by the marketing promotions. The peak capacity of the plant is significantly higher than the average consumption. This means that the investment in property, plant, and equipment is far too great, as are maintenance and personnel costs. Another great cost is the money tied up in channel inventories. Notice that production is much higher than actual shipments to the distributors, occasioning excess costs of warehousing.

Variation in delivery time is just as evil as any other kind of variation. The impact of imposing huge demand swings on a factory causes massive congestion and delay in the whole supply chain. The major takeaway from the example above is that *these costs are self-inflicted and hence can be removed.*

Conclusion: the pull system should be implemented across the

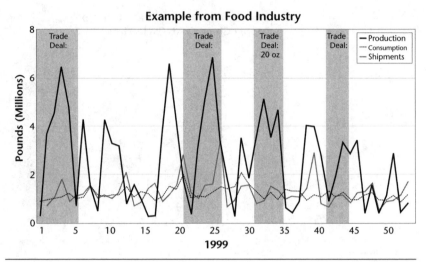

Figure 13-7. Effect of marketing promotions on production and delivery

entire supply chain. Only the actual consumption of products down to a strategic kanban trigger level should create a demand on the factory. This in turn should ripple through to suppliers in the same manner. Suppliers should receive a forecast of demand for their own planning purposes, but should be encouraged to create a flexible supply system to minimize both parties' inventories and costs. A framework that has been very effective in achieving this goal is discussed in Part B (below). The logistical considerations are covered in the next chapter.

Lesson #1: No One Can Really Predict Demand. With few exceptions, my experience shows no one can accurately predict future demand—which means our strategy should be to improve our flexibility instead of depending solely on forecasting algorithms.

My personal reason for believing in flexibility rather than forecasts is knowledge that was "bought not taught."

When I was the CEO of International Power Machines (later acquired by Rolls-Royce), we built large uninterruptible power systems (UPSs). Out of a total of hundreds of possible voltage, frequency, and power level combinations—each of which represented an SKU—we built 20 to 30 per month. The subassemblies within a system were also highly dependent on these combinations.

While marketing was pretty good at forecasting total dollars and units, it was terrible at forecasting the information critical to manufacturing: the specific voltage, frequency, and power rating for a given

UPS. I was so irritated by this that I sat down and called two dozen customers who had placed orders that month to find out why they had not bought what was forecasted (a primitive form of CRM). The answers were revealing: "the electrical contractor had changed transformer voltages," "the drawings were wrong," or "new loads had been added, which increased power level," etc., etc. In other words, the customer often did not know what specific product was needed until the last minute and product specifications often changed *after* orders were placed.

These interviews convinced me that the only rational course of action was to discontinue the floggings of marketing. The only way to improve morale was to create a highly responsive manufacturing organization. Through operations improvement, we reduced manufacturing cycle time from six weeks to one week. That meant that we could wait until just two weeks *before delivery* to launch kits into the line and had a lot more time to make sure all components were available.

The result was a company with very little WIP, fewer finished goods, and superb on-time delivery. Typically, the customers gave us two to three months of lead time and we used this to plan the deliveries from suppliers that needed that lead time. Raw material was fungible among many SKUs—we could use it on a wide range of products—so therefore represented very little inventory risk.

You might think that very high demand for a more limited population of SKUs would lead to more accuracy in mathematical forecasting. I agree with the principle, but examples from Nike that would appear to fit that description have not been successful. So I have come down on the side of believing that the cost of becoming flexible is a relatively small investment with great returns. At the minimum, it is a great insurance policy in case supply chain forecasting falls short of promises.

Non-Repetitive Manufacturing. The solution to unpredictable demand lies in coordinating the marketing forecasts and sales promotions with the process lead times and capacity of the supply chain. We discussed an example of this process in Chapter 4. Now we have a better understanding of all the parameters that affect lead time and how to reduce them and continually reduce variation.

But what about companies that do not produce SKU, i.e., their product is highly customized? The basic components are shown in Figure 13-8, which depicts the cycle for a fabrication and assembly operation for a discrete manufacturer.

The system is put together by working backwards from the point

Planning Time Fences

Changes Accepted Based on Lead Time	Changes Minimal Only Short Lead Items	Schedule Frozen	Assembly

E	D	C	B	A
Generic Unit Add	High Cost Commitment	Schedule Frozen	Line Start	Ready Ship

A - Unit is ready to ship
B - Unit has started production; therefore, no changes
C - Unit has been scheduled for line start; therefore, no changes
D - Majority of unit cost occurs here, so commitment level is high
E - Deadline for adding units to schedule without risk

Must Establish Time Fence(s) for Material and Options

Figure 13-8. Integrating Marketing and Sales with production control

where an assembled product is ready to ship to the customer:

- Operations (Engineering, Master Scheduler, Manufacturing, Purchasing) has to define the timeframes within which volume and mix changes are acceptable (that is, the amount of time Operations needs to react to changes in volume or product mix). It must also commit to Marketing to continually reduce these timeframes, so the company will be better able to beat the competition.
- Operations then works with Marketing to create a process view with *time fences* (milestones in the design-to-shipping process) that are related to the manufacturing cycle time. They work back from the actual fabrication and assembly steps (C-B-A on the diagram) to identify how much lead time is needed to finalize designs and order materials and parts.
- Long lead time items that are generic to the product family and therefore can be used for a number of products (or, in the lingo, are fungible among SKUs) may be ordered at point E.
- By point D, the company must commit to the production items so that any changes afterwards in design, bill of material, and quantity will be minimal.

This system will work only if Sales and Marketing conduct their promotions within the time and capacity bounds defined by Operations. But that doesn't mean they should refrain from pressuring Operations to abide by the Olympic motto: Higher, Faster, Stronger. The interval of C to B is a period of fabrication and subassembly build and is usually longer than assembly. If fabricated parts are highly fungible or low cost *and* have few part numbers, a stocking strategy may be used to gain additional time flexibility by specific SKU at point B. However, the goal of Lean Six Sigma is to compress the time between C (when the schedule is frozen) and A (shipping), thus eliminating the variation within the value-added process. Looking again at Figure 13-8, we want to move the variation into the planning horizons of E-D and, to a lesser extent, D-C.

PART B: EXTENDING THE ENTERPRISE TO SUPPLIERS

Everything we have done so far is really treating a symptom by protecting our manufacturing system from variation and long lead times. Lean Six Sigma can dramatically reduce the lead times, inventories, etc., within your factory and the downstream distribution system. However, long supplier lead times are the root cause of the excess raw material inventory, shortages in material, lost productivity, and resulting long lead times to your customer.

From a Lean perspective, the safety stocks discussed above are actually just a trap of invested capital, cost, and stockroom expense that is non-value-added. In order for you to become a Six Sigma supplier to your customers in terms of quality, lead time, and cost, your suppliers must embrace Lean Six Sigma.

The suppliers' role in most supply chains has increased, as many firms have outsourced all but their high-value-added, core competence processes. As a result, the goal of delivering products and services with six sigma quality and lead time is held hostage by the performance of suppliers.

The first thing to remember is that many of our problems with suppliers are our own fault! The traditional practice of building in large lot production imposes all the evils of variation on our suppliers.

Because of immediate potential cost reduction, many companies have approached the problem of minimizing material spend by entering pools or web exchanges.

The major opportunities for working with suppliers lie in two areas:

- Minimizing raw material inventory dollars using a supplier pull system. Lean Six Sigma enters the process by providing the "pull demand" and by using the lead times defined by the suppliers in establishing kanban replenishment and supplier-replenished "point of use" inventory levels.
- Encouraging suppliers to use basic Lean Six Sigma methods to improve quality and delivery. Most firms that use Lean Six Sigma

offer lead time improvement assistance to their suppliers. By sharing Lean Six Sigma training and coaching with long-lead-time, high-value, A-level suppliers, the inventories of both the firms and their suppliers can be significantly reduced.

Strategic purchasing organizations focus on managing vendor relationships, maintaining vendor scorecards, monitoring buying performance, tracking overall purchasing effectiveness, etc. But operationally, they separate *strategic* procurement from *tactical*:

- The tactical purchasing group is focused on purchasing parts and material (buying, planning, expediting) and, most importantly, dealing with the daily firefighting.
- The strategic purchasing group focuses on maintaining good vendor relationships, negotiating better pricing, pursuing alternate sources, and managing overall material spend. Its efforts reduce the number of suppliers and focuses buying—to reduce cost and gain better leverage.

Since more than 80% of material cost is "designed in" by product development, an effective strategic procurement effort requires dedicated standards and evaluation engineers who understand the mission-critical importance of the initiative. Strategic procurement creates a link to the Design for Lean Six Sigma efforts, such that necessary engineering initiatives are supported by black belt projects. In addition, strategic procurement guides the implementation of raw material dollar reduction and Lean Six Sigma implementation within the supplier base.

Taking the Supplier Plunge

Before you get into the mechanics of trying to get suppliers on a pull system, you have to first acknowledge how much effort will be needed on both sides. Hence you have to be able to show that the *rewards* will also be great, on both sides—something you'll be better able to do once you have successfully implemented pull in your own organization.

When you're ready to begin working with your suppliers, where do you start? I have worked with companies that invited all their suppliers in for a "supplier day" and gave them a pitch on Lean Six Sigma. One multibillion dollar company had me speak to about a hundred suppliers in a Norman Chateau in New Jersey. The problem is that many firms went through the motions by sending their local sales rep, but there was absolutely no follow-up. This large forum is not an effective way to begin the process.

Instead, you'll have a better chance of success if you select a very few key suppliers and put a focused effort on them with full black belt and green belt support. When the pull system is up and running with these suppliers, *then* you have a "supplier day" where these pilot suppliers speak of their experiences, as well as of your internal successes in operations. The suppliers must understand that faster lead times are going to make them more money and get them more of your business as well as that of other customers.

We do not recommend that Lean Six Sigma implementation be directly coupled to price concessions. This approach has caused a lot of ill will when attempted in a heavy-handed way in the automotive world. Rather, we recommend allowing the normal market forces to drive costs down as fewer suppliers, with lower cost bases, compete for larger contracts. If a cost reduction goal is imposed, suppliers should receive credit for innovations in design that achieve the goal. You should plan to spend three months in the planning and implementation stages of the pilot and six months of focused implementation on a few suppliers.

Identifying the Pilot Candidates. The essence of strategic purchasing lies in the understanding that we source a variety of types of product from a variety of companies. The buy strategy and business relationship should be based on a supplier segmentation analysis, which relies on a thorough understanding of the dependencies that exist between the buyer and vendors. This analysis should also form the Lean Six Sigma supply base initiative. For those parts or items where there are plenty of qualified suppliers, the goal of strategic purchasing should be to re-source the business to vendors that are already implementing or wish to implement Lean Six Sigma principles. On the other hand, when there are few if any alternatives for the desired item, strategic purchasing needs to establish an atmosphere of co-makership with the supplier. It is in the buyer's best interest to sponsor Lean Six Sigma training and projects at these critically vital business partners.

Segmentation analysis need not be a burdensome effort. There are quick-and-dirty ways to determine likely Lean Six Sigma supplier candidates. For example, plot the cumulative spend of your vendors, starting with the vendor that has the largest percentage of your business and going down to the vendors with the smallest. You'll no doubt discover another Pareto effect: typically, 20% of your vendors will represent 75% to 95% of your material costs. So once again, it's Pareto to the rescue! Your challenge is less daunting because you're able to focus your efforts on a small number of your vendors and still maximize potential savings.

We always recommend that clients perform a similar Pareto analysis in which the suppliers are graphed versus the sigma level of their quality and on-time delivery. This will show you which vendors are the most reliable and which need the most help. An estimate of the cost impact of supplier problems is also important. If one of the suppliers that need help is also near the top of the Pareto chart in terms of percentage spend, you have an obvious starting point for your efforts.

Another very quick way to prioritize the supply base opportunity is to use the cause-and-effect matrix of Chapter 11 (p. 193). Rate each vendor on a scale of 1-10 on critical-to-quality features, on-time delivery, and dollar spend. The weighting of the factors across the top might be 100 for critical-to-quality features, 70 for dollar spend, and 50 for on-time delivery. You then multiply each vendor's scores against the weights for each factor and summarize the values for a total score. This process will reduce the list to fewer than a dozen targets.

As you and your suppliers become more accomplished in Lean Six Sigma implementation, you may choose to perform an annual Lean Six Sigma assessment of your major suppliers. This practice is quite common in the automotive and aerospace industries. This assessment can be used to not only identify prime vendor candidates for a Lean Six Sigma project, but also more accurately focus the energies of the project in those areas where the supplier has the most to gain. The Integrated Supply Chain & Material departments of Lockheed Martin and Honeywell Aerospace (formerly AlliedSignal) sponsor Lean Six Sigma development projects with their major strategic suppliers. In fact, Lockheed and Honeywell have even teamed up to sponsor a Lean Six Sigma project at a manufacturing vendor in Southern California that supplied sheet metal fabrications to both companies.

Whichever method you use to identify high-potential targets, the strategic procurement team needs to make a final judgment about where success is most likely, using criteria such as the following:

- The supplier is important (per the C&E matrix or Pareto analysis).
- The supplier is strategically desirable in the long term.
- Your volume constitutes more than 10% of the supplier's revenue (the "stick").
- You wish to cut an alternate supplier (the "carrot").

- Top management wishes to embrace Lean Six Sigma or has already implemented Lean Six Sigma or Lean.
- You have defined goals for quality and lead time improvement and have buy-in from the supplier.

Steps in the Pilot Implementation

For the suppliers chosen:

- Provide their top management with the two days of Lean Six Sigma training that mirrors what your executives receive.
- Assuming they elect to move forward, extend training to the rest of the plant.
- Develop a funding scheme. One approach that works well is to have your firm pay the cost of training and implementation in these pilots, to be refunded out of future savings on your product on a mutually agreeable schedule. The supplier should keep the balance of the savings.

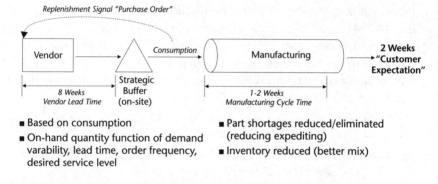

- Based on consumption
- On-hand quantity function of demand varability, lead time, order frequency, desired service level

- Part shortages reduced/eliminated (reducing expediting)
- Inventory reduced (better mix)

Figure 13-9. The purchased parts pull system

The process of implementing a pull system between a supplier and a customer has some logistical implications. Do *not* impose a kanban pull system on your suppliers at the outset—all that does is force them to hold excessive amounts of inventory. This strategy has been tried by some auto manufacturers and has resulted in ill feelings. The goal is to make this a success to be replicated throughout your supplier base.

The purchased parts pull system diagram (Figure 13-9) is modeled after the basic pull system shown earlier.

Just as you do internally, when working with suppliers you want to focus your efforts on the big-dollar items and free up time for purchasing to become involved in the process. If you perform a Pareto analysis of your material spend by part number, you will generally find that 10%-20% of the part numbers account for 80% of the dollars. (Pareto again!) You want to put these "A" items on daily releases *if* the vendors' lead times and distances are such that this ideal can be achieved. If not, you'll have to invest in inventories adequate to sustain manufacturing demand during the suppliers' lead time, plus safety stocks as discussed above.

On the other end of the spectrum, 50%-80% of the part numbers may account for only 5%-10% of the dollars. These "C" items should be stored at the point of use and be replenished every 10 days, preferably by the supplier. These actions typically reduce raw material inventory dollars by 15% and purchasing transactions by more than 50%. We now have the visibility and focus to help our key suppliers dramatically reduce their lead times and lead time variability and improve quality by process improvement.

The minimum kanban buffers and triggers are calculated using the same method described above. The key here is that you will maintain the *strategic buffer* at your site to allow your manufacturing system to operate at high cycle efficiency by preventing stock-outs and avoiding any effects of variability of arrival times while your suppliers begin to improve their own systems. As was true of your determination of internal strategic buffers, the amount of material depends on a number of parameters:

- **Lead time,** time from order release to the supplier until parts are received.
- **Release frequency,** how often parts are released (so you can sustain production between arrivals).
- **Safety stock,** to compensate for variation in lead time, demand, weather, etc., as was described above.

Creating a kanban system on these high-priority ("A") items will create the visibility to reduce both inventory and shortages. Nevertheless, I recommend that you work with the suppliers to identify their time traps and to reduce their delay using Lean Six Sigma tools. These high-dollar buffers will be considered as a priority issue when the pilot and subsequent suppliers are chosen. As the supplier reduces lead time etc., the buffer can be reduced in size.

The Pull Formula for Supplier Parts

We are now in position to develop a rational approach to raw material and supplier inventories that will keep manufacturing supplied

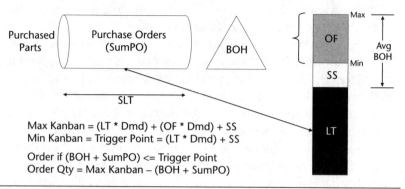

Figure 13-10. Formulas of the purchased parts pull system

and point the way to improving key suppliers, using the formulas in Figure 13-10.

If these formulas look suspiciously familiar, it is because they are! The factors represent issues already addressed in this chapter:

LT = lead time
SLT = supplier lead time
OF = order frequency
SS = safety stock
Dmd = Demand
BOH = batch on hand

The vertical box on the far right of Figure 13-10 represents the total inventory buffer.

The top portion represents order frequency times the average demand. This component fills up the buffer when an order arrives and triggers a new order when inventory falls to the minimum level.

As the order is placed, we will confirm that the supplier can ship on time and that usage is not fluctuating upward, then place an order to replace the consumed inventory. While awaiting the arrival of the new release, we are eating into the safety stock (SS) portion of the buffer (the middle segment of the bar). If we hit the 75% point of the safety stock, we go into an expedite mode.

If the buffer continues to drop, we'll reach the lead time segment of the vertical bar. That means we are immediately using all the parts on hand and are in trouble if there are any delays. If this happens, a red alert comes on at the plant manager level. Why? Because if that vendor fails to ship or if demand fluctuates upward, we will face a shutdown! But if we react just as the level of the buffer reaches the top of that lead time segment, we still have time to take corrective action (time that was built into the safety stock calculations).

The variation in consumption demand on the supplier is reduced if the customer frequently produces in small batches, as opposed to the infrequent production of big batches. We saw in Chapters 1 and 3 that delivery time variation falls in proportion to the reduction in average lead time. Thus the safety stocks are dramatically reduced when a fast and reliable supplier serves a fast customer's manufacturing process.

Seasonal fluctuations affect the demand and hence the buffer sizes using the above formulas. Buffer sizes should be recalculated on a monthly basis if demand changes by 20% or more. Historical demand can provide an estimate of demand and will provide the lead time to advance or delay a reorder. The suppliers should receive an update of forecasts at least monthly.

Rolling out Supplier Deployment

With the success of the pilot, you are in position to deploy Lean Six Sigma throughout the supply base. To champion and coordinate this work, many firms have created a *supplier advisory council*, consisting of the corporate Lean Six Sigma champion (or someone who works closely with him or her) and representatives from strategic procurement, corporate training, three or more suppliers, and a consultant. The council's job is to use lessons learned during the pilot to develop the methodology, metrics, communications, and training and development process. The goal is to institutionalize the process as part of the routine efforts of the strategic procurement organization.

The first step is to recognize the importance of obtaining buy-in from the balance of the important suppliers. To obtain interest and commitment to move forward, the council should host events like the "supplier day" and ongoing discussion forums, publish newsletters on the Web, etc. Because the suppliers will typically sell products and services to one or a few business units, the appropriate champion should be involved in their project selection process and make his or her Lean Six Sigma implementation available to the appropriate suppliers. The council will be responsible for the development and delivery of appropriate training curriculum and provide on-site support. Each supplier will provide a champion to lead the deployment and will be responsible for developing the training and implementation schedule ... because this is the suppliers' program, not yours. Most suppliers have

---

Caterpillar 6 Sigma Supplier Survey
(for suppliers already pursuing 6 Sigma)

Caterpillar is deploying 6 Sigma, and we would like to gain a better understanding of how you are deploying 6 Sigma and lessons you've learned.

Supplier Background: _____

Supplier Name: _____ Supplier Code: ____

Estimated Annual Sales: _____ Number of Employees: ____

Supplier Contact Name:_____

Address: _____

Phone Number: _____ E-Mail Address: _____

Why did your organization decide to pursue 6 Sigma?

What is your overall 6 Sigma objective?

__ Problem Solving—Fixes specific areas of high cost, rework, or delays (e.g., reducing parts shortages in central region, shortening application processing time).

__ Strategic Improvement—Targets key strategic or operational weaknesses or opportunities (e.g., building e-commerce capabilities, speeding up product development).

__ Business Transformation—A major shift in how the organization works, a culture change (e.g., creating a customer-driven, process-foused attitude; abandoning old structures or ways of doing business).

__ Other. (Please describe.)

What are the scope and approach for your 6 Sigma deployment (e.g., company-wide vs. targeted area; top-down vs. bubble up; mandated vs. voluntary participation; process improvement and/or process creation methodology)?

What targets or stretch goals have you set for your deployment (e.g., # or % of Black Belts / Green Belts / Deployment Champions in a specific time frame, and are these full-time or part-time positions)?

When did you begin your 6 Sigma deployment and where are you now in relation to the targets you've set?

How are you deploying 6 Sigma within your organization (e.g., hired your own Master Black Belt; using an external consultant for training, coaching and/or program management support)?

What type of formal training are you providing for 6 Sigma (Deployment Champion, Black Belt, Leadership, etc.)? Please describe (include # of days/weeks for each type of training and any coaching support).

Figure 13-11. Sample supplier survey

Are you using any type of software to support your 6 Sigma deployment (e.g., statistical analysis, project tracking, collaboration)? If so, please describe.

How has the executive leadership team been involved in your 6 Sigma deployment?

Do you have incentives and recognition tied to your 6 Sigma deployment? If so, please explain.

In general, what are some of your foremost "lessons learned" in regards to 6 Sigma?

What would you do differently as you look back on your deployment? Is there one thing that really stands out?

What are some of your 6 Sigma success stories? Are there a few key things that really contributed to a successful deployment?

Are you involving (or planning to involve) your suppliers in your 6 Sigma deployment? If so, please explain.

Thank you for sharing your experience with 6 Sigma!

Figure 13-11. Sample supplier survey, continued

heard of Six Sigma and are even more attracted to Lean Six Sigma; some may already have such a process in place. In such a case, installing a pull system is all the easier. You could even use a form similar to that used by Caterpillar to survey your suppliers. (See Figure 13-11.)

In terms of identifying suppliers for joint Lean Six Sigma projects, we have not mentioned evaluating/assessing suppliers via an audit, though such audits are extremely common in both the automotive and aerospace industries. For example, Boeing and Lockheed Martin require that their major suppliers perform a self-assessment on an annual basis.

PART C: THE DOWNSTREAM PULL SYSTEM

A vital input to the sales and operational planning process is a system that institutionalizes the measurement of real demand: the down-stream pull system. If we can radically reduce the lead time of the factory, the amounts of inventory held downstream of the factory can be reduced while improving service levels.

A lot of money is wasted in carrying finished goods inventories in company warehouses, in consignment inventories, and by the hapless distributor or dealer who has invested money in slow-moving inventory. As an example, a wall-covering client spent 4% of revenue in company-owned warehousing facilities, including personnel, rent, and 10% cost of capital on PP&E and inventory. This did not count the obsolescence cost, which was not being measured and written off. These costs exceeded the cost of direct labor to produce the product. This slow-moving inventory is subject to the same obsolescence, damage, and rework issues as WIP within the factory. On the other hand, there are valid reasons for carrying inventory that are related to meeting customer lead time demands. The downstream pull system provides a rational means of ensuring a high level of service with minimal inventories.

To determine rational downstream inventory levels, simply use all the pull system methodology described above—in reverse! The distribution inventories by SKU are a discrete kanban buffer from which demand is drawing. We obviously want to replenish the inventories to keep up with consumption and not miss any orders. The same pull formulas used above apply to downstream inventories:

Maximum Inventory Quantity =
(Lead Time * Avg Demand) + (CTI * Avg Demand) + Safety Stock etc.

Minimum Inventory Quantity =
Trigger Point for Reorder = (Lead Time * Avg Demand) + Safety Stock

The terms are the same, but their definitions are changed. Lead time to the first downstream distribution point now must explicitly contain the transportation time. If it takes 10 days to transport a product, we obviously must maintain a buffer equal to 10 days' usage to cover usage during this interval. Within the four walls of the factory, this amount of inventory is usually negligible. But outside the factory, it can become significant. So we will write:

Lead Time$_{downstream}$ = Factory Lead Time + Transport Time

The order frequency is now related to the "batch size" of the transportation system. Can you order small or carload quantities? The safety stock formula can simply be modified to include this lead time. Actual customer consumption driving a pull system will allow a dramatic reduction in the cost and the inventory levels of distribution.

Total Supply Chain Acceleration

The Three Laws of Supply Chain Acceleration were introduced in Chapter 3; let's revisit them now with a broader eye.

First Law:

Customer Demand Rate =
Batch Size$_{Min}$ / Minimum Workstation Turnover Time

Implication: Reducing workstation turnover time allows you to reduce batch size while maintaining a flow demand (production) rate.

Expansion: Change "workstation" to "factory" and this principle holds for the total supply chain. If you can speed up an entire factory, for example, you allow everyone in the supply chain to operate "Lean."

Second Law:

When the process cycle efficiency is less than 5%, 80% of the process lead time delay is caused by just 20% of the activities or workstations.

Implication: You don't have to improve every procedure in every step in a process to achieve your goals. Rather, leverage your efforts by focusing on those workstations that contribute the most to delays.

Expansion: You don't have to improve every supplier in the process, just those that contribute the most to delays.

Third Law:

Process velocity and lead time are driven by the number of "things in process."

Process Velocity =
Number of Activities in the Process / Process Lead Time
= Completions per hour * Number of Activities / Number of
"Things in Process"

Implication: You can speed up a process and reduce lead time by reducing the number of "things in process."

Expansion: You won't really be able to achieve significant reductions in work-in-process until you no longer have to accommodate variation in delivery and quality from your suppliers.

By the time you consider undertaking an effort to improve your total supply chain, you will no doubt have a lot of experience with Lean Six Sigma in your own organization. Knowing how much effort it took *internally* should give you a good idea of how much *more* effort it will take when you have to interact with people and organizations that don't share your company's processes or culture.

But if you want to achieve the biggest gains in shareholder value, you don't have any choice but to look beyond your corporate boundaries. Work in process, delays, scrap ... these are all systemic viruses infecting your supply chain. And just as you can't cure a human infection by treating only an arm or leg, you can't cure delays and excess inventory by just looking at one part of the supply chain. You need to improve the *entire* system.

Notes

1. Spreadsheet calculations available from www.profisight.com.
2. The EOQ (Economic Order Quantity) is derived in all the production control books. It will assign the same batch size to two workstations, no matter that one only produces 10 different parts and the other 100. The consequence on lead time is obvious from the inflexibility diagram (Figure 3-6).

Chapter 14

Lean Six Sigma Logistics

By Robert Martichenko of Transfreight[1]

The previous chapter described how you could bring both suppliers and distributors/dealers into your "extended supply chain" and make even further gains in process speed and quality of information and performance. Given faster lead times and lower inventories, you now have an opportunity to reduce the cost and improve the quality of performance of your logistics network. What capabilities do you think Lean Six Sigma offers to the logistics network? Do you think Lean Six Sigma ...

1. Is a strategy to bring raw materials into a manufacturing facility exactly as the facility is running out of that particular part?
2. Is actually a distribution function, producing only what has been ordered and replenishing inventory levels to replace only what has been sold?
3. Could help you level out the demand on your resources and reduce inventories at all stages of the supply chain?

Well, if you answered "all of the above," then we are off to a great start! However, I wonder today how many companies believe they are practicing Lean techniques when in fact all they are doing is postponing the ordering of raw materials? You might recall the example given in Chapter 3 (p. 34) from a visit I made to a company that thought it was great how the supplier's truck would appear just as the manufacturing line ran out of supplies. Unfortunately, that truck was bringing two months' worth of supplies!

Such practices are what many people thought was the beginning and end of just-in-time (JIT). The adoption of the word Lean to replace JIT was in part an attempt to use a more descriptive term so that people would understand that JIT should be broadly construed. That's why we have used the word Lean throughout this book.

The first thing we need to recognize is that Lean, JIT, "Efficient Consumer Response," and "Quick Response" inventory strategies go a lot farther than simply receiving raw materials just as you are running out. Similarly, it's not fair to say you are practicing these techniques just because your finished product arrives at the retailer just as the last item is purchased from the shelf.

How do you actually implement a Lean logistics program? Like a lot of Lean thinking, much of the answer is logical though counterintuitive. The answer to these questions lies in the analysis of inventory and how a firm uses inventory to meet strategic goals.

INVENTORY AND STRATEGIC GOALS

Several times in this book we've discussed the impact of ROIC on shareholder value (see p. 12, for example). Since ROIC is the ratio of profit to invested capital, it is obvious that reducing inventory will reduce invested capital and improve ROIC. Less obvious is the fact that lower inventories will reduce cost and improve profit. Through an analysis such as what we'll follow in this chapter, a company will be able to demonstrate how its inventory strategies have direct implications for the company's revenue, cost of production, and ultimately profitability.

Over the years, many opinions have surfaced over how to calculate inventory carrying costs, in particular how the cost of capital should be calculated in order to recognize the opportunity costs of holding inventories. In the automotive industry, for example, which at times is plagued with inventories of raw materials, these inventories can result in high costs of production and hence can undermine an automotive manufacturer's position in the market. Consequently, to remain competitive in today's markets, manufacturers need to understand the implications that inventory and related inventory costs have in terms of the firm's revenue, cost of production, and ultimately profitability. Previous chapters have discussed the costs of inventory internal to factories; in concert with the process view of a business, we will now integrate that discussion throughout the extended supply chain.

Why Do We Hold Inventories?

To begin our analysis of how inventory affects a firm's overall performance, it is important to consider the reasons why a company holds inventory in the first place. Relative to inbound logistics supporting a Lean Six Sigma manufacturing facility, a company will hold raw materials for any or all of the following reasons:

1. **Safety stocks:** Raw materials kept on hand in order to avoid inventory risk and shortages due to unpredictable production schedules, long lead times, and supplier undependability.

2. **Cycle stocks:** Inventories resulting from a firm's strategic decisions about production batch sizes, raw material lot sizes, and constraint (long time delay) workstations within a production process.

3. **In-transit inventories:** The necessary inventories that cover transportation lead times *from* suppliers and *to* customers. These inventories are at least equal to the demand per day times the days of transit.

4. **Work in process (WIP) stocks:** Inventories that are actively being used in the production process, both by the manufacturer and by the suppliers.

5. **Speculative stocks:** Inventories used to support business operations such as marketing promotions, potential raw material shortages, purchasing discounts, or concerns such as strike protection.

Understanding why firms hold inventory—and the reasons they must in fact hold a certain amount of inventory—allows us to comprehend the economic and financial implications of this necessary business practice.

However, the goal of any Lean logistics network is to eliminate safety and speculative stocks and to minimize lead times, WIP, and cycle stocks to optimal levels. The question, though, is why go to all this trouble? The answer to this question is seen in the way inventory affects the firm overall.

INVENTORY AND THE COST OF PRODUCTION

From a simplistic point of view, a firm must optimize costs in order to achieve maximum profitability. Therefore, focusing on controlling and lowering costs is instrumental to a firm's long-term profitability. In the automotive industry, for example, competitive pressures have put downward pressure on retail prices, which means that profit margins can be increased only through decreased costs. Additionally, those companies that can maintain competitive pressures on their competitors will in fact see increased sales, which will result in more efficiency through the realization of economies of scale in terms of overhead cost spreading. In essence, companies that gain competitive cost advantage will continue to maintain competitive advantage overall. However, inventory control, and its financial impact, can be challenging for many firms, as it affects the components of both explicit and implicit costs.

■ **Explicit costs** are defined as historical costs or actual costs that are tangible and allocated on a firm's financial statement. With respect to inventory, these costs can be seen in items such as storage of inventory, transportation, and material handling costs, including all the personnel, warehouse, and PP&E costs. Other explicit costs associated with holding inventory include those costs due to scrap and rework (which are proportional to WIP), shrinkage, obsolescence, taxes, insurance, and damages to the inventory.

Even though firms recognize that explicit costs exist with inventory, many companies rationalize that these costs are necessary evils and say they should simply be considered a cost of doing business. Even though reducing these explicit costs can appear to be daunting, doing so can truly separate the top performers in any competitive industry.

■ **Implicit costs** are those costs that do not involve actual payment by a company but represent lost opportunity that results from allocating money in one area, thus ultimately abandoning other potential projects. The opportunity cost of such decisions is the return that the abandoned projects may have generated on the invested capital.

There are many schools of thought on how to calculate the cost of lost opportunity; however, most financial managers will agree that the financial losses fall somewhere between the actual cost of capital and a firm's required risk-adjusted rate of return on its equity (the weighted average cost of capital) for that industry. Regardless of how a firm calculates the opportunity cost of holding inventory, there is no question that the cost exists and must be taken into consideration when making strategic decisions.

As you can see, explicit costs are not reflective of the whole story relative to inventory. Implicit costs of holding inventory tell the true story of how inventory can have significant financial implications for the firm.

Much has been written and many opinions exist on how to calculate the true cost of holding inventories. Most sources will break the calculation of inventory carrying costs into the following categories:

A. Capital Costs
   – Inventory investment

B. Inventory Service Costs
   – Insurance
   – Taxes

C. Storage Space Costs
   – Plant warehouses
   – Public warehouses

D. Inventory Risk Costs
   – Obsolescence
   – Scrap and rework
   – Cost of change orders
   – Damage
   – Shrinkage
   – Relocation costs

A. Capital Costs. Whether inventories are tied up as raw materials or as finished goods, there is an explicit cost to the firm for holding these inventories. For raw materials, money has been paid out in order to cover the cost to suppliers; for finished goods, both raw materials and the variable costs of production have been sunk into the inventory. The two potential costs of capital associated with these inventories are:

1. The cost of financing the inventory.
2. The opportunity cost of tying up capital in the form of inventory rather than using the capital for other purposes. The opportunity cost of the capital should be calculated using the required rate of return on the capital deployed.

B. Inventory Service Costs. Inventory service costs are typically in the form of taxes and insurance. Taxes may include inventory taxes assessed by certain states on inventories in a firm's possession at some particular point in time. This tax typically varies with the level of inventory and therefore could be considered to be part of a company's short-term variable cost elements. Insurance costs relative to inventory may be in the form of property, fire, and theft insurance. These costs may not necessarily vary with inventory levels and therefore could be considered a fixed overhead cost in the short and long term. Consequently, reducing inventory in the supply chain will not eliminate these costs immediately.

C. Storage Space Costs. Storage costs can also be considered an incremental or unnecessary cost due to holding inventories. The costs that we should consider as part of inventory carrying costs are those that necessarily vary with the level of inventory. For example, if a firm is forced to use an outside warehouse to store safety stock, then the handling and storage costs associated with this warehouse are considered costs directly attributable to holding this inventory. In a Lean environment, the strategy is to reduce the raw material, i.e., "things in process," to accelerate the velocity of the process. By doing so, we keep raw materials moving at all times and minimize any points in the supply chain where storage may be required.

D. Inventory Risk Costs. Inventory risk costs include such items as inventory obsolescence, inventory damage, inventory shrinkage, and relocation costs associated with needing to move unwanted inventory to new locations for storage. These are real costs associated with inventory and can be calculated using activity-based costing (ABC) techniques, which in turn can be accurately represented on a company operating statement. Since ABC can be an onerous "activity trap," some companies perform these analyses on only a few samples. In general, a correlation exists between the overhead cost associated with inventory and the speed with which that inventory moves through the process. This would suggest focusing the ABC analysis on the slowest-moving inventories first. These costs are variable with the level of inventories and therefore are considered part of a firm's variable cost curve in the short term.

One area where we see the dramatic impact of inventory obsolescence is when manufacturers have product changeovers or build-outs. Under these circumstances, it is still common for manufacturers to be sitting on millions of dollars of raw materials that are of no use as the parts will not fit the new products being manufactured. Only through Lean logistics inventory control techniques will these situations begin to disappear from industry.

Costs in the Short Run

The short run is defined as a business cycle where managers can make strategic changes to only the variable components of the business. Typically for most businesses, the short run is considered to be less than one year.

Companies may decide to maximize profitability in the short run by analyzing and reducing variable costs such as labor, raw material inputs, resource allocation, and general overheads. Inventories—such as raw materials, in-process stocks, and finished goods—represent both variable costs and fixed costs in the short run and therefore need to be managed effectively:

- Variable costs associated with inventories include material-handling labor, short-term financing, and short-term public warehousing.
- Fixed costs in the short term include short-term leases for material-handling equipment and short-term leases on warehouses.

One metric that inventories can affect and that most firms are aware of is short-run marginal cost. This is defined as the rate of change of short-run total costs with respect to the level of output. Common sense would dictate that any profit-maximizing firm should want to increase output (assuming output equates to revenue) at a faster rate than cost will increase.

As discussed previously, the associated costs with holding inventories would be recognized in the short-run marginal cost curve. Therefore, if a firm decides to increase output, the inventory strategy of Lean Six Sigma will reduce inventories at all levels and will decrease the marginal cost curve and ultimately improve the company's overall financial performance. The advantage of Lean Six Sigma is that it allows significant reductions in inventory and marginal cost simultaneously. The reduction of raw material inventory can be achieved only if the lead times of the suppliers are reduced, as discussed in the previous chapter. The cost of excess inventories due to such suppliers must be counted into the total cost of ownership along with the actual purchase cost of the material.

Costs in the Long Run

Similar to short-run costs, inventory management is crucial when analyzing long-run cost strategies. The long run is considered to be the period of time when strategic changes can be made to fixed inputs (such as facilities and new technologies) as well as the variable inputs discussed above. This timeframe is typically considered to be greater than one year.

In the long run, a firm must focus on investment in resources and facilities to ensure long-term profitability in order that the firm succeed over time. Consequently, in the long run, the firm would not be concerned with managing current variable operational costs, but rather focusing on the most effective way to optimize revenue, reduce costs, and retain profits in order to invest into the future. This would include calculating the economic profit of businesses, product lines, customers, etc. But any business will have long-term assets whose return must be questioned. Unfortunately for many firms, these investments will typically include warehouses, distribution centers, and other facilities that are critical to management of slow-moving inventory, but many of which would not be required if lead time could be reduced 50% to 80%. Therefore, strategic inventory planning is critical to decreasing fixed and variable costs and increasing profits in the long run.

Now that we have examined the costs of inventory at a high level, we need to drill one step down and look at logistics costs drivers and prove the necessity to move to Lean logistics practices throughout the supply chain.

Lean Six Sigma Inventory Practices

The advantages underlying a Lean environment involve optimizing the supply chain while reducing costs and becoming more flexible to meet the customers' needs. But we must remember that a transition to a Lean environment affects all functional areas within a company, including all major logistics functions. However, not all functional areas or logistics functions may realize cost reductions individually, as Lean relies on the premise of optimizing an entire process and not simply micro-managing a particular department.

This need to look across the business as a whole unit is the number-one adjustment for companies when going to a Lean logistics strategy. Simply stated, most companies today still have functional barriers that do not allow them to properly optimize costs across intra-company departments. To do this—and to understand the benefits of implementing a Lean system within the context of logistics functions specifically—one must understand the activity and cost drivers behind specific logistics activities.

Once this information is available, an analysis can be performed summarizing the individual cost drivers so it can be compared with the optimal cost that would result if the activity drivers were integrated within a Lean network.

After basic logistics fundamentals are taken into consideration, we must then look at inbound logistics systems relative to Lean logistics principles. These include many of the parameters that drove the discussion of safety stock in Chapter 13:

1. Delivery frequency per supplier to the plant.
2. Lot size per part number.
3. Returnable packaging.
4. Leveled flow of each part number into the plant.
5. Pipeline visibility and contingency planning.
6. Logistics measurement systems and continuous improvements.

In order to have a world-class inbound logistics system, a company must take these Lean logistics principles and build its logistics networks using the Lean principles as the foundation of the network.

FUNDAMENTAL LOGISTICS COST DRIVERS

Recently my colleagues and I came up with an idea for a bumper sticker: "What in the World *Isn't* Logistics?" I really like this slogan because logistics has been the orphaned child in most industries, when it should easily be front and center.

What makes logistics so important? From a Lean manufacturer's point of view, inbound logistics cost drivers are seen in the following areas:

1. Demand forecasting
2. Inventory control
3. Material handling
4. Order processing
5. Packaging
6. Transportation
7. Warehousing and storage
8. Quality
9. Obsolescence
10. Cost of expediting, shortages, etc.

As we can see from the diversity of these inbound cost drivers, it is essential for a firm to understand its "total cost" picture relative to these logistics activities. To this end, the goal must not be to optimize each activity *individually*, but rather to optimize the entire equation, using *the total sum of all costs* in reaching strategic decisions.

In order to do this, each activity driver must be analyzed relative to the cost drivers within the activity. To exemplify this philosophy, a firm can choose some of these logistics cost drivers to analyze and understand their interrelationships. The hard part with this is that it requires cross-functional cooperation and high-level understanding of the issues because you may run into instances where one area should *increase* its costs in order to reduce *overall* system costs. For example, even though most companies are aware of how much it costs to carry inventory, they continue to optimize transportation costs and try to move raw materials in truckload quantities. This is shortsighted, backward logic because the costs associated with holding the inventory will most likely *exceed the savings* achieved from optimizing transportation costs.

Consequently, the real challenge for companies is to develop an algorithm or management method that focuses on optimizing total logistics cost. To perform this, someone must own the logistics process—have you ever considered having a Chief Logistics Officer?

The primary goal of all inbound logistics systems is to get the right product, in the appropriate quantity, to the right place at the right time, in the right condition, and at the right cost. Typically in a non-Lean environment, firms carry too much inventory and consequently may not possess accurate data for available raw materials or may lack materials that the plant requires at line side.

Taiichi Ohno, the founder of Lean (originally called just-in-time or the Toyota Production System) at the Toyota Motor Manufacturing Corporation, has stated that "the more inventory a company has, the less likely they are of having what they need." Therefore, Lean manufacturers need to understand their manufacturing demand patterns in order to level out production and streamline their inbound network.

Typically, just-in-time (Lean) manufacturing is thought of as a manufacturing and inbound procurement strategy. However, the first step to implementing a Lean system is having control over your demand planning. Lean relies on leveling production and maintaining a state of leveled production. Just-in-time focuses on leveling demand and aligning production to meet actual demand, therefore reducing inventories and all associated costs of poor demand planning. *In short, do not manufacture what has not been sold and replenish only what has been used* (the definition of pull!). This, of course, assumes that the factory can operate with the very short lead times discussed in previous chapters.

With this in mind, to truly understand Lean logistics, we must continue our study of logistics cost drivers and how each driver affects total cost.

LEAN MANUFACTURING, RAW MATERIALS, AND INVENTORY MANAGEMENT

Management of raw materials is a major undertaking for many industries. Any company that can reduce the costs of holding raw materials will gain a competitive advantage in its industry, from a viewpoint both of lower cost structures and of increased manufacturing flexibility. Lower cost structures will ultimately increase pressure on competitors, while manufacturing flexibility will allow for shorter lead times to market, resulting in greater customer satisfaction and ultimately increased market share.

Lean logistics systems must focus on eliminating the four main wastes that arise in a mass production environment. These four main wastes are typically itemized as:

1. Excessive production resources (excessive workforce, excessive facilities, and excessive inventory).
2. Overproduction.
3. Excessive inventories.
4. Unnecessary capital investment.

All four of these fundamental areas of waste are related to inventory management. When these elements of waste exist, all they do is increase costs and add zero value to the manufacturing process. Hence, they contribute to an upward sloping of the marginal cost curve for the firm.

Also, each of these wastes are intertwined:

- Excessive resources result in overproduction. This is evident when firms continue to manufacture product even though demand and marginal cost curves would logically indicate they should stop operations.
- Overproduction results in excess inventories, which then require additional manpower, equipment, and floor space.
- Excessive inventory will, over time, result in unnecessary direct

costs/capital investments in the form of:
1. Building warehouses to store excess inventory.
2. Hiring workers to transport and handle the excessive inventory.
3. Purchases of material handling and transportation equipment.
4. Hiring of inventory control personnel and purchases of inventory control information systems.
5. Personnel and associated costs to deal with inventory obsolescence, damages, and shrinkage.

And that's not all: a firm must also take into consideration the costs associated with capital financing, opportunity costs, depreciation, and administrative costs that surround the issue of inventory—costs that are not required to support the manufacturing process.

Consequently, a firm must ensure that all processes are designed to control overproduction. This means that these processes must support manufacturing that is designed to produce only relative to the demand pull of the market.

One approach that companies take toward the management of raw material inventory is to implement just-in-time inventory systems. Lean systems are designed to ensure that raw materials are produced and delivered only when they are needed and only in the quantities that are required to support the upstream manufacturing process. Executed properly, Lean will result in a reduction of overall inventories and all related inventory carrying costs and an increase in raw material quality, as suppliers will be forced to ensure that quality is perfect. This happens in part because the upstream process will not have large buffer stocks to rely on in the event that quality issues surface or that delivery promises are not met.

Now that we have built a case for why inventory management is crucial, we must look at the primary focus areas to implement a Lean inbound logistics program.

IMPLEMENTING LEAN LOGISTICS

Once a company embraces Lean manufacturing, it will undoubtedly need to implement a pull system for raw materials supporting the manufacturing process. The main points to take into consideration when designing this logistics network are:

1. Transportation design and delivery frequency.
2. Lot size per part number.
3. Returnable packaging.

4. Leveled flow of each part number into the plant.
5. Pipeline visibility and contingency planning.
6. Logistics measurement systems.

Focusing effectively on these key components across the entire supply chainwill allow a Lean manufacturer to realize its goal of minimized inventory levels, leveled flow of raw materials, increased flexibility, and ultimately reduced costs.

1. Transportation

Transportation costs are significant for most businesses and certainly for all manufacturers. In the past, inbound transportation has been considered a necessary evil and simply a cost of doing business. However, Lean manufacturers are now recognizing that Lean inbound transportation networks can in fact be strategic and are pivotal to support the flow of raw materials into a Lean plant.

Thus, we need to focus attention on the following areas of inbound transportation to reduce safety and cycle time related stocks:

A. Increasing delivery frequency per supplier.
B. Reducing interplant transfers.
C. Reducing trailer and raw material sleep time in the plant trailer yard.
D. Eliminating multiple and inefficient channels of distribution.
E. Reducing and preventing transportation damages.
F. Implementing leveled, consistent deliveries into the plant.
G. Reducing transportation equipment due to better asset utilization.

Increased delivery frequency in particular plays a pivotal role in a Lean environment because Lean principles rely on numerous sequenced deliveries to realize the goal of zero inventories. Ultimately, this means that manufacturers must break old habits of moving raw materials in truckload quantities. Increasing delivery frequency reduces the space requirements at the plant by the number of deliveries. For example, if a particular supplier currently delivers to a plant once per day, the manufacturer may require 1000 square feet of space to store the parts. This space is held captive as it will again be required to store the same supplier materials the following day. Increasing this supplier's delivery frequency to twice per day will reduce the space requirements by two; increasing the delivery to four times per day will reduce the space requirements by four. This logic is used in Lean environments today to the point where Lean manufacturers may have suppliers deliver as many as 20 times per day. At that point, very little space is used to store the raw materials and the material can generally go from the trailer directly to line side. This obviously will free up space for the manufacturer that can be used for revenue-generating activities rather than the non-value-added costs associated with the storage of raw materials.

A second benefit of increased delivery frequency is better quality, in terms both of quality assurance and of contingencies in the event of poor quality. With respect to quality assurance, reducing raw material inventories and increasing delivery frequency will provide faster feedback to our supplier about quality problems that might have remained hidden for some time if delivered in a single large shipment. This quick feedback will help the supplier implement Lean Six Sigma, mistake-proof its processes, and respond to problems with faster lead time. (Meanwhile, though, we must use safety stock buffers.)

If materials are being delivered two or even 20 times a day, doesn't that mean transportation costs will skyrocket? To help reduce transportation costs caused by smaller lot sizes and high frequency of deliveries in a Lean system, manufacturers are locating closer to customer markets and closer to their supplier bases. There is no question that Lean manufacturers are now dealing with inbound supplier pipelines measured in hours—as opposed to days or even weeks, which was previously the norm. This reduction of transit times results in a reduction of inventory and all associated costs. For example, supporting high-frequency deliveries is now used as a negotiation lever between Lean manufacturers and suppliers.

Lean logistics relies on leveled, sequenced deliveries, which means that transportation networks are typically structured route systems, if not completely dedicated closed systems. In some respects, trucking companies servicing a Lean manufacturer will act more like an airline than an over-the-road carrier because schedules are set, pickup windows of time at suppliers are predetermined, unload dock times are specific, and all material handling is completed by a standardized work schedule. It is common now to see the use of "milk runs," where loads from multiple suppliers will be picked up on systematic, consistent routes. This allows a company to utilize private fleets more effectively, negotiate more competitive rates with common carriers, and achieve overall cost reductions in transportation costs.

2. Lot Sizes

Increasing delivery frequency for all suppliers in a Lean logistics network will result in smaller lot sizes being shipped to the manufacturer. Although this seems logical, reducing lot sizes proves to be very challenging for some manufacturers. Notwithstanding this challenge, it is imperative that lot sizes of raw materials be reduced to the level where Lean manufacturers can order the exact quantity required for small production runs.

Why is reducing lot size so challenging and why is it so important?

The main challenge with reducing lot sizes is within the manufacturers, in the functional barriers between purchasing and production control departments. Generally speaking, purchasing departments believe that larger lot sizes produce volume discounts and transportation economies. Consequently, all functional areas within a Lean environment need to be educated on "total cost" relative to the procurement of raw materials. It is myopic to look at transportation costs by themselves, as shareholder value will be optimized only when the costs for the system as whole are minimized.

Second, reducing lot sizes is extremely important because it reduces variation in demand patterns from the manufacturer's and the supplier's perspectives. For example, if a supplier is required to ship 50 parts per day and the minimum lot is 75 parts, the supplier will not have leveled demand as they will see orders fluctuating between one and two lots each day. Due to this fluctuation, the supplier will probably decide to build safety stock, as they'll suspect that the variation in demand will have even more dramatic swings. The direct and indirect costs of this variation will increase overall costs of the supply chain. Reducing the minimum lot size to 25 parts will allow the manufacturer to order exact daily requirements and the supplier will have consistent, leveled demand to effectively plan its manufacturing resources. Safety stocks will not be required and both the supplier and manufacturer will create stability in the supply chain. This stability is ultimately what drives all forms of waste and costs out of the entire system.

3. Returnable Packaging

As manufacturers begin their journey to becoming Lean, one area that is generally overlooked and definitely understated is the use of returnable packaging for inbound raw materials. Truth be told, returnable packaging is one of the fundamental tools to achieve flow of parts through the supply chain and the manufacturing process.

Without returnable packaging, design of optimized inbound transportation routes is virtually impossible because effective route design begins with exact knowledge of cubic requirements from each supplier. To achieve this level of accuracy and high cubic utilization of trailer space, all loading characteristics need to be known for each part number. These loading characteristics include:

1. Parts per lot size and number of lots per pallet.
2. Stackability of packaging and susceptibility to damage.
3. Compatability of parts and packaging to other parts and packaging.

In the end, returnable packing allows for consistent network design, trailer loading configuration, and effective protection for the raw materials. For example, it is virtually impossible to design a milk run with five suppliers to reach 90% cubic trailer utilization if the packaging characteristics are unknown or if the packaging is made of corrugate that will not allow for stacking of parts on the trailer.

The true challenge of packaging relative to Lean logistics is in the development of the packaging file itself. Although moving from one-way packaging to returnable packaging is a significant endeavor, the real work is to maintain the packaging database once the conversion is completed. In order to prevent the packaging database from becoming outdated and corrupt, there must be excellent communication among purchasing, production control, and the logistics provider to ensure that packaging changes are being updated and that logistics network design is taken into consideration when packaging designs are conceptualized.

When you look at the three logistics factors we've just discussed, you can see how they are all related. Lean manufacturing relies on leveled production, sequenced delivery, and small lot sizes to accommodate changes in demand without having stale and obsolete inventory. Second, it requires a dedicated transportation network where shipping routes are predetermined and load configurations are designed from an engineering point of view. To facilitate effective load configuration, product packaging must meet strict guidelines with respect to size, stackability, and durability. Only through consistent packaging can lot sizes be determined, load configurations designed, and product protected while in transit and during material-handling activities. Once the packaging is consistent, costs will be driven out of the system that are typically related to poor trailer utilization, large inventory lot sizes, and product damages.

4. Leveled Flow

Lean manufacturing relies on a steady and consistent flow of raw materials being pulled through the production process. Pull is also crucial when designing a Lean inbound logistics network.

Drawing on our discussions so far, Lean logistics relies on small lot sizes and high frequency of deliveries into the manufacturing facility. To meet the demands of the pull system, inbound shipments of raw materials need to be leveled out through the production cycle. For example, if a particular supplier delivers eight times per day over a 16-hour production day, then this supplier should deliver into the Lean facility every two hours. Only through leveled deliveries will space requirements be optimized, material handling minimized, and overall costs reduced.

Pull is also very important for the suppliers as well. From a supplier's perspective, higher delivery frequency may result in higher pickup frequency at its facility. For example, if a particular supplier has a plant delivery frequency of 10 times per day, this could mean a pickup frequency at the supplier of five times per day. Through the use of a cross-dock, the five supplier pickups per day will result in 10 deliveries to the manufacturing facility. This is accomplished by consolidating shipments from multiple suppliers at the cross-docks and reloading the parts into trailers bound for the manufacturing plant. With this high-velocity method, parts should continue to move and the plants will receive inbound trailers that could have as many as 50 suppliers represented in one trailer. *This one trailer may represent one hour of production inventory from each of the 50 suppliers.*

Fundamentally, what this means is that a supplier that is used to loading one trailer per day may now be required to load as many as five trailers each day. Consequently, pull is important to suppliers, as they will maximize resource utilization if they are able to level the loading of the trailers throughout the day. Also, it allows the suppliers to set their own production schedules to build using Lean techniques, as opposed to mass production techniques, because parts will be pulled from the suppliers gradually throughout the day instead of fulfilling a large order once per day.

Overall, leveled demand will lead to consistent demand patterns, high frequency of deliveries to the plants, and optimized logistics costs at all nodes of the supply chain.

5. Pipeline Visibility

Lean manufacturers require information as to when raw material will arrive at their facility and where it is in the supply chain at any given time. For most firms it is necessary to know where their inventory is, in terms of both raw materials and available finished goods. A number of available technologies and systems allow them to manage these functions. Satellite systems with Global Positioning Systems and radio frequency warehousing networks are examples of the new technologies available to facilitate pipeline visibility between vendors and customers.

Paradoxically, these technologies are developed to *manage inventory* at a time when firms should concentrate on *reducing inventory*, thus reducing the need for technology costs and all related inventory costs! Lean tries to prevent the need for advanced systems and consequently all related technology costs are avoided. However, in a Lean environment where raw material inventories may be as low as six hours of production inventory on site at the plant, manufacturers absolutely need to have full visibility of inventory at all steps in the supply chain. Web-enabled tools allow manufacturers to have this visibility, which allows them to make operational decisions dynamically as circumstances change from day to day.

For example, a production control employee may realize that the manufacturer has a shortage of parts from a particular supplier. Through Web-enabled systems run by a third-party logistics provider, the employee can gain visibility of the entire pipeline, assess the criticality of the situation, and create a contingency plan directly through the Internet. Only through these types of technologies are Lean manufacturers able to reduce raw material inventory levels to absolute minimums.

Pipeline visibility is important internally for the Lean manufacturer. In fact, it is equally important for all players in the supply chain. Suppliers, logistics partners, and manufacturers need to know what is inbound to the plant, what is at the plant, and what is available at the supplier at any given time. Without this visibility, going Lean logistically may put a manufacturer in a position of suboptimization, as reducing inventories without pipeline visibility will likely result in raw materials shortages at some point in time.

6. Logistics Measurements

So far in our journey into Lean logistics we have discussed the reasons for holding inventories, the implications of holding inventories, and the action items required when implementing a Lean logistics network. No logistics network will be complete, however, until you have a measurement system in place.

To ensure quality in a logistics network, the measurement system must reflect the overall goals of the particular Lean strategy. The measurement system must also provide information that can be used to continuously improve upon the logistics network design. To meet this end, the following measurements should be in place in order to continue the drive toward Lean logistics:

1. Delivery frequency per supplier.
2. Lead time from supplier receipt of order to delivery to plant line side.
3. On-time delivery by supplier.
4. Lot size by supplier.
5. Delivery pitch by supplier.
6. Trailer, tractor, and driver utilization.
7. Space requirements for raw materials at both supplier and manufacturer.
8. Overall inventory in supply chain.
9. Raw material sleep time at plant trailer yard.
10. Order fill rate by supplier.

By measuring these 10 key components, the logistician will be able to isolate the logistics variables that deal with the Lean aspects of the inbound network. Although other, more traditional logistics measurements should also be generated, the above metrics focus specifically on the Lean aspects of the system. Through the effective use of these measures, all parties involved will be able to isolate improvement opportunities and prioritize the areas to address first.

CHALLENGES OF LEAN LOGISTICS

Going Lean is no easy feat internally; the same is true for implementing Lean logistics. Some people may argue that Lean benefits are not what they seem to be.

One example is the argument that a downstream manufacturer may simply push the requirement to hold inventories to upstream suppliers, therefore not actually reducing any costs overall. Ultimately, these costs will be transferred through to the cost of the product, therefore forcing the manufacturer to absorb the costs of the inventory at some point in the transaction.

This criticism is valid, which is why we spent so much time in the previous chapters discussing the rollout of Lean Six Sigma to suppliers and treating them as partners. The key objective is to have all supply chain partners practicing Lean principles to truly squeeze all logistics costs out of the system.

To achieve this end, many companies look for innovative ways to keep inventory moving at all times. As mentioned, to eliminate the need for warehouses, some Lean manufacturers will design and operate cross-docks, which facilitate the fluid motion of inventory and allow a manufacturer to achieve small lot sizes of inbound raw materials at a high frequency of delivery. By producing a fluid motion of inventories, companies avoid sitting inventory and therefore eliminate warehousing needs. Other techniques, such as milk run design, increased delivery frequency, and smaller lot sizes, have all been discussed; they are essential for the Lean network to actually benefit all participants in the supply chain.

When implemented throughout the supply chain, Lean Six Sigma will drive costs out of a company's cost structure in all functional areas. Many activity drivers and associated costs fall into the category of logistics functions. Logistics plays a pivotal role in all industries and its importance cannot be overemphasized. Progressive companies realize they are no longer competing at the manufacturing and marketing levels, but are now competing at the supply chain level. Lean Six Sigma systems attempt to optimize logistics functions by reducing inventories and therefore reducing the many costs that are associated with holding inventory. Once a firm truly integrates its supply chain from suppliers straight through to customers, costs will be reduced, quality will improve, and profitability will increase.

Note

1. Robert Martichenko is the General Manager of Business Development for Transfreight LLC, based in Erlanger, Kentucky. Transfreight is an integrated, full-service, third-party logistics provider backed by the strength of two world leaders. Transfreight, a joint venture between Mitsui & Co. Ltd. and TNT Logistics, provides dedicated supply chain management services. Robert can be reached at Robert_Martichenko@transfreight.com.

Chapter 15

Design for Lean Six Sigma

With Ken Jacobson[1]

Design for Lean Six Sigma (DLSS) applies all the Improve methods and tools described in Part II to the product development process. The objective of DLSS is that products go into production meeting customer performance and cost goals, with robust performance and with defects prevented. The DLSS process should make further rapid improvement possible as market and cost demands change with time.

Chapter 11 described a number of tools that contribute to these goals. For example, Figure 11-6 shows how asymmetry can be *designed* into a product to prevent assembly errors. An example of Robust Design (an application of Design of Experiments) was shown in Figure 11-25, showing how customer critical-to-quality parameters can be met despite external noise factors. These tools and many others ensure the Six Sigma quality of a product. We need to now address two additional issues: the speed of the design process itself and the reduction of product cost to attain the goals of DLSS.

If you have ever worked with a company that relied heavily on supplying new product to market, the situation faced by the following engineers will sound familiar to you. Each of the 21 design engineers at a manufacturer had been assigned 12 "must" projects, plus 12 lower-priority projects they were also supposed to accomplish! You know overall manufacturing lead time is directly proportional to the amount of work in process inventory. The same is true of product development lead time: it is directly proportional to the average number of projects in process. Is it any wonder that the overall cycle time needed to get designs to market was computed as greater than a year? But what could they do? Revenue varied from "flat" to "down" each month, everything had to be sold now, there was no time to plan or analyze—just get new product out to the market!

If you have read other chapters of this book, the cause of this company's problem should leap out at you: having too many "things in process" was slowing cycle time! (The Third Law of Lean Six Sigma.)

This organization made two significant changes in a relatively short period:

1. They reduced the number of projects in process to just the four with the highest net present value (NPV) (an estimate of contribution to shareholder value).
2. They reorganized from a functional structure to "product" or "platform" teams. As a result, cycle time for their design process was cut by 60%.

Here's another example. A construction equipment manufacturer usually took 36 months to get to market with a new model. Their competitor had released a product that was stealing their market share at an alarming rate. After identifying this product as the highest-NPV project and reorganizing into dedicated, focused product teams, a new model was introduced to market in 11 months. The cost of the new model was 25% less than the model it replaced, allowing the manufacturer to remain competitive in the market, while maintaining their gross margins. Both the process and the product were successfully "Leaned" (see Figure 15-1).

The lesson is clear. Lean Six Sigma principles apply equally to the product development process (and other transactional processes) as they do to the manufacturing process. There are many challenges a company faces with respect to developing new products: time-to-market, product quality, customer satisfaction, productivity/efficiency of the development process, product margins, costs.

Over the last 30 to 40 years, product development capability has evolved considerably:

- We've seen a shift from functional development to concurrent engineering or integrated product development with cross-functional teams.

Reduced Product Cost by > 25%
Product Development Velocity Increased 300%

- Brought to market in 11 months, compared with 36 months.
- Enabled recapture of lost market share in highly competitive product segment while maintaining strong gross margins.
- First cross-functional team, replaces three existing models, greatly simplifying current operating processes.
- Improved customer satisfaction while implementing over 150 cost reduction ideas (50 units sold in advance of actual production).
- Platform for three other ratings, reduced family part numbers by 40%.

Figure 15-1. Example of product development acceleration

- Many companies have implemented formal stage-gate development processes.
- Program management training and tools have helped teams better manage cost and schedule.
- Recently, we've seen a shift to enterprise-wide product strategy to include product portfolio planning and pipeline management to ensure that companies are developing the right products and developing them right.

In this chapter, we'll look at ways in which you can apply Lean Six Sigma principles to your product development process, contributing to factors that directly influence shareholder value: faster time-to-market through faster design velocity and reducing product line complexity. We'll also discuss Design for Lean Six Sigma (DLSS), a powerful combination of tools and methodology to not only help accelerate time-to-market for new products, but also drive down product cost and improve design quality.

THE CASE FOR APPLYING LEAN SIX SIGMA TO THE DESIGN PROCESS

Actual stock market data shows that only companies with differentiated products and services can sustain "above market" profit margins.

Differentiation can take on many forms. It may consist of superior quality, shortened lead times, efficient distribution, or lower costs. Yet, apart from patent protection, differentiation generally has a limited life. Eventually an early adopter will copy what you offer and the product or service becomes a commodity—leaving any price premium in jeopardy.

What are the dangers of being a commodity producer from the shareholder's perspective? Here are a few quotes from a very successful shareholder, taken from several Berkshire Hathaway Annual Reports:

Producers of relatively undifferentiated goods in capital intensive businesses must earn inadequate returns except under conditions of tight supply or real shortage. As long as excess productive capacity exists, prices tend to reflect direct operating costs rather than capital employed. (1978)

One of the ironies of capitalism is that most managers in commodity industries abhor shortage conditions—even though those are the only circumstances permitting them good returns. Whenever shortages appear, the typical manager simply can't wait to expand capacity and thereby plug the hole through which money is showering upon him. (1987)

In a business selling a commodity-type product, it's impossible to be a lot smarter than your dumbest competitor. (1990)

If you think I am belaboring the point, I'm speaking for the shareholder. The lesson is: if you are in a commodity business, you need to become:

- The fastest, lowest-cost, highest-quality producer (which has been the subject of the book thus far) *or*
- Differentiated such that customers will pay for your value proposition *or*
- Both, if possible—and create a wider moat around your economic castle.

The alternative is to earn your cost of capital, which means that wise shareholders will shun your company as a money pit. However, even if you create differentiation, as John Chambers of Cisco has wisely said, "Products will commoditize so quickly that in the end the only differentiation you can sustain is brand, speed, and talent."

Lean Six Sigma has a lot to offer in terms of speed, quality, and cost with which you can empower your talent and build brand.

As noted, any innovation, no matter how clever, is subject to rapid adoption by an alert competitor. While competitors will copy your products and match your capital expenditures, our experience has shown that they are much slower in copying improvement processes such as Lean Six Sigma. Thus, speed and quality are more sustainable advantages. The value of delivering differentiated products and services rapidly to the market place is depicted in Figure 15-2. The figure demonstrates that getting to market faster enables companies to:

1. Establish higher prices before the competition is able to "commoditize" the marketplace.
2. Gain additional revenues from increased market share.
3. Generate revenues for more of the product life cycle.

These factors combine to decrease the time to reach break-even or capture your return on investment. The old adage "time is money" is critical—by reducing the development time of differentiation, a substantial increase in economic profit results.

Decreased Cycle Time Drives the Capture of Greater Market Share and Higher Margins for More of the Product Life Cycle

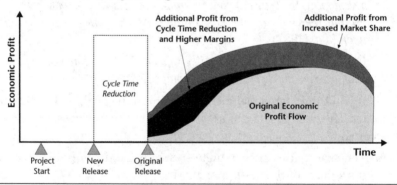

Figure 15-2. Value of faster product development

Leverage Through Speed and Better Products

How much is a price premium worth? The bar chart in Figure 15-3 shows the impact on operating profit in a typical manufacturing company by effecting a 1% improvement in any of the items that contribute to a firm's economic profit. Shown on the right is an example of a company's income statement and balance sheet. In a $10B company, a 1% price increase across the board will generate an additional $100M in operating income per year, while a 1% increase in sales volume generates $40M.

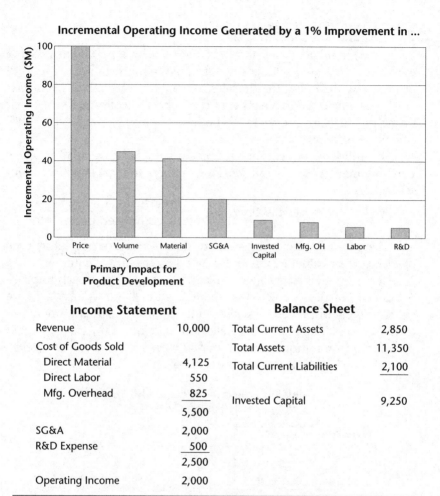

Figure 15-3. Leverage from 1% improvement

It is quite clear that price, material cost, and sales volume have the greatest leverage on operating profit. Higher-quality products, higher customer satisfaction, increased innovation, and faster time-to-market all result in the ability to command higher prices and maximize sales volume. Material cost is primarily addressed through better designs. Product line complexity drives much of the manufacturing overhead cost and labor. This chapter will principally focus on differentiation and speed to attain higher prices, rationalizing products to attain lower costs and increase manufacturing volume, and designing higher-quality products that meet critical customer needs to generate profitable growth.

IMPROVING DESIGN VELOCITY

Being the *second* company to reach market with a particular product means that you are in danger of entering the market as a commodity producer, with all that that implies for shareholder value. All companies, yours included, have only a finite capacity to create, improve, or prune products and services. To be first to market, you have to allocate these resources wisely.

The following equation—the basic lead time calculation—tells you how many projects you *dare* launch to get to market within a prescribed time.

$$\text{average lead time } = \frac{\text{Projects in Process}}{\text{Projects completed per month}}$$

Each effort competes for scarce resources and the completion time of each project is ineluctably determined by the above equation.

Here's another way to look at this. The typical approach to product development is depicted on the top left of Figure 15-4. There are eight projects in process and the finite capacity is spread among all eight. It takes 80 weeks to complete all the projects: projects completed per month (throughput) is eight per 80 weeks (or one per 10 weeks). The average lead time is therefore 80 weeks.

**Aligning Projects-in-Process with Resource
Capacity Lowers Cycle Time**

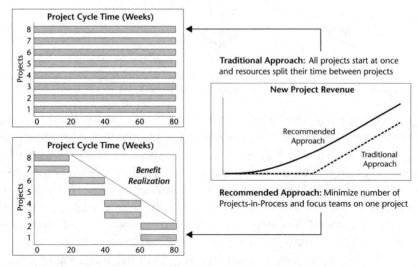

Figure 15-4. Changing the resource allocation mindset

The bottom left of Figure 15-4 illustrates the Lean approach to resource allocation: we have "gated" the projects in process to focus on the *two* projects with the most promise (highest NPV). As soon as the first two projects are completed, the next two projects go online, much as a pull system releases material to a workstation. We've reduced the number of projects in process from eight to two. Notice that we haven't accounted for any throughput improvement—it still takes 80 weeks to complete all eight projects—although it is usually an added benefit of limiting the number of projects in process. However, instead of taking 80 weeks to complete, the most critical projects are completed in just 20 weeks (a reduction of 75%), the next two most critical projects are completed 50% faster, and so on. This results in the generation of revenues much sooner, as shown by the comparison of both revenue streams on the right side of Figure 15-4.

There are three steps in resource allocation for product development projects:

1. Create the cycle time baseline.
2. Value the potential projects.
3. Gate the projects.

1. Creating the Cycle Time Baseline. The first step in the process is usually a real eye-opener: listing all of the projects in process, their manpower requirements, and the available manpower per month. You will no doubt be appalled to realize the extent of which your development resources are overloaded.

The average cycle time is simply the sum of the total manpower requirements divided by the available manpower per month:

$$\text{average cycle time} = \frac{\Sigma \, (\text{Project})_i(\text{Manpower})_i}{\text{Total Manpower per Month}}$$

This equation does not account for delays related to "skill bottlenecks"—the inability to have people with specific skills working on two projects at once—but you can refine the calculation if needed. But even without that refinement, what you'll find is that the projects in process generally drive lead times far beyond the market's acceptable window.

2. Valuing the Projects. Much of Chapter 8 was devoted to a method for valuing potential projects. That same analysis can be applied to potential product development efforts. The basic principle is to find those design projects with highest NPV.

3. Gating the Projects. Once you have a list of all the projects and some estimate of the value of each design project based on NPV, you can rank the projects in preparation for gating. The impact of these two pieces of data is essential to begin pruning down the list of projects, each of which will have its advocate! With the list of projects ranked, as a project team completes its project and becomes available, you may assign it a new project, one that both maximizes NPV and matches the team's skill base. The gating process should involve the P&L manager and representatives from Product Development, Marketing, and Manufacturing.

Be cautious, in that teams will be anxious to begin a new project. Do not allow critical team members to leave a project to get started on the next project, hoping that the remaining team members will finish things up. Make certain that the team members ensuring the new product's success through manufacture and roll-out have the skills and the organizational power necessary to achieve the NPV goals of the project.

Reducing Projects in Process: The Tough Decisions

Some years ago, when I was the CEO of a manufacturing firm, I learned a very valuable lesson related to improving design velocity. My company built uninterruptible power supplies (UPSs) for refineries and nuclear power plants. Every UPS was different, as each engineering firm (Bechtel, Brown and Root, etc.) had its own specifications. Thus we had a plethora of projects in process and no focus or reusability in our designs. We saw a light at the end of the tunnel:

- IBM was pushing real-time computing.
- Its customers would need a source of uninterruptible power.
- Its customers were used to buying standard products.

This situation appeared to offer a way out of our break-even performance, but it required a lot of engineering to develop a standard product line. We would have to abandon all new engineering efforts for nuclear power plants, etc. This was a huge decision: it meant abandoning our roots and all of our carefully built-up customer relationships to go into the unknown! Our current performance was bad and the future beckoned, so I decided that we would go for it.

Fate has a strange way of testing our resolve. No sooner had I made this commitment to our marketing and engineering staffs than an old customer, TVA, called us. They asked us to bid on a multimillion-dollar order for their new series of nuclear plants.

What helped me through this dilemma was a bit of wisdom that some unknown person had once given me: "A commitment is a commitment only if you are willing to suffer to keep it."

We informed TVA we would not be bidding and we focused all our engineering resources on developing a standard product. Making this decision to reduce projects in process was difficult but liberating. Everyone was focused, we felt we had a chance, and the results proved it.

I cited Andy Grove earlier in the book. He went through a similar gut-wrenching set of decisions in pulling Intel out of its roots in semiconductor memories and positioning the company as a specialist in microprocessors. This ordeal is discussed in his book *Only the Paranoid Survive*. This book shows that it takes judgment and character to execute what people know is the right thing to do. The supporting data and NPV calculation provide a rational basis for action, but ultimately it's a matter of judgment. As Churchill said: "The King's First Ministers are not called upon to make easy decisions."

Reducing Product Line Complexity

It's a well-established guideline that 100% of the economic profit is typically concentrated in less than 50% of a company's products. Why? Because the proliferation of products into your company's product portfolio is inevitable. Companies tend to try to address all aspects of their customers' preferences. In doing so, the number of variants of platform products increases over time, resulting in a highly complex product line. The end result is that a lot of capital is tied up in value destruction—and the added complexity of these value-destroying products adds costs to *all* products. Such complexity costs arise from increases in variability and in transactions across marketing, planning and scheduling, shop floor control, and product development activities.

Figure 15-5 is essentially a Pareto analysis of EBITDA (Earnings Before Interest, Taxes, Depreciation, and Amortization) contribution for a particular company. It shows that a minority of product families (far left on the graph) contribute the majority of profit. In other words, more than half of the company's products add cost to the business but are failing to contribute profit!

The issue of complexity is related to how requirements evolve during a product's life:

- In the infancy stage, market requirements lack clarity and standardization and also tend to be in an environment of rapid technological development.
- In the pursuant growth phase, requirements tend to develop into a

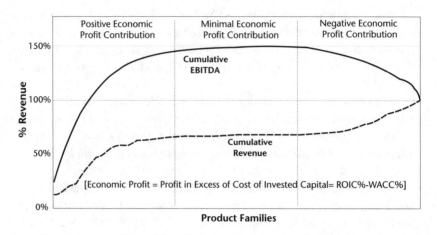

Figure 15-5. Locating high-leverage product families

set of standard "platforms" but with an increase in products/ options in an effort to cover all aspects of market preferences.

- In the maturity phase, requirements are usually focused around a set of fewer established "platforms," with greater emphasis on improving reliability and delivery.

Usually firms enter the growth and maturity phases without a structured approach to portfolio management and thereby are faced with the maintenance of all the products developed in prior phases. Sales and Marketing typically favors covering all aspects and tastes of the market. If this can be achieved without complexity, it is a tremendous bonus. However, mature markets often desire a value proposition that offers competitive pricing (which necessitates lower costs from the supplier), a high emphasis on quality and reliability, and rapid and predictable delivery cycle times. A highly proliferated portfolio prohibits Sales and Marketing from providing such a value proposition. It is virtually impossible to precisely capture costs across a broad product portfolio, let alone allocate them. This leads to inaccurate product costing and skewed pricing policies in which value can be unknowingly destroyed.

Reduce Complexity to Enhance Lean Effectiveness

Learning curves have been studied for many decades and findings show a significant correlation between *direct cost* and learning in terms of cumulative experience. The late Bruce Henderson, founder of the Boston Consulting Group, was a student of learning. He noted that learning increases and cost declines in direct proportion to the repetition of the product line and inversely with its breadth. This reveals another pitfall of product line complexity: our ability to achieve high-quality, rapid processes is based on the level of repetitiveness of our manufacturing processes. On a non-repetitive product line, manufacturing engineering cannot provide adequate work instructions and process sheets. Instead, the operators do it from memory or "unofficial" instructions, leading to increased cost.

Less understood is the impact of complexity on *indirect* costs. Yet, since manufacturing overhead is often three times as great as direct labor, we need to give it the proportional consideration. One of Lean Six Sigma's principal goals is to reduce manufacturing overhead and quality costs by 20%. A narrower product line makes the implementation of pull scheduling (Chapter 13) far more effective:

- Higher-repetition products can employ a simple card pull system.
- Less-frequent usage can use an electronic pull system, which uses the MRP data to create a pull from scratch. The cycle times are not as fast as with a card system, but they are predictable and do not congest or delay the higher-volume usage.

Most importantly, with narrower product lines, the cost of planning and scheduling is greatly reduced and expediting is nearly eliminated. Product development maintenance costs are dramatically reduced by eliminating proliferation, and the punch and power of the engineers rises as the portfolio is narrowed.

Lessons Learned the Hard Way

There were a lot of other lessons I learned when I was a CEO. Let me give you a personal example of what complexity really costs. When I founded International Power Machines, the uninterruptible power supply business was in its infancy. As the market grew, the power ratings we supplied also grew from 5KW … to 50KW … to 500KW … with a total of 30 separate power ratings in between! Each new design used the then-best choice of silicon-controlled rectifier (SCR) power switches. The ratings between 10KW and 80KW had evolved into five separate mechanical designs, all with unique heat sinks, SCR, wiring diagrams, terminal blocks, etc. The complexity of the product required a separate bill of material, kitting procedure, and purchasing and expediting activities for each design. This manifested itself in high manufacturing overhead cost and long delivery lead times. Because material spend was fragmented among many different products, purchasing had very little leverage with suppliers, leading to a high material cost as a percent of revenue.

The gross profit margin was 10% and the company was sinking fast! The products that finally shipped had frequent problems when first used in the field. These quality problems cost us tremendous warranty charges and customer ill will.

But then the marketing opportunity I described earlier emerged. IBM was making a big push to move its customers from batch processing to real-time, online processing. The power consumption of its systems was moving down into our power range due to new technology. Their customers were used to buying standard IBM products and they would need continuous power.

We had been trying unsuccessfully to cost-reduce the existing designs. This was very difficult because every order was different. We suddenly thought of a common redesign: we would build a specific model for each IBM system and sell standard products in high volume. To do this required the difficult decision to reduce the number of projects in process, as described above. But once we were free of this burden, our forces were focused on building a cost-effective standard design. This meant that we would build an 80KW mechanical design and use it from 10KW to 80KW. Though the 10KW unit had heat sink and SCR four times the needed rating—and were more expensive than those originally used—this new approach allowed purchasing to order in quantities four times as great and virtually eliminated all expediting efforts.

We created a standard wire harness, standard routings, lengths, cutting tables, etc. A common set of work instructions was developed. Purchasing and scheduling became simple, because the volumes flowing through each part number were four times greater. The variation in demand throughout the process dropped by about 50% (as statistics would lead you to expect). You will recall from previous discussions that variation greatly adds to lead time and delay. With less variation, units went into test with virtually no wiring errors and test time and total lead time decreased by 70%. This had a major impact in reducing manufacturing overhead cost.

Better still, when the new designs flowed through to the income statement, the gross profit margin jumped from 15% to 30% and, with continued refinement, eventually reached over 40%. The product line was also more reliable in the field. We began shipping "disassembled" units overseas, where they were reassembled with local transformers and cabinets, wired up, … and ran *perfectly*! This was a goal I had set, in the midst of our problems, when I read Ernest Hemingway's *For Whom the Bell Tolls:*

> *His eyes, watching the planes coming, were very proud ... and he watched their steady, stately, roaring advance.... They had come, crated on ships, from the Black Sea, through the Straits of Marmora, through the Dardanelles, through the Mediterranean and to here, unloaded lovingly at Alicante, assembled ably, tested and found perfect and now they were flying high and silver in the morning sun to blast those ridges....*

This overseas volume eventually became 40% of sales and 50% of profit. Our competitors didn't "get it" and remained mired in complexity and high cost or competed savagely at higher power ratings. We were generating 18% pre-tax margins, took the company public, and sold it to Rolls-Royce. When our margins became public, our competitors quickly figured out what we had done and we were suddenly in a commodity business with plunging margins—remember the quote at the beginning of this chapter about the need for speed, brand, and talent?

I must admit I never dreamed that complexity cost so much! Here again is another lesson I bought instead of being taught. You need to look hard at quantifying the costs of product complexity in your own business and balance those costs against the needs of the customers you sell to. The product lines to the right side of Figure 15-5—the ones not contributing profit—need to be given critical thought in terms of their value to the firm. Although there are many factors to consider (market segments, customer needs, competition, complementary products, etc.), products that add to complexity but do not earn an economic profit need to be either simplified through standardized products, modules, or components or eliminated from the portfolio.

DESIGN FOR LEAN SIX SIGMA

We've talked a lot about Lean Six Sigma and "Leaning" the product development process to improve time-to-market. Design for Lean Six Sigma (DLSS) is the next logical step to take value creation to a new level. DLSS is all about designing in quality rather than addressing quality problems down the road. Many companies are now employing DLSS to help them better execute the development process to improve their time-to-market, better understand their customers' needs, increase innovation, drive down costs, and improve product quality.

As is widely known, GE is one of the pioneers of Six Sigma—at least in terms of the success it's had with it. It was also one of the first companies to embrace DLSS:

> *The first major products designed for Six Sigma are just now coming into the marketplace and beginning to touch some of our customers. ... [They] are drawing unprecedented customer accolades because they were, in essence, designed by the customer, using all of the critical-to-quality performance features (CTQs) the customer wanted in the product and then subjecting these CTQs to the rigorous statistical Design For Six Sigma process.*
>
> *...Every new GE product and service in the future will be "DFSS"— Designed For Six Sigma. These new offerings will truly take us to a new definition of "World Class."*
>
> —Jack Welch, 1998 GE Annual Report

DLSS encompasses many of the same characteristics that have made Six Sigma initiatives so successful. It is based on a structured methodology and a comprehensive toolbox of product development techniques. It builds on existing development capabilities and provides teams with the knowledge and discipline to apply effective techniques to help them better execute the development process.

Among the large number of techniques addressed by DLSS, three key tools stand out as having the biggest impact for product development teams: Quality Function Deployment (QFD), the Theory of Inventive Problem Solving (TRIZ), and Robust Design using Taguchi Methods (see Figure 15-6).

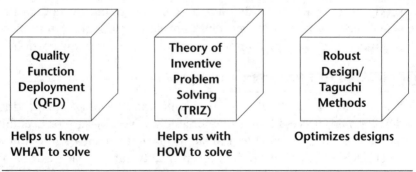

Figure 15-6. Key DLSS tools

Quality Function Deployment

How well a company captures the Voice of the Customer and defines requirements has a big impact in the overall success of its products in the marketplace. Up to 70% of a product's cost is determined prior to detailed design, during requirements definition and conceptual design. The up-front requirements process is often shortchanged—with costly results. Few companies allocate significant resources to projects until they are well into the detailed design phase. The key to success in the marketplace is a thorough understanding of your customers' key buying factors and the effective translation of desired features and functions into specific design requirements.

QFD is a highly evolved technique for capturing customer requirements for a product (or service) and translating them into required product/process design changes. Describing QFD in detail could easily consume a whole book by itself, but you can get a flavor for what's involved by revisiting the cause-and-effect matrix described in Chapter 11 (pp. 189-190). This matrix is a simplified version of the House of Quality, a complex form used in QFD to track the linkages from product performance requirements to design features and process characteristics.

Applied correctly, QFD is effective in ensuring that customer needs are prioritized, design requirements are established to address all customer needs, design requirements are prioritized to help focus the design effort, and performance targets are established. In short, *QFD helps teams know exactly* what *to solve.*

Theory of Inventive Problem Solving (TRIZ)

TRIZ helps increase innovation during the design process by helping teams address technical challenges and resolve contradictions, as opposed to making design compromises or trade-offs.

There are three ways in which designers deal with technical problems:

1. Ignore them and hope they go away.
2. Make trade-offs or compromises.
3. Resolve them.

TRIZ is a structured, technology-based methodology for resolving technical problems. It was developed by a Russian scientist, Dr. Genrich Altshuller, who spent years studying patents worldwide with two objectives in mind:

- How can the time to invent be reduced?
- How can a process be structured to enhance breakthrough thinking?

He studied over 400,000 patents and realized that similar problems in different industries using different science and technology have all been solved by similar solutions.

Altshuller determined that a finite number of principles were used to solve problems or conflicts within a finite number of technical parameters. If you could define your problem in generic terms to match conflicts between two of these design parameters (size, weight, speed, stress, temperature, etc.), you could learn how others have solved conflicts between the same two parameters and apply the solution to your own problem.

For example, have you ever wondered how sunflower seeds are shelled? A manufacturer of artificial diamonds had a problem: their process often yielded diamonds with fractures. In order to be able to sell the diamonds, they would split the diamond at the point of fracture in an attempt to create two perfect diamonds. However, the splitting process would often create more fractures and they'd have to split the diamond again. Obviously, the more they split the diamond, the smaller the diamonds became, thereby decreasing the market value.

This company needed a way to split the diamonds apart without causing more fractures. Using TRIZ, they defined the problem as "how to make objects explode or fly apart." They came upon a patent for shelling nuts and sunflower seeds. Seeds are put in a pressure cooker and the pressure raised to several atmospheres. The shells break at the weakest points and water seeps in. The pressure is quickly reduced, causing the water to expand and break the shells apart. The diamond manufacturer now places the crystals in a thick-walled, airtight vessel, increases the pressure to several thousand atmospheres, and then drops the pressure quickly. The sudden change in pressure causes the air in the fractures to expand and break the diamonds apart without creating more fractures.

Here's another example. A company's automotive division was having difficulty competing in a market for golf cart brake systems. Their problem was cost. They were applying designs of automobile braking systems. Using TRIZ, they instead applied the principles of a bicycle braking system and reduced the number of parts by 67% and cut cost by 50%.

TRIZ helps problem solvers combine their knowledge with the knowledge of thousands of inventors.

Robust Design

Robust Design can significantly improve product quality by designing products that are immune to various noise factors. Dr. Genichi Taguchi defines *robustness* as "the state where the technology, product, or process performance is minimally sensitive to factors causing variability (either in the manufacturing or user's environment) and aging at the lowest unit manufacturing cost." The goal is to predict and prevent problems that may occur during production and in the marketplace after a product is sold to a customer. There are many causes of variability—noise factors—that impact product quality and performance: customer usage, manufacturing environments, supplier part quality, etc. By establishing and designing to the right design parameters, one can optimize the design to minimize the effect of these noise factors.

Earlier in the book we talked about the effectiveness of Design of Experiments (see pp. 217-222). This methodology enables us to design in quality to "prevent fires" rather than "fight fires" after the fact. It enables the development of six sigma quality products and allows us to optimize designs early in the development process (where changes are inexpensive) to prevent downstream problems in manufacturing and customer usage (where changes are very expensive).

DLSS

The subject of Design for Lean Six Sigma could also be an entire book in itself. But the key message is that DLSS enables us to develop six sigma quality products. GE's CEO Jeffrey Immelt had tremendous success with DLSS during his tenure leading GE Medical Systems.

> *GE Medical Systems delivered record financial results in 1999, with revenue and earnings growth exceeding 25%. …We introduced seven products in 1999 using Design for Six Sigma (DFSS), with more than 20 to be released in 2000. These products are different—they capture customer and patient needs better and can be brought to market faster than ever before. …We will sell more than two billion dollars' worth of DFSS products by the end of 2000.*
> —Jeffrey R. Immelt, 1999 Annual Report

FINAL THOUGHTS ON LEAN SIX SIGMA AND PRODUCT DEVELOPMENT

This chapter described a number of ways you can apply Lean Six Sigma principles to the product development process to speed time-to-market through faster design velocity and reducing product line complexity. Once you can deliver a product quickly, Design for Lean Six Sigma is the next logical step to drive down product cost and improve design quality. In his book, *Common Stocks and Uncommon Profits*, Philip Fisher gives this advice:

> *It does mean that a company with research ... (which develops products) like a cluster of trees around each of these divisions, each growing additional branches from its own trunk, will do much better than a company working on a number of unrelated products which, if successful, will land it in several new industries unrelated to its existing business.*

This homey advice really summarizes all of the points I have been making. You should apply the concepts of Lean Six Sigma to build upon your existing development capabilities and provide your design teams with the knowledge and tools to help them generate more profitable products faster to grow your business.

Note

1. Ken Jacobson leads the Design for Lean Six Sigma (DLSS) Product Development Practice for George Group Consulting. He holds a B.S. degree in Electrical Engineering from Tufts University and an M.S. in Management from the MIT Sloan School of Management. His expertise is in the design and implementation of performance improvement systems related to new product design, strategic planning, program management, manufacturing, and support operations. He has led multiple Six Sigma initiatives, trained several hundred black belts, and consulted with companies in many industries.

Index

A

Activity-based costing (ABC), 275
Adjustments, eliminating, 213–214
Advanced Planning programs, 202, 248
AlliedSignal, 158
Altshuller, Genrich, 305–306
Analysis, in kaizen, 208
Analysis of variance (ANOVA), 200–201
Analyze phase
  overview, 25, 174–175
  tasks in, 26, 171, 172
  tools for, 172, 175, 199–203
ANOVA, 200–201
Assessment, in kaizen, 208
Asymmetry, 205–206
Asynchronous pull systems, 243
Automation of Lean Six Sigma metrics, 230
Awareness training, 108

B

Backup capacity, 211
Balanced scorecard, 133
Barriers to implementation, 122
Barton, Glen, 66–67
Basic lead time, calculating, 296
Batch size calculations, 246
Batch sizes
  software for calculating, 202–203, 246
  workstation turnover time and, 46, 47–48
Belbin, R. Meredith, 159

Belts, defined, 102. *See also* Black belts
Benefit/effort criteria, 147–148, 154–155
Benefit/effort graphs, 127–129, 154–155
Benefit index scores, 154
Best practices, documenting, 109–110
Big buckets of money, 137
Black belts
  as full-time positions, 228
  importance of leadership skills, 24, 157–158, 163–165
  overview of role, 104–105
  rewards and recognition, 114–115
  role in kaizen, 209
  role in Six Sigma, 22–23
  selecting, 21, 83–84, 102, 126–127
  tool and process training principles, 181
  training, 25–26, 95, 106
  transitioning projects to, 169–170
Bonuses, for black belts, 114
Book value, impact of ROIC, 11–12
Bottom-up project selection, 131, 132, 144–146
Bowl Championship Series, 148
Brainstorming
  focused, 147
  in kaizen, 208
  as Measure tool, 174
  procedure, 192
Brazing experiments, DOE example, 27–29

Breakdowns, preventing, 214–217
Brink of chaos processes, 198
Buffers
  purpose, 240
  recalculating, 264
  with supplier pull systems, 262,
    263–264
  total inventory, 263
  types, 241–242, 251–252
Buffett, Warren, 71–72, 73–74, 86, 144
Built to Last, 63
Burning platform, 88–89
Business case, documenting, 91
Business planning, 231
Business strategies
  aligning project selection with,
    131, 134–136
  importance of implementation,
    79–80
  integrating Lean Six Sigma, 81,
    230, 231
  inventory and, 271–272
Business unit champions, 21–22,
  103–104. *See also* Champions
Business unit managers. *See* Profit
  and loss (P&L) managers
Business value-added processes,
  52–53. *See also* Value streams

C

Capital costs of inventory, 274
Career development
  for black belts, 114, 127
  Lean Six Sigma roles and, 103, 106
Carnegie, Andrew, 15–16
Caterpillar
  institutionalizing Lean Six Sigma,
    227
  Six Sigma gains, 66–67
  supplier survey, 265–266
Causal analysis tools, 199–201
Cause-and-effect diagrams, 193
Cause-and-effect matrices, 189–190,
  260

Champions
  defined, 102
  as full-time positions, 228
  learning business strategy, 134
  selecting, 21, 83–84, 102
  Six Sigma roles, 21–22
  training, 106–108
  transitioning projects to black belt
    teams, 169–170
Chaos processes, 198
Check-in time example, 42–45
Checksheets, 194
Chief executive officers (CEOs)
  awareness of quality improve-
    ment tools, 29
  expressions of support from,
    114–115
  fostering company-wide vision,
    123
  infrastructure process role, 100
  need for engagement, 19–20,
    85–87
  role in Lean Six Sigma, 63–64,
    66–71
  Transforming Event presentations
    by, 119
Churchill, Winston, 70
Cigar butt theory of investing, 86
Coefficient of variation, 242
Collaborative thinking, 164
Collateralization, 93–94, 98
"collection of brilliance" approach,
  159
Commitment, from management,
  83–84, 88, 227–228. *See also* Chief
  executive officers (CEOs);
  Executive support
Commodity producers, 293
Common cause variation, 196, 198,
  224
*Common Stocks and Uncommon
  Profits*, 308
Communication, supporting Lean
  Six Sigma through, 229

Company champions, 102–103. *See also* Champions

Company-wide approach, 123, 277–278

Compensation, 113–114

Competitive advantage, 273, 292–294

Competitive position, market attractiveness versus, 134–136

Completer Finishers, 160

Complexity, Comply, Commit, Embed, Encode, 227–228

Confirmation of data, 169–170

Congestion, reducing, 210–211

Consultants, 93

Control charts, 196–198, 223

Control limits, 197

Control phase
overview, 25, 176–177
tasks in, 26, 171, 172
tools for, 172, 176–177, 222–224

Coordinators, 160

Core processes, analyzing, 142–144

Corporate champions, 21–22

Corporations, assessing sigma levels, 31–32

Cost levers, 138

Cost of poor quality (COPQ), 8

Critical to quality (CTQ) requirements
defined, 18
mistake proofing and, 206–207
role in project development, 22
in SIPOC diagrams, 185

Cross-docks, 286, 289

Cross-training, 211

Culture
incorporating Lean Six Sigma, 234
of Six Sigma, 17, 32, 62

Customer centricity, 17–18

Customer inquiry system example, 180

Customers
defining, 190
gathering requirements data, 139–142

Lean Six Sigma for, 231

Customer value-added processes, 52, 53

Customized products, 255–257

Cut runs, 41

Cycle efficiency
applying Lean to all processes, 40–42
defined, 130
measuring, 187–188
overview, 36–38
in service industry, 42–45
sources of cost reductions, 38–40

Cycles of learning, 40

Cycle stocks, 272

Cycle time baseline, 297

Cycle time interval buffers, 241, 251–252

D

Data accuracy tools, 194–195

Data analysis, in DMAIC model, 25, 26

Data collection, in DMAIC model, 25, 26

Data collection tools, 193–195

Defects
cost of, 18
identifying at enterprise level, 31–32
preventing. *See* Improve phase tools
variation and, 17. *See also* Variation

Defects per million opportunities, 16–17

Defensiveness, 165

Define-Measure-Analyze-Improve-Control (DMAIC). *See* DMAIC model

Define phase
DMAIC model, 150–151
overview, 25, 173–174
tasks in, 26, 171, 172
tools for, 172, 173, 183–185

Delays
  effects on quality, 4
  impact of scrap on, 207
  techniques for reducing, 210–211
Delivery frequency, increasing,
    282–283
Demand, predicting, 254–255
Deming, W. Edwards, 20
Deployment champions, 23, 30
Deployment plans
  building support for, 231–232
  components and timelines, 94–95,
    96
  measures, 110–113
  organizational structures, 98–110
  process focus, 96–98
  rewards and recognition, 113–115
  tools to support, 115–116
  Transforming Event presenta-
    tions, 120
Design/deployment teams, 90–91,
    120
Design for Lean Six Sigma (DLSS),
    290, 303–307
Design of Experiments (DOE),
    26–29, 217–222, 307
Design process
  differentiation, 292–294
  improving velocity, 296–303
  Lean Six Sigma for, 231, 290–292,
    303–307
Destruction of shareholder value,
    74–76
Diagnostics, 130
Diamond splitting, 306
Dictatorial team leaders, 164–165
Differentiation, 143, 292–294
Discovery, in kaizen, 208
Discussions for process mapping,
    188
Distribution centers, consolidating, 53
DMAIC filter, 177, 178
DMAIC model
  breadth of application, 167–168

context of improvement, 168–170
filtering, 177, 178
keys to training in, 181
overview, 24–26, 170–173
sample gains, 178–181
step-by-step application, 173–177
tools, 172
DNA, Lean Six Sigma in, 228
Documentation tools, 173
Downstream pull systems, 266–269
Downtime, 57–58, 214–217
Dynamic batches, 203

E
Economic order quantity (EOQ), 48,
    269
Economic profit %, 152
Economic profit, leverage from price
    premiums, 294–295
Effort index scores, 154
80/20 rule, 51
Embedding Lean Six Sigma, 228
Empirical correction of process
    velocity, 248–249
Employees
  introducing Lean Six Sigma to,
    122–123
  project selection ideas from, 146
  reassignment to value-added
    roles, 38, 55
Encoding Lean Six Sigma, 228
Endorsement, management engage-
    ment versus, 19–20
Enterprise Resource Planning (ERP)
    systems, 247–248
E-tracking systems, 30
Excessive production resources, 280
Exciting quality, 141
Execution infrastructure, 17, 21–23
Executive launch, 94
Executive support
  CEO role, 63–64, 66–71
  commitment, 83–84, 88, 227–228
  communicating commitment,
    232–234

endorsement versus engagement, 19–20
project selection ideas, 145–146
securing, 62–66, 85–89
Existing strategy lens, 134–136
Expected quality, 141
Expert coaching, 106
Explicit costs, 273
External noise, 221
External setup, 212–213

F

Factory velocity, 237–238
Failure Modes and Effects Analysis (FMEA), 190–191
Final project selection, 153–155
Financial analysis lens, 136–139, 151
Financial measures
    impact of Lean Six Sigma, 10–12
    project selection criteria, 71–76, 136–139
    refining, 151
    in Six Sigma culture, 17, 19
    tracking, 110–113
    See also Net present value (NPV); Return on invested capital (ROIC)
Finished goods safety stock, 252
First Law of Lean Six Sigma for Supply Chain Acceleration, 47, 268
Fishbone diagrams, 193
Fisher, Philip, 308
5S method, 217
Five-year goals, 89–90
Fixed costs, inventory as, 276
Flavors of the month, 226
Flexibility, forecasting versus, 254-255
Flowcharts. *See* Process mapping
Focused brainstorming, 147
Focused factories, 243
Focus/prioritization tools, 188–191
Follow-up, in kaizen, 208
Food distributor supply chain example, 253
Ford, Henry, 33, 50–51, 59
Forecasting, 254–255

Formal strategies, 134
Four-step rapid setup method, 211–214
Frequently Asked Questions, 123
Functional organizations, 97, 98, 277–278
Fundamental logistics cost drivers, 278–280
Future problems, 224

G

Gage repeatability and reproducibility, 194–195
Gantt charts, 155
Gap analysis, 91
Gas mileage simulation, 217–221
Gate reviews, 30
Gating projects, 297–298
GE, 304
GE Medical Systems, 307
Giuliano, Lou
    comments on Lean Six Sigma, 29, 67–69
    involvement in launching projects, 70
    on selecting projects, 71
Goals
    confirming with data, 169–170
    inventory and, 271–272
    setting, in initiation stage, 89–90
Green belts, 22, 23, 105
Grinding operation, mistake proofing, 204
Group champions, 102–103. *See also* Champions
Grove, Andy, 299

H

Hidden Factory
    elements of, 8
    as high-priority project area, 169
    lead times and, 238
    revealed in value stream mapping, 54
    wait time in, 36
High-potential-NPV value streams, 129–130

Holistic approach to improvement, 123, 277–278
Honeywell Aerospace, 260
Hotel check-in example, 42–45, 210
House of Quality, 305
Hybrid MRP/trigger pull systems, 248–249

I

Idea-generating and -organizing tools, 191–193
Ideal state processes, 198, 199
Ideas, screening, 146–148
Ideas, seeking. *See* Project selection
Immelt, Jeffrey, 307
Imperial Chemical Industries, 159
Implementation, in kaizen, 208
Implementation stage
  monitoring, 155
  overview, 62, 93–94
Implementation streams of Lean Six Sigma, 81
Implementers, 160
Implicit costs, 273–274
Improvement tools. *See* Tools
Improve phase
  overview, 25, 176
  tasks in, 26, 171, 172
Improve phase tools
  Design of Experiments (DOE), 26–29, 217–222, 307
  kaizen, 207–210
  mistake proofing, 5, 25, 203–207
  overview, 172, 176, 203
  queuing methods, 210–211
  rapid setup method, 47–48, 211–214
  Total Productive Maintenance, 57–58, 214–217
Inbound cost drivers, 278–279
Inbound transportation costs, 282–283
Increasing Leadership Effectiveness workshops, 165, 166
Indirect costs, 301

Individual performance, understanding, 158–159
Infancy stage of product life cycle, 299
Informal strategies, 134
Infrastructure development, 93–94
Infrastructure tools, 115–116
Initiation stage
  commissioning design/deployment team, 90–91
  documentation, 91–92
  establishing, 87
  goal setting, 89–90
  leadership engagement, 87–89
  overview, 62, 85–87
Inquiry skills, 164, 165
Insignificant factors, identifying, 220
Institutionalization, 226–234
Insurance, 275
Intel, 299
Interactions, learning from, 109
Internal customers, 190
Internal setup, 212–213
International Power Machines, 254–255, 301
In-transit inventories, 272
Inventory
  calculating costs, 273–278
  costs of, 33, 266–267
  strategic goals and, 271–272
  types of excessive costs, 280–281
  See also Logistics networks; Supply chain acceleration; Work in process (WIP)
Inventory risk costs, 274, 275
Inventory service costs, 274, 275
Iomega, 20
Iron making, 15–16
Isaac, Max, 157, 166
ITT Avionics, 40
ITT Corp., 67–69

J

Jacobson, Ken, 308
Jumpers, 41
Just-in-time (JIT), 271, 279

K

Kaizen, 207–210
Kanban systems, 57, 240–243, 261.
    See also Pull systems
Kano analyses, 140–142
Key buying factor analysis, 139
Key process input variables (KPIVs),
    177, 223

L

Launch preparations, 122, 231–232.
    See also Deployment plans
Leadership skills
    importance for black belts,
        157–158, 163–165, 229
    for Six Sigma teams, 24
    understanding individual per-
        formance, 158–159
Leading indicators, 110
Lead time
    costs of, 238
    measuring, 187
    for product development, 291
Lead time reduction
    benefits, 39, 239
    importance to Lean Six Sigma,
        8–9
    ITT Avionics example, 40
    for product development, 296–303
    role in cycle efficiency, 36–38
Lean
    applied to all processes, 40–42
    applied to service industry, 42–45
    basic objectives, 33, 35
    common perceptions, 34–35
    cycle efficiency overview, 36–38
    elements of, 35–36, 60
    major tools, 56–59
    sources of cost reductions, 38–40
Lean Six Sigma
    basic purposes, 79
    combined with ERP systems, 247
    competitive advantage, 76–78
    defined, 7
    executive support, 62–70

finding waste, 51–56
First Law for Supply Chain
    Acceleration, 47, 268
implementing. *See*
    Implementation stage
importance of overhead reduc-
    tion, 8–9
institutionalizing, 226–234
leveraging learning, 108–110
measures, 110–113
principle of, 4
process overview, 62, 80–82
Second Law for Supply Chain
    Acceleration, 51, 168
targeting value streams for
    improvement, 71–76, 100
Third Law for Supply Chain
    Acceleration, 49–50
value proposition, 9–13, 61
Learning, 108–110, 300–301
Least preferred roles, 163
Leveled raw materials flow, 286
Levels, in designed experiments, 218
Leveraging learning, 108–110
Line managers, 99–100, 101
Little's Law, 49
Lockheed Martin, 260
Logistics networks
    inventory and strategic goals,
        271–272
    inventory costs, 273–278
    Lean implementation, 270–271,
        281–288, 288–289
    measurement in, 287–288
    raw materials management,
        280–281
    total costs in, 278–280
Long-run inventory costs, 277
Lot sizes, 284

M

Machinery
    reducing downtime, 57–58,
        214–217
    reducing setup time, 211–214

Robust Design, 221–222, 307
Main effects plots, 219–220
Manageable roles, 163
Management engagement. *See* Chief
    executive officers (CEOs);
    Executive support
Manufacturing lead time buffers,
    241
Manufacturing overhead, 8–9, 301
Manufacturing Resource Planning,
    246
Mapping value streams, 51–55
Market attractiveness, 134–136
Marketing promotions, 253–254
Martichenko, Robert, 34, 289
Mass production environments,
    waste sources, 280
Master black belts, 23, 24, 104
Materials Requirements Planning
    (MRP) systems
    batch size calculations, 48
    debates over, 245
    identifying delays, 5
    importance to Lean Six Sigma, 13
    origins and evolution, 245–247
    in synchronous pull systems, 244
    use in value stream mapping, 53,
        54
Maturity phase of product life cycle,
    300
Measurement in logistics networks,
    287–288
Measure phase
    overview, 25, 174
    tasks in, 26, 171, 172
Measure phase tools
    data collection/accuracy, 193–195
    focus/prioritization, 188–191
    idea-generating and -organizing,
        191–193
    process characteristics, 186–188
    summarized, 172, 174
    variation, 195–199
Micro-stops, 216–217

Milk runs, 283, 285
Minimum batch size, 202–203
Minitab, 200–201
Mistake proofing
    in DMAIC model, 25
    elements of, 25, 203–204, 206–207
    examples, 204–206
    in tier-one auto supplier case
        study, 5
Monitor Evaluators, 160
MRP systems. *See* Materials
    Requirements Planning (MRP)
    systems
MRP/trigger pull systems, 248–249,
    250
Multivoting, 192–193

N
Neighborhoods, on benefit/effort
    graphs, 154–155
Net present value (NPV)
    components of, 11–12, 13, 73–74
    as criterion for improvement pri-
        orities, 12, 13, 153
Nominal group technique (NGT),
    192
Non-repetitive manufacturing,
    255–257
Non-value-added processes
    identifying in value stream map-
        ping, 53–55, 188
    redeploying workers from, 38, 56
Normal quality, 141

O
Obsolescence, 275–276
One-factor-at-a-time approach,
    217–218
Only the Paranoid Survive, 299
On-time delivery improvement
    example, 64–66
Operating profits
    e-tracking systems, 30
    leverage from price premiums,
        294–295

Six Sigma requirements, 16, 19
Opportunities, 130, 147
Opportunity costs, 273–274
Order point logic, 247
Organizational structures, 98–105
Organizations
  assessing sigma levels, 31–32
  functional versus process, 97, 98
Outsourcing, 257–266
Overhead, 8–9, 301
Overproduction, 280, 281

P

P&L managers. *See* Profit and loss
  (P&L) managers
Packaging, returnable, 284–285
Pareto charts, 188–189
Pareto principle
  origin, 189
  with suppliers, 259–260, 262
  wide applicability of, 5
Parking lot, in kaizen, 208
Persistent pains, 132
Pet projects, 130, 132
Pilot supplier pull project, 259–264
Pipeline visibility, 287
Plants, 160
Pooling, 210–211
Preferred roles, 24, 159–163
Preliminary proposals, 91–92
Presentations, in kaizen, 208
Pre-testing solutions, 211
Price concessions, 259
Price premiums, 294–295
Printed circuit board example, 41–42
Priorities for improvement
  benefit/effort criteria in setting,
    155
  customer value-added processes,
    53
  examples, 169
  net present value (NPV), 12, 13,
    153
  tools for determining, 188–191
Process analysis lens, 142–144

Process capability analysis, 198–199
Process characteristics tools, 186–188
Process cycle efficiency, 130. *See also*
  Cycle efficiency
The Process Edge, 143
Process factors, optimizing with
  DOE, 27–29
Process flows, improving, 178–180
Process focus, 96–98
Process mapping, 174, 178–179,
  186–187
Process owners, 101
Process velocity
  applied to all processes, 40–42
  effects on cost, 33
  effects on quality, 4
  number of WIP items and, 49–51
  See also Lean
Product development
  Design for Lean Six Sigma, 290,
    303–307
  differentiation, 292–294
  improving velocity, 296–303
  Lean Six Sigma for, 231, 290–292
Production control, WIP and, 245–251
Production costs, inventory and,
  273–278
Product line complexity, 243,
  299–301
Profit and loss (P&L) managers
  commitment to Six Sigma, 21–22
  initial skepticism, 117–118
  in Lean Six Sigma organizational
    structure, 100–101
  tactical focus, 85–86
Profits. *See* Economic profit;
  Operating profits
Project definition forms (PDFs),
  149–151, 183, 184
Project identification balanced score-
  card, 133
Project planning and execution, Six
  Sigma model, 21–23
Projects, defined, 130

Project selection
  approaches, 129
  basic questions, 155–156
  benefit/effort graphs, 127–129,
    154–155
  bottom-up approaches, 131, 132,
    144–146
  criteria for, 71–76
  final ranking, 153–155
  grouping and screening ideas,
    146–148
  introducing P&L managers to
    concepts, 122
  in Lean Six Sigma deployment
    timeline, 95
  project definition and scoping,
    148–153
  responsibility for, 100, 130–131
  terminology, 129–130
  top-down approaches, 131, 132–144
Projects in process, reducing, 298–299
Project sponsors, 22, 23, 30
Project-tracking software, 149, 230,
  231
Promotional buffers, 241
Proposals, preliminary, 91–92
Publicizing improvements, 229
Pull systems
  automating, 249–251
  downstream, 266–269
  leveled raw materials flow, 286
  narrow product lines and, 301
  overview, 7, 56–57, 240–244
  rise to popularity, 247
  for suppliers, 258–266
Purchased parts pull systems, 261
Pursuant growth phase of product
  life cycle, 299–300

Q
Quality
  delivery frequency and, 283
  designing into products, 303–307
  effect of delays on, 4, 13–14
  impact of machine downtime,
    215–216

Quality circles, 207
Quality Function Deployment, 139,
  305
Quality improvement tools. *See*
  Tools
Queuing methods, 210–211
Quick hits, 130

R
Rapid setup method, 47–48, 211–214
Raw materials management, 280–281,
  286
Recognition, 114–115
Regression analysis, 200, 201
Remedial training, 108
Repeatability of measurements,
  194–195
Repetitiveness, 300–301
Replenishment schedules, 262
Reproducibility of measurements,
  194–195
Resource availability risk, 154
Resource commitment
  for product development, 296–298
  in Six Sigma culture, 17, 21
Resource Investigators, 160
Response surface, 221
Results, publicizing, 229
Returnable packaging, 284–285
Return on invested capital (ROIC)
  impact of Lean Six Sigma, 10–11,
    66
  shareholder value growth and,
    11–12, 64, 71–76, 152–153
Revenue growth, 11–12, 72–73
Rewards and recognition, 113–115
Rework, 207
Risk Priority Numbers (RPNs), 191
Risks, 154, 274, 275
Roadmaps, 4–5
Robust Design, 221–222, 307
Route systems, 283
Run charts, 195–196
Runs, 218

S

Safety stock
    calculating, 251–252
    lot sizes and, 284
    as reason for inventory, 241, 272
Safety time stock, 249
Sales and operations planning,
    252–257
SCA software. *See* Supply chain
    accelerator software
Scatter plots, 199–200
Scrap, 207
Screening criteria, 147–148
Seasonality buffers, 241, 264
Second Law of Lean Six Sigma for
    Supply Chain Acceleration, 51, 268
Segmentation analyses, 259–260
Selection stage, 62
Self-assessments by suppliers, 266
Self-censorship, avoiding, 131
Semiconductor diode chip misorien-
    tation case, 204–205
Senior managers. *See* Executive sup-
    port
Service industry applications, 42–45
Setup time
    effects on delays and inventory,
        215
    Lean systems for limiting, 57
    rapid setup method, 211–114
    workstation turnover time and,
        46, 47–48
Shapers, 160
Shareholder value, 11–12, 71–76
Shiseido, 251
Short-run inventory costs, 276
Short-run marginal cost, 276
Shut height, 214
Sigma levels, 16–17
Sign-offs, 41–42
Simulations, 120–121
SIPOC diagrams, 183–185
Six M's, 193
Six Sigma
    culture of, 17, 32, 62

overview, 16–17
    as process versus enterprise met-
        ric, 31–32
    success and failure, 23–24
    tools, 24–30
Skill bottlenecks, 297
Slow-moving inventory, 266–267
Soft benefits, weighing, 154
Software
    for ANOVA, 200–201
    for assessing team balance,
        162–163
    DOE, 218–219
    educational, 109
    pipeline visibility, 287
    project tracking, 149, 230, 231
    supply chain, 201–203, 237–238, 239
    for what-if scenarios, 211
    See also Materials Requirements
        Planning (MRP) systems
Sorting ideas, 147
Special cause variation, 196, 198,
    223–224
Specialists, 160
Speculative stocks, 272
Springback, 213
Standardization
    of improvement processes, 181
    in kaizen, 208
    of products, 298–299, 301–303
Statistical process control, 223–224
Stock-keeping units (SKUs), 243
Storage space costs, 274, 275
Strategic buffers
    components, 241–242
    defined, 240
    with supplier pull systems, 262
Strategic planning
    implementation and, 79–80
    integrating Lean Six Sigma, 230,
        231
Strategic purchasing, 258
Strategies. *See* Business strategies
Streamlining internal setup, 212–213

Stretch goals, 89–90
Structured routes, 283
Supplemental training, 108
Supplier advisory councils, 264
Supplier days, 258, 259
Supplier lead times, 251–252. *See also*
    Lead time; Lead time reduction
Supplier Lean Six Sigma initiatives,
    231, 257–266
Supplier material safety stock, 252
Supplier surveys, 265–266
Supply chain acceleration
    downstream pull systems, 266–269
    extending to suppliers, 257–266
    overview, 237–239
    pull systems, 240–244
    safety stock calculations, 251–252
    sales and operations planning,
        252–257
    WIP controls, 245–251
Supply Chain Acceleration laws
    First Law, 47, 60, 268
    Second Law, 51, 60, 268
    Third Law, 49–50, 60, 268
    Zeroeth Law, 60
Supply chain accelerator software,
    201–203, 237–238, 239
Synchronous pull systems, 244

T

Tacit knowledge, 212
Tactical focus, 86
Tactical purchasing, 258
Takt time, 244
Taxes, 275
Team leaders. *See* Black belts
Team Roles at Work, 159
Teams
    effectiveness factors, 159–163
    success in Six Sigma, 23–24
    transitioning projects to, 169–170
Team Workers, 160
Technical problems, resolving, 305–306
Technology-based education, 109

Terminology, as everyday language,
    231
Testimonials, 120
Theory of Inventive Problem
    Solving, 305–306
Third Law of Lean Six Sigma for
    Supply Chain Acceleration, 49–50,
    268
Threshold processes, 198
Tier-one auto supplier case study
    cycle efficiency, 37
    DOE example, 27–29
    financial gains, 10
    identifying CTQ defects, 18
    lead time reduction, 38–39
    overview, 3–7
    process capability analysis,
        198–199
    time traps, 5-6
Time delays, 4–6, 13–14
Time fences, 256
Timelines for project deployment,
    94–95
Time traps
    analysis tools, 201–203
    DOE solutions, 27–29
    identifying, 45–47
    as Lean targets, 36
    revealed in value stream map-
        ping, 55
    tier-one auto supplier analysis, 5–6
Tollgate reviews
    Analyze phase, 175
    Control phase, 177
    Define phase, 173–174
    Improve phase, 176
    Measure phase, 174
    purposes, 170–173
Tools
    Analyze phase, 175, 199–203
    Control phase, 222–224
    Define phase, 173, 183–185
    deployment, 115–116
    Improve phase. *See* Improve
        phase tools

Lean overview, 56–59
Measure phase, 174, 185–199
Six Sigma overview, 24–30
Top-down project selection
   "existing strategy" lens, 134–136
   "financial analysis" lens, 136–139
   overview, 132–133
   "process analysis" lens, 142–144
   "Voice of the Customer" lens,
      139–142
Total costs, optimizing, 278–280
Total inventory buffer, 263
Total lead time, 36–38
Total Productive Maintenance,
   57–58, 214–217
Total Quality Management (TQM),
   19, 20
Total supply chain acceleration,
   267–269
Toyota Production System, 34
Traffic light metric, 69–70
Training
   of champions, 106–108
   cross-training, 211
   emergence of personal shortcom-
      ings during, 127
   implications of team roles on,
      165–166
   importance for black belts, 25–26,
      106, 157–158
   in kaizen, 208
   in Lean Six Sigma deployment
      timeline, 95
   leveraging learning, 108–110
   for suppliers, 261
   tool and process principles, 181
Transactional processes, 40–42, 230
Transforming Events, 70, 118–123
Transportation costs, 279, 282–283
Transport time buffers, 241
Triaging, 211
Trial-and-error improvement methods, 217, 218

Triggers
   order point logic, 247
   in pull systems, 240, 242
   in synchronous pull systems, 244
TRIZ, 305–306
Two-year goals, 89–90

U
Unscheduled downtime, 57–58

V
Value-added time, 36–38
Value-Based Six Sigma, 68–69
Value creating processes, 143
Value delivered, 111–112
Value destroying processes, 143
Value driver tree, 137
Value mountain, 12, 152
Value proposition, 9–13, 61
Values, reinforcing, 230
Value streams
   defined, 129, 142
   impact on NPV, 12, 13
   mapping to find waste, 51–55, 188
   process focus, 96–98
   targeting for improvement, 71–76,
      100, 122
   See also Project selection
Valve cap example, 206
Variable costs, 276
Variation
   as cause of defects, 17
   coefficient, 242
   impact of machine downtime, 215
   in measurements, 194–195
   product line complexity and, 243
   reducing in products, 299–303
   relation to lead times, 238
   relation to wait times, 57–58
   in safety stock calculations, 252
   tools for eliminating, 195–199,
      210–211
Vendors. *See* Supply chain acceleration
Videos, 123

Visionary leadership, 63
Vision, company-wide, 123
Voice of the Customer (VOC), 18, 139–142

W

Wait time
   importance of reducing, 8–9, 35–36
   variations and, 57–58
Warranty reduction projects, 221–222
Waste sources, 280
Wenninger, Fred, 20
White belts, 105
Work in process (WIP)
   capping, 239
   costs of, 38, 40
   effects on process velocity, 49–51
   Lean systems for limiting, 56–57
   measuring lead time from, 187
   production control and, 245–251
   as reason for inventory, 272
Workstation congestion, 210–211. *See also* Lead time reduction
Workstation turnover time, 46, 47
World-class cycle efficiency, 37–38
World Wide Web e-tracking systems, 30

Z

Zeroeth Law of Lean Six Sigma for Supply Chain Acceleration, 60

ABOUT THE AUTHOR

Michael George is the founder and CEO of George Group Consulting based in Dallas, Texas. Established in 1987, George Group pioneered the deployment of Lean methods in the United States and created and deployed the first integrated Lean Six Sigma process. The company designs programs to meet specific operational goals of the CEO, and provides support to the client by delivering sustained improvements in operational performance and shareholder value. George Group clients include Caterpillar, ITT, GE, United Technologies, Ingersoll-Rand, Johns Manville, etc.

Prior to founding George Group, Mr. George was the founder and president of International Power Machines, a manufacturer of large uninterruptible power supplies, which protect critical computers from power failure. Mr. George took the company public in 1980 and sold it in 1984 to a division of Rolls Royce. Mr. George then visited Japan to study the Toyota Production System and in 1987 authored the popular book America Can Compete. He is also the holder of US Patents relating to cycle time reduction.

Mr. George began his career as an integrated circuit engineer at Texas Instruments. He holds a bachelors degree in physics from the University of California and a master's degree in physics from the University of Illinois.